D1252198

CHESS REVOLUTION

by

Richard Moody

DORRANCE
PUBLISHING CO
EST. 1920
PITTSBURGH, PENNSYLVANIA 15238

Dorrance Publishing Co
585 Alpha Drive
Suite 103
Pittsburgh, PA 15238
Visit our website at *www.dorrancebookstore.com*

ISBN: 978-1-6453-0636-8
eISBN: 978-1-6453-0652-8

CONTENTS

PREFACE

Every revolution starts with a concept. In the case of the author, RM, it was the desire to become a top-flight theoretician in chess. Since RM had no talent as either a player or a theoretician, this was a grandiose goal. Having an enormous reservoir of good ideas is useful as a theoretician. RM, however, had an enormous reservoir of bad ideas that had to be treated like wheat and chaff.

When RM first began an intensive study of chess in 1984, he realized he needed someone to help steer him in the right direction. Enter Grandmaster Lev Alburt. This began a rewarding professional relationship (for both men!) that has lasted for over thirty-five years. Even though it is possible for Fritz 8 to play and analyze at a world-class level, it is amazing to RM that GM Alburt is still relevant to the analysis of chess theory. He routinely sees resources both the computer and the author overlook.

At the start, GM Alburt would simply take out his copy of *Encyclopedia of Chess Openings*, look up the appropriate page, and write back to RM in a timely fashion. Lev is an excellent businessman. He soon realized that if he disagreed with his analysis, RM would send him more letters defending whatever analysis Lev was refuting on that occasion. If Lev's analysis confirmed his theory, RM would stop sending questions on that topic. By consistently playing devil's advocate, Lev helped create opening theory of a reasonable quality because both the pros and cons of each opening were thoroughly analyzed with best play being constructed concept by concept and, in many occasions, move by move. (This was in the day when RM would use a Par Excellence computer and a Sphinx Legend, two 1700 computers, to do "research." When RM wrote the book *Universal Chess: The Search for Truth and Beauty*, he had graduated to a Mephisto Berlin, a master-strength computer but still well below the playing strength of Fritz 8, a 2700+ level computer, which he uses today).

By a distillation process, RM, over the span of years, would put together decent original theory. This process took years and sending hundreds of letters to Lev. Every few days, the author would send letters to Lev. (He is listed in the pages of *Chess Life*.) With no opening library, the author starting sending questions that Lev would simply research and answer easily. After asking questions that were covered routinely in chess literature, Lev suggested that if RM was interested in opening theory, perhaps he should buy some books on opening theory. RM then began to collect a small library of opening books.

Lev would suggest that perhaps he could be more useful to research if RM would provide questions familiar with Lev's praxis. This offer was declined because it was RM's opinion at that time that only king-pawn openings mattered. Lev rarely plays the white side of king-pawn openings and has been known to play the Alekhine Variation with black.

At a very early stage in his analysis, RM viewed the Evans Gambit as critical to chess. (He intuitively understood that the Two Knights Defense was unclear, a position validated in this book.) It was his opinion at that time that double king-pawn openings were a win for white. To test this, he started out to prove that the Evans Gambit was unsound and sent dozens of letter to Lev on this opening. Lev would respond routinely with ideas and analysis overlooked by RM. His most common comment: "White has full compensation for the pawn."

An interesting aside here is the question posed in an internet article by Timothy Y. Chow. He asked, "Is chess ripe for foundational exposition/research?" This question, in view of this book, could not be more timely. According to the RM, the answer is a resounding yes! Here is a hypothesis offered by RM: "Is the Two Knights Defense a forced win for white in all variations?" It will be established in this book that the modern main line of the TKD, the Berliner Variation, is, indeed, a forced win for white in all variations. According to theory offered by RM in terms of the lines leading up to the "main" line, most variations of the Fritz are wins for white at a theoretical level, i.e., if a human world champion were to take on the strongest computers in the world, he/she would win 100 percent of the time from the starting position, provided each screwup in play can be retracted and better moves be substituted. The starting moves which are +- on a theoretical level.

Perhaps correspondent chess players are better at getting at the truth, but if world champion Berliner cannot be counted on to produce accurate theory, even with the aid of the strongest computer in the world, maybe even this is not possible.

It is suggested here that a clearing house of chess theory be established not to test moves, but to test ideas. Perhaps we should have all proponents of all strengths from both sides plead their case, either that the position is a win for white or that the position is a win or draw for black. It is argued here simplistically that all double king-pawn openings are a win for white, assuming best play by both sides. In this book, you will find practical tests of the Latvian Gambit, the Damiano the Philidor, the TKD, and the Petroff against Fritz 8, a world-class opponent. The balance of the Italian game, the Evans Gambit, has been addressed in a number of publications but favorable to white in many variations. If the Evans Gambit is unsound, then test all the quiet alternatives to the Evans.

If players want to do this with the Ruy Lopez, then start with the Marshall Gambit. The ultimate question to be posed by the proponents of white having a forced win on black's first move of the game is this: Is the weakening of the f7 square caused by black's first move fatal? Probably the most definitive answer is the Wilkes-Barre Traxler Variation (WBT). Here black engages in the most violent attempt to seize the initiative, and, indeed, in the sharp variations, black does well. For those of you who like dessert before the main course, skip to the chapter on the WBT to see a big plus for white.

It is here that the first shot is fired that all double king-pawn openings, especially the Italian game, are wins for white. The alternatives are even worse. Black's hope in the Italian game is that white's spatial advantage in the Evans Gambit Declined is offset just enough by his overextended pawns and his more active piece play. Black should follow the example of GM Alburt and try to exploit the overextended pawns just as Lev has been known to do in the Alekhine Defense against GM Nigel Short. (Unfortunately Lev's good technique escaped him here, and he let the wins slip through his fingers due to practical play, not theory.) White should fight to use controlled space in the manner that RM used against the computer in "Magic."

Getting back to the Evans Gambit, in the words of a sage, "If you can't beat 'em, join 'em." Thus began several years' worth of study of the white-side ideas of the Evans Gambit, culminating in RM's book published by Ken Smith of *Chess Digest* called, *The Evans Gambit Revolution*. When RM approached Ken about writing the book, RM suggested he team up with a grandmaster to coauthor the book. Ken suggested that he write it himself. This seemed incredible! RM is only a Class B player, and to be offered the opportunity to publish a book on his favorite opening was a dream come true. (RM is the Walter Mitty of class players because good Class B players become Class A players, while good Class A players become Experts, etc. RM, on the other hand, has been mired as a Class B player for decades.) He has had national masters Steve Taylor and Alon Bochman help him with his analysis. In tournaments where he was a competitor, his opponents would come up after the games and ask him if he was the same Richard Moody who had written a letter in *Chess Life* in GM Larry Evans's column, and we would retire to a room and go over the opening in question.)

GM Andy Soltis, of the *New York Post*, gave the Evans Gambit book a good review, but the Brits, relying on the work of Tim Harding, panned it viciously. When Ken saw the reviews, he promptly cancelled our contract to write a second book on the Two Knights Defense. Then the author simply wrote an eight-page rebuttal of his critics, which Ken promptly tried to sell for $3.95 and agreed to renew the contract, which was declined at that time by RM. We never came to a meeting of the minds after that.

Much of the Evans Gambit book was unnecessarily critical of the pioneering work done by Tim Harding. It just seemed to be inaccurate but could have (and should have) been addressed more diplomatically. After all, it was the classic book by Cafferty and Harding that rescued the Evans Gambit from the obscurity of nineteenth-century chess. What is not generally recognized about the Evans Gambit is that Steinitz, even though he was world champion and anxious to try out his new opening theories, was crushed routinely by Chigorin on the black side of the Evans Gambit.

When GM Joel Benjamin of *Chess Life* received letters on the Evans Gambit where RM came up with improvements for white, his comment was, "When was the last time you saw a grandmaster lose on the black side of the Evans Gambit?" Just at the time RM's book was being promoted, world champion Kasparov began to win some brilliancies against world-class professionals in the Evans Gambit. Ken was so thrilled he devoted half the outside back cover of his catalogue and the entire inside back cover to a promotion of the Evans book.

One thing RM has done in recognition of the value of "technique" is to play entire games against Fritz 8 out to the point it resigns at a time limit of either 120'/25 or 120'/40 or 120'/50, or the computer evaluates the game as +-. This represents a valid rest of RM's theories because there are perhaps a dozen players in the world rated higher than Fritz 8. This rating, though, is based on Fritz's entire game, not just the sharp middle games played by RM. RM has Class B endgame skills, so he has no other choice but to outplay Fritz 8 in sharp middle games. In these middle games, where the computer sees every legal continuation six to eight moves deep, it probably plays at world-champion level. Twice it overstepped the time limit when it saw, but didn't play out, a draw by repetition, so there are major programming problems with computers still. What will knock three hundred to five hundred rating points off computers in the future is that they will become schizophrenic if they are programmed to play both universal chess and classical chess at different stages of the game.

In his book, *Universal Chess: The Search for Truth and Beauty*, RM detailed what is meant by a Universal Position (UP). First of all, they are incredibly common at the highest level of play because RM counted over fifty of them in one issue of *Inside Chess* alone. A UP is defined as any situation where all of a player's pieces are behind his farthest advanced pawn. There can, at most, be one open file.

When supercomputers of the future encounter a typical human opponent, it will be clueless because it will never know what school of chess to follow. What human competitors will do is jump back and forth between the various schools of chess and whipsaw the computer because it is helpless evaluating UPs and consistently misevaluates them. If it can't evaluate them properly, it is never going to know what options to play. As long as computers don't know what a practical win is for human players, they will have lousy technique in UPs.

The computer, prior to its first move where it "thinks," is required to regurgitate theory for the first few moves. This gives it extra time to reach the first time control. This is not beating a dead horse; computers of this strength are notorious for punishing human players for tactical mistakes. For instance, in a highly complex middle game in the Berliner Variation, RM played thirty-two moves without a single tactical oversight yet turned a clearly winning position into an inferior endgame because of a single mistake. (RM decided to get four connected passed pawns! See game on the Berliner Variation.) This is why computers are so brutal; they punish tactical oversights with lethal effect. Just one missed tactical shot will turn an easy win into a dead loss.

To prove that the position was really a win for white, RM returned to the point of the blunder and inserted an obvious alternative. The resulting middle game saw Fritz 8 try to stop three connected passed pawns. When one reached the seventh, Fritz 8 sacrificed two rooks for bishop and pawn and wound up in a losing endgame of bishop and two connected passed pawns versus king and slow pawns. (During the course of the game, RM had sacrificed the double exchange in order to obtain the bishops; they escorted the passed pawns on their march to the 8th).

Although computers are viewed as "monsters" in the middle game, RM, in at least ten to twelve sharp games, has been able to outplay the computer consistently, winning a half dozen and drawing at least a half dozen. The only exceptions where RM has won games against Fritz 8 were on the black side of the Sicilian Defense and one white side of one Sicilian Defense. All the other king pawn wins are on the white side of double king-pawn openings.

OPENING PRINCIPLES

For the basis for much of this theory, see Moody, R. 1999. *Universal Chess: The Search for Truth and Beauty*. Is chess art, science, or sport — or something else? Clearly it is not science. (World champion Steinitz a "scientist"? This is comparable to calling medieval alchemists scientists.) Merely codifying one's beliefs does not make one a scientist. As far as space is concerned, Steinitz thought that the world was flat. Here is a quote from Estrin, *The Two Knights Defence*, page 117, 1983 edition: "Take a look at the board now, after my awkward retreat 13.Ng1. I have six pawns on their original squares, which, according to my theory, is a great advantage..." This is one of the most bizarre, twisted theories of all of chess. It makes sense if we assume that the only kind of player who plays chess is a classical chess player. Steinitz was willing to be a human punching bag who assumed that the only kind of attack was a direct frontal assault. In other words, Steinitz could deal effectively with attempts to overrun his position quickly. How would he fare against former world champion Karpov? If you asked world champions Kasparov and Karpov whether we should keep most of our pawns on their original squares during the course of the game, they would laugh at you.

Steinitz was a big fish in a very small pond. Here are two games of "world-class" caliber that could easily be mistaken for a skittles game between class players. Bird played three games at about ELO 1600; dismiss these three games where Bird played horribly, and he outscored Steinitz during the rest of the 1866 match. So Steinitz, the original world "champion" (worst among equals?), beat an opponent in two games whose play would be an embarrassment for a class player. Here are the score of these two ridiculous games: Steinitz-Bird, London, m/9. 1.e4 e6 2.d4 d5 3.Nc3 dxe4 4.Nxe4 Nf6 5.Nxf6 Qxf6 6.Nf3 Nc6?? 7.Bg5 Qf5 (this is why early queen moves get their

1

bad reputation) 8.Bd3 Qg4 9.h3 Qxg2 10.Rh2 Qxh2 11.Nxh2 Nxd4? 12.Bb5ch 1-0.

Remember, Bird outscored Steinitz +5-4=5 in those games he didn't play like a turkey. To show how consistently poorly Bird could play and still be in this match is the second game, i.e., Steinitz-Bird, m/17. 1.e4 e6 2.d4 g6 3.Nf3 Nc6 4.d5 Nce7 5.dxe6 dxe6?? 6.Qxd8ch Kxd8 +- 7.Nc3 Nc6 8.Bf4 f6 9.O-O-Och Bd7 10.Bb5 h5 11.e5 f5 12.Rd2 Ke8 13.Rhd1 Rh7 14.Ng5 Bh6 15.Bxc6 bxc6 16.Na4 1-0. Truly a "classic" battle between the titans of that era.

Steinitz's theories in the opening can best be described as a long-running gambit, i.e., when they are first tried out, they may score well, but as the theory becomes known, they score poorly. Taking Steinitz seriously as an opening theoretician is on a par with my endorsing the Flat Earth Society as a geologist. In the world of Steinitz, the earth is flat, and RM dismisses out of hand any individual who passionately believes that the earth is flat. For this reason, he rejects the teachings of Nimzovich, who obsessed over pawn chains, which can only be constructed if both sides cooperate. Would anyone care to pigeonhole the game Magic? There was a pawn link that was borne out of absolute necessity in view of the nature of the odds game; however, the author was willing to "destroy" his pawn structure just to eliminate the pawn link. Is this classical, romantic, or hypermodern chess — or something else?

We place way too much stock in the teachings of Steinitz and Nimzovich. It is now time to address *My System* by Nimzovich. Fred Reinfeld, p.v. "...could not have arrived at such a position in the world of chess had his 'law' been based on false philosophy, or his 'way' led to barren ground." This statement reflects the widespread belief that winning games correlates directly with the theoretical soundness of one's ideas. Computers win lots of games; does this mean we should all learn chess theory from computers? There is a wide assortment of reasons why players win games that have absolutely nothing to do with the soundness of their theories. Isn't it a fact that a player with an axe to grind is more likely to be persistent in testing his theories and will, like the Avis, commercials, "try harder"? Aren't most games in the nineteenth and twentieth centuries won simply because one player was stronger than another, having a good day, or simply wanted to win more? Here is a simple test to demonstrate why technical skill, not opening theory, will rule chess of the future. Have a strong computer make any of the twenty legal moves that are available at the start of the game. Have the computer take on a strong grandmaster with either white or black, and I predict that the computer, without any opening theory, i.e., just crunching moves, will win +10-5=10 against any grandmaster. This could be construed as a test of opening theory when, in fact, it is a test of technical accuracy. Even the great Bobby Fischer was seduced by the theories of Steinitz and played the bizarre Steinitz variation of the TKD against GM Arthur Bisguier (1.e4 e5 2.Nf3 Nc6 3.Bc4 Nf6 4.Ng5 d5 5.exd5 Na5 6.c6 bxc6 7.Be2 h6 8.Nh3??) Bobby could make even the Garbage Gambit work. This is not theoretical soundness; Bobby, for a long time, was a spectacular competitor who could beat anyone, any time with any opening system.

By the way, GM Bisguier, who at a ranking of fifth in the nation, almost lost to RM on the white side of the Damiano Gambit in a simul because RM couldn't win a knight, rook and pawn endgame versus a rook and busted pawn structure endgame. This is one reason the author "hates" endgames. The only other grandmaster he played against, this time in a blitz game over the phone, was against Lev on the black side of the Blumenfeld Countergambit. According to Lev, black was winning during most of the middle game and accepted a draw offer in a superior position. (Do you really believe a grandmaster would offer a draw to a Class B player in a winning position?)

Back to theory: One of the most important things said by Nimzovich in *My System* on p. 3 was, "The line shown in Diagram 1 we call the frontier: 'line' is, of course, to be taken in its mathematical sense, not its chess sense." This is typical of the pseudo-scientific balderdash given in this book. By using the word "mathematical," Nimzovich hopes to equate his theories with the rigor of a mathematical treatise. As an MS in geology, I see this sort of nonsense all the time (see: Moody, R.H. Jr. 2007, "Beyond Plate Tectonics: 'Plate' Dynamics". *Infinite Energy*. 74:12-24.). Scientists who have little to contribute to the discipline of geology often couch their phrases in mathematical certainty. In the above case by Nimzovich, math is being used as a substitute for concept. Mathematics is the refuge of scoundrels.

Nimzovich, p. 4, ibid., then compounds this mistake with the assertion that both sides should rush their pieces and pawns into the center as quickly as possible. This is absurd.

Next Nimzovich, ibid., claims for development to make sense "...that all pieces be developed." This is an absurd comment and makes no provision that undeveloped pieces can serve a useful purpose without being developed. Again, in Magic, black never tried to develop his king rook until late in the game because it was needed for defensive purposes, not attacking purposes.

Nimzovich compounds his mistaken theories with the observation that only piece moves count as development. What about pawn moves that permit other pieces to move? Shouldn't they be considered "development"? According to Nimzovich, the following move sequence confers a developmental edge to black: 1.e4 Ne6 2.d4 Nf6. According to RM, white still has a lead in development based on his first-move advantage, and, specifically, his bishops are freed. This also counts as development. Nimzovich didn't have a clue that pawn moves can gain time.

On page 4 as well, Nimzovich, ibid., states, "...the pawn is not a fighting unit." This is highly suspect. Apparently Nimzovich has never heard of Noah's Ark trap or the phrase that connected passed pawns on the sixth are worth a rook. Aren't connected passed pawns a fighting unit?

Nimzovich then goes on to state that flank pawns shouldn't be moved. How about the Italian game, e.g., the Evans Gambit? Here in a romantic opening, white hits the king bishop with b4. What Nimzovich didn't realize is that b4 hits the opposing bishop, giving white the option of Bb2 without loss of time. To arbitrarily state we should not move flank pawns in the opening is just bad theory. However, all open positions should favor white because he has the first-move advantage. The white horses are faster than the black horses.

"Section 3 — To be ahead in development is the ideal to be aimed at." This is a highly dubious observation and applies only to situations where the center is blasted apart and both players are throwing their pieces into the center as fast as they can. But even here, Nimzovich completely overstates this point. What if black grabs a pawn and gives white a three-tempo lead in development in an open position, e.g., the Smith-Morra Gambit Accepted (1.e4 c5 2.d4 exd4 3.c3 dxc3 4.Nxc3)? Should players of the black pieces automatically avoid this position because of the open center? It is the quality of development that matters, not the quantity. A player whose pieces don't coordinate well may stand worse despite having a lead in development. Here again, king safety is often more important in open positions than a lead in development.

Some of Nimzovich's games are instructive, but not for the reasons Nimzovich gives. They show us that Nimzovich, like Steinitz before him, was an opportunist, not a theoretician. Consider the game Lee-Nimzovich, Ostend, 1907. The game proceeded: 1.d4 Nf6 2.Nf3 d6 3.Nbd2 Nbd7 4.e4 e5 5.c3 Be7 6.Bc4 O-O 7.O-O? Nimzovich never questioned this knee-jerk reaction. Just 7.Bb3 is +/=. Now black's cheap tactical trick doesn't work, i.e., 7...exd4 8.cxd4 d5 9.e5 +1-. It is not a good idea to use bogus examples to bolster one's theories.

Nimzovich doesn't distinguish between useful development and merely moving pieces away from their original squares. According to Nimzovich, black should never steer for this position because white is ahead in development or that white should never play the open variations of the Two Knights Defense because black may get the initiative.

The next statement is so absurd that it is laughable: "Never play to win a pawn while your development is yet unfinished." Nimzovich,

p. 18. I guess white should stop playing the Ng5 variation of the Two Knights Defense. Perhaps someone should tell world champions Bobby Fischer and Garry Kasparov to stop playing the black side of the Poisoned Pawn Sicilian, i.e., 1.e4 c5 2.Nf3 d6 3.d4 exd4 4.Nxd4 Nf6 5.Nc3 a6 6.Bg5 e6 7.f4 Qb6 8.Qd2 Qxb2!

"The beginner should decline the King's Gambit..." p.19, ibid. If Nimzovich had given the variation 1.e4 e5 2.f4 d5, his statement might make sense. Instead he gives the variation 1.e4 e5 2.f4 d6 3.Nf3 Nc6 4.Bc4? Be6 5.Bxe6 fxe6. No mention is made of 1.e4 e5 2.f4 d6 3.Nf3 Nc6 4.d4! In the only variation involving 2...d6, GM Korchnoi, writing for the *Encyclopedia of Chess Openings*, p. 190, evaluates the final position as +1-. Nimzovich is steering beginners toward losing positions.

Nimzovich, p. 19, ibid., says similar rubbish about the Evans Gambit. The Declined variation, 1.e4 e5 2.Nf3 Nc6 3.Bc4 Bc5 4.b4 Bb6, "4...13b6 has by no means lot, a tempo...4.b4...was unproductive...it does not bear a logical connection to the center." What about the resource Bb2? Does this have any relevance to the center?

Chapter Two on open files contains a great deal of relevance to chess. However, Chapters Seven and Eight are pretty trivial. Do we really need a chapter on pins and how we use them or, even less significant, "Discovered Check" and their utility? Any player who does not know what to do with a discovered check should take up checkers.

One of the faults of *My System* is the use of extraordinary, or otherwise impractical, examples. Nowhere is this better displayed than Nimzovich's work on pawn chains. First of all, it is doubtful that Nimzovich knew what a pawn chain was because he uses the term "chain" that clearly contradicts its meaning the way he describes them. According to Nimzovich, a pawn chain consists of "...two consecutive series of pawns abutting on one another in consecutive diagonals, divides the board diagonally into two halves:" Nimzovich, ibid., p.132. There can be no misunderstanding what Nimzovich meant by pawn chain. He used the term "series" in his definition. Series means more than two.

Precision in the use of terms is important, so the author is going to include a definition of chain as defined in *Webster's New International Dictionary of the English Language, Second Edition, Unabridged,* p.443. There chain is defined as "a series of links or rings." Another definition is "a series of things linked together." In both cases, the operative word is "series." A link would be the joining of two elements. Thus chains and links are different animals.

Nimzovich includes a very high percentage of diagrams that do not contain pawn chains in his chapter on pawn chains. This includes diagrams 111, 112, and 115-122, where pawn links, not pawn chains, are presented. In fact, Nimzovich does not include a single pawn chain in his chapter on pawn chains, except for the arbitrary examples given in connection with his definition! This is just low-quality work when the author doesn't even understand the terms he is using.

As far as pawn chains are concerned, the following game illustrates how to avoid pawn chains: Marcuson-Moody (Postal: 1994): 1.d4 g6 2.e4 Bg7 3.Nc3 e6 4.f4 Ne7 5.Nf3 O-O? (premature) 6.Be3 d5! 7.e5 b6 8.Bd3 Bb7 9.Qd2 Nd7 10.O-O (O-O-O c5) c5 11.Nb5 Nc8! 12.c4 a6 13.Nc3 Ne7 14.a4 Rc8 15.b3 f6 (see diagram)

16.exf6 Bxf6 17.Ne5 Nf5 18.Bxf5 exf5 19.cxd5 cxd4 20.Bxd4 Nxe5 21.Bxe5 Bxe5 22.fxe5 Qc7 23.Rf3 Qxe5 24.Re1 Qg7 25.Re6 b5

26.axb5 axb5 27.R3e3 f4 28.R3e5 Qc7 29.Nxb5 Qc5ch 30.Nd4 Bxd5
(centralization! — see diagram)

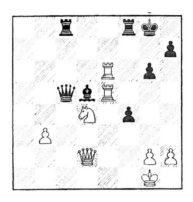

31.Qf2? Qc1ch! 32.Re1 Bxe6 33.Nxe6 Rf6 34.Qe2 Qe3ch 35.Qf2
Rxe6 36.Rxe3 fxe3 0-1

What can we learn from the game Marcuson-Moody? Looks are
deceiving. It seemed that all of white's moves were logical, but eventually he lost the thread in a tactical middle game. As a practical
matter, this is reason enough to give black's move order a try.

Steinitz's theories vary from interesting to wildly unsound and
should be viewed with skepticism. Nimzovich is viewed as one of the
greatest theoreticians in chess, but it is clear that many of his ideas
are outmoded, poorly formulated, trivial (like his chapter on discovered checks), and wildly off the mark. Nimzovich gave two clear examples of what he meant by pawn chains and promptly ignored his
own definition when presenting examples of this! That Nimzovich,
just like Steinitz, codified a series of incorrect theories seems true, but
this does not make him a scientist. It makes him an anecdotalist or,
perhaps, a Scientologist. Many of Nimzovich's key ideas are suspect,
his examples flawed, his rationale dubious, and his methodology un-
scientific. We would do well to consign his theories to a previous gen-
eration and move on.

CREEPER QUEEN MOVES

When we think of early queen moves, it is almost universally thought that the queen do something extravagant like going far afield and chasing after pawns. (The best way this works is if you are former world champions Bobby Fischer or Garry Kasparov on the black side of the Poisoned Pawn Sicilian!) But there is a known concept that applies in the opening: the "creeper" queen move of former world champion Botvinnik. We are told to use a piece of lesser value to guard a pawn; in other words, if a player has a choice between defending a pawn with a queen or a knight, he is supposed to defend it with the knight. This is a completely misguided principle. The pawn should be defended with whatever piece fits most consistently with a player's overall strategy. If your queen is doing nothing useful other than guarding a pawn, and your knight can be maneuvered to a better square, then the queen should guard the pawn.

The quintessential creeper queen move is Qe2 prior to the deployment of the king bishop in double king-pawn openings. Qe2 in the French defense is known as the Chigorin variation (1.e4 e6 2.Qe2); it is here that it is most poorly used! Thus after 1.e4 e6 2.Qe2 c5., black transposes to a Sicilian where white has nothing better than 3.f4 with about an equal game. The game presented below is, perhaps, the best example of a "creeper" queen move.

PETROFF DEFENSE: 1.E4 E5 2.NF3 NF6 3.QE2

The Petroff Defense (1.e4 e5 2.Nf3 Nf6) has a reputation of being solid and drawish, but 3.Qe2 upsets black's hopes of tranquility. White simply defends e4 with the threat of 4.Nxe5. (Note that black cannot copy white's moves indefinitely, i.e., Moody-NN skittles game: 3...Qe7 4.d4 d5 5.dxe5 dxe4 6.exf6 exf3 7.fxe7 fxe2 8.exf8ch +-).

In the game Moody-Klein, postal 1994 (see also, *Inside Chess*, v.10, issue 3, p.3), black tried the obvious 3...Ne6. GM Alburt, as an alternative, suggested that perhaps black could try a Philidor with 3...d6, but just 4.c3/d4 is +/=, and a Pirc with 3... g6 4.c3 Nbd7 4.d4 Bg7 5.Qc2 +/=. Black could also try to punish the alignment of king and queen, i.e., 3... Bc5 4.Nxe5 O-O 5.Nd3 Bb6 6.f3 Re8 7.Nf2 d5 8.d3 +/-.

The best try is 3...Ne6 to restrain 4.d4, but in Moody-Klein, we see 4.d4! simply offering a sham sacrifice (white is always guaranteed to regain the pawn). The only question though: Does it confer an advantage? (e.g., 4...Nxd4 5.Nxd4 exd4 6.e5 Nd5 7.Qe4 c6 8.Qxd4 d6! 9.Bc4 unclear.) It gets really weird after 4...Nxd4 5.Nxd4 exd4 6.e5 Nd5 7.Qe4 c6 (recommended by Fritz 8 after several minutes of thought) 8.Bc4! Bc5 9.Bxd5 cxd5 10.Qg4! (see diagram) with a complex position, which is as far from the placid waters of the Petroff as one can get!

11

At this point, the game Moody-Klein (Postal 1994) will be presented on a move-by-move basis with only the white moves displayed in the diagrams (as a concession to space requirements). In as much as the game involves a major theoretical novelty on move 4, a flawless middle game by white, and a unique ending, this seems justified. This is an exemplary example of how to use the first-move advantage all the way into the late endgame. The starting moves are 1.e4 e5 2.Nf3 Nf6 3.Qe2 (see diagram). This is how to use a creeper queen move to defend the pawn. According to a database of over three million games of Colin Leach, there were eight examples of this move order. The next move sequence is 3...Nc6 (trying to restrain 4.d4) 4.d4! (TN).

The idea of 3.Qe2 in the Petroff is so new that the editorial staff of *Inside Chess* did not even classify the move order as a Petroff! Despite this we believe that 3.Qe2 will become the main line of the Petroff eventually for one very good reason: It greatly increases white's ability to safely unbalance the position with the sham sacrifice 3...Nc6 4.d4! Once black accepts a busted pawn structure or a lag in development, white will have good endgame prospects in several variations. White's queen is very powerfully posted in the center on e4. White has good middle-game prospects so 3.Qe2 appears to be a new weapon against one of the oldest openings in chess.

Somewhat surprisingly, 4.d4! appears to be a TN — at least it was not in a database the author got from Colin Leach. The two choices that are tried here are 4.c3 and 4.g3. Neither looks good for equality. With regard to 4.c3, we see, Lanni-Bhat, Concord, 1993; Murillo-Barcarola, 1991; Vujovic-Bex, Biel, 1990; Bauer (2525)-Marciano (2470), French champ., Narbonne, 1997; and Lehtinen-Kobrin, European champ. U18, Tallin, 1997. In response to 4.c3, black scored 2½ out of 3 with 4... d5, the correct response. The game Bauer-Marciano is a fairly high-level test. White reacted cautiously with 5.d3 reinforcing the center. 5...dxe4 6.dxe4 a5? to anchor the bishop on b4? This has nothing to do with the game. Just 6.Bd6/O-O is good for at least equality, demonstrating that 5.c3 is a bust theoretically.

White can also meet 4.g3 with Bc5 as in Marino-Mader, Bolzano Open, 1991. This should be good for at least equality, e.g., 5.Bg2 d6 6.c3 Bg4 = to =/+. Cartagena (2505)-Braun (2502) proceeded with 4...g6 +/=.

Here is a peripheral line: 3.Qe2 (analysis below) Nc6 4.d4 Nxd4 5.Nxd4 exd4 6.e5 Nd4 7.Qe4 Nb4 8.a3 Nc6 9.Bd3 Be7 10.Bf4 b6 11.c3 dxc3 12.Nxc3 Bb7 13.Rd1 Na5 14.Ne4 +/-

Mr. Klein tried a different approach (see diagrams): 4...exd4 5.e5 Nd5 6.Qe4 Bb4ch?! (better than Nb6 +/=) 7.Bd2 Bxd2ch 8.Nbxd2 (White just picked up a tempo.) Nde7 9.O-O-O (White just picked up a second tempo should black decide to castle kingside.) d5! (Black fights for time.) 10.Qh4 Bf5 11.Nb3! (White finally regains his gambit pawn.) Ng6 12.Qxd8ch Rxd8 13.Nbxd4 Bg4?! (A waste of a critical tempo; black must improve here.) 14.Bb5! (Nothing more sophisticated than "winning" the pawn structure. This is still a purely developmental attack.) 14...Nge7 15.Rhe1 O-O 16.Nxc6 Nxc6 17.Bxc6 bxc6 18.Rd4! Bc8 (Mr. Klein doesn't like the look of 18...Bxf3) 19.gxf3 a5!? (This is a suggestion of GM Alburt. But — 20.c4! Rfe8 21.c5 +/-) 19.b4! (White freezes the queenside.) Rfe8 20.Re3! (Note the difference in the activity of their respective rooks, a residual effect of a lead in development) 20...f6 21.Kd2 fxe5?! (Alburt suggested Kf7, but it is still +/=) 22.Nxe5 Bb7 23.Nd3 Rxe3 24.Kxe3 Ba6 25.Kd2 Bb5 26.Rf4 Rf8? (Black's only hope is to swindle; this loses all options.) 27.Rxf8 Kxf8 28.Kc3 Ke7 29.Kd4 Kd6.

What we are about to see is one of the most unusual maneuvers in all of chess. The author knows of only one other naturally occurring "knight wheel" besides this one, the one annotated by Chernev in *Capablanca's Best Endings*, p.155. Instead of winning a pawn, white wins a "squeeze." 30.Nc5 Be2 31.Nb7ch Kd7 32.Kc5 Bb5 33.Na5 Ba4 34.Nb3 Bb5 35.Nd4 Ba4 36.c3 a6 37.a3 g6 38f4 h6 39.Nf3? Ke6 40.Nd4ch Kd7 41.g4 g5 42.f5 Bd1 43.Nxc6 Ke8 44.Ne5 Bb3 45.Kc6 Kd8 46.Kb7 Ba4 47.Kxa6 1-0.

Here are the diagrams with white to move in all forty-seven moves. 1.e4 e5 2.Nf3 Nf6 3.Qe2 Nc6 4.d4 (see diagram). This could be considered a complete game, not a brilliancy or, in the words of GM Anand, a well-played game.

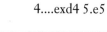

3...Nc6 4.d4

4....exd4 5.e5

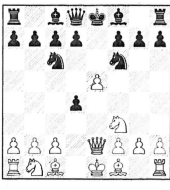

5...Nd5 6.Qe4

6...Bb4ch 7.Bd2

7...Bxd2ch 8.Nbxd2

8...Nde7 9.0-0-0

9...d5 10.Qh4

10...Bf5 11.Nb3

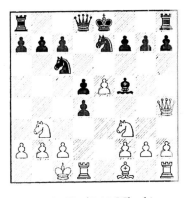

11...Ng6 12.Qxd8ch

12...Rxd8 13.Nbxd4

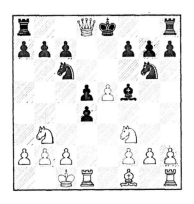

13...Bg4 14.Bb5

14...Ne7 15.Rhe1

15...O-O 16.Nxc6

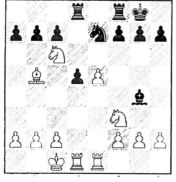

16...Nxc6 17.Bxc6

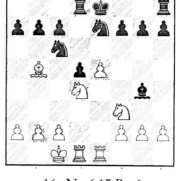

17...bxc6 18.Rd4

18...Bc8 19.b4!

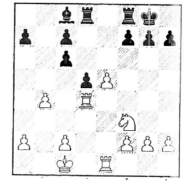

19...Rfe8 20.Re3!

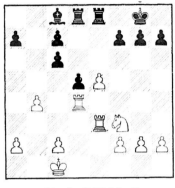

20...f6 21.Kd2

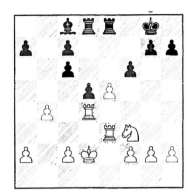

21...fxe5 22.Nxe5

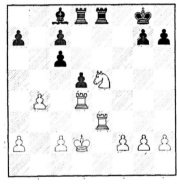

22... Bb7 23.Nd3

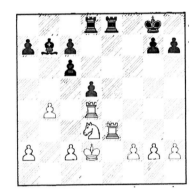

23...Rxe3 24.Kxe3

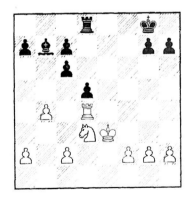

24...Ba6 25.Kd2

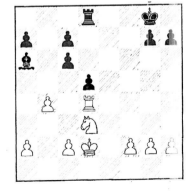

25...Bb5 26.Rf4

26...Rf8 27.Rxf8ch

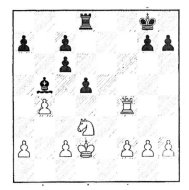
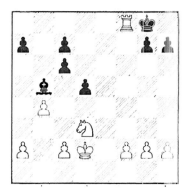

27...Kxf8 28.Kc3

28...Ke7 29.Kd4

29...Kd6 30.Nc5

30...Be2 31.Nb7ch

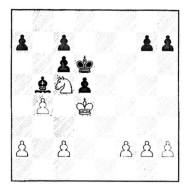
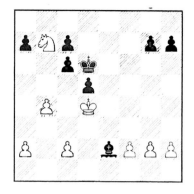

31...Kd7 32.Kc5   32...Bb5 33.Na5

 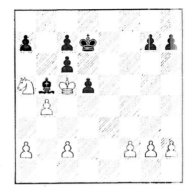

33...Ba4 34.Nb3   34...Bb5 35.Nd4

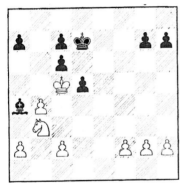 

35...Ba4 36.c3   36...a6 37.a3

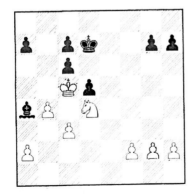 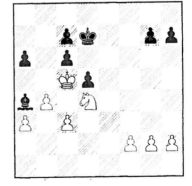

37...g6 38.f4

38...h6 39.Nf3

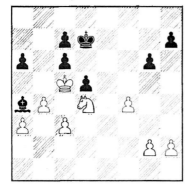

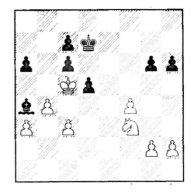

39...Ke6 40.Nd4ch

40...Kd7 41.g4

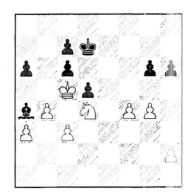

41...g5 42.f5

42...Bd1 43.Nxc6

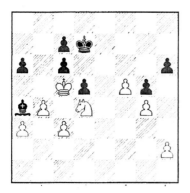

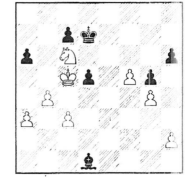

43...Ke8 44.Ne5

44...Bb3 45.Kc6

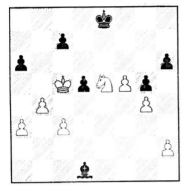

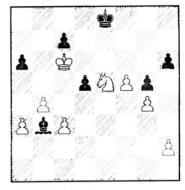

45...Kd8 46.Kb7

46...Ba4 47.Kxa6 1-0

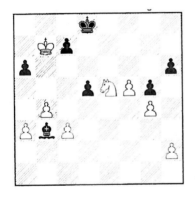

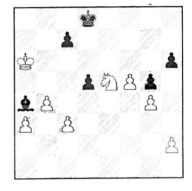

MAGIC ODDS

The starting position is called Magic because it is a sleight of mind rather than a sleight of hand. On the surface, it appears that white has an overpowering position based on conventional concepts of classical chess. According to the principles of universal chess, all the white pieces are on the wrong squares. For example, the minors block the advance of the c or f pawns, and, once the center is closed, the rooks are useless on e1 and d1. What is deceptive about this position is how quickly white can stand worse with completely logical moves, e.g., 2.Kb1, 3.Bg5, 4.Bh4, 5.e5 =/+, and just like that, white is fighting for a draw because black can castle queenside and has two center pawns. Based on this one line of analysis, it is clear that once black gets two pawns to the six before white gets in d5 or e5, the position is balanced. The better player will win.

Here are a few of the concepts addressed by the author:

1) Knights before bishops. Not necessarily.
2) Castle early and often. If the king is a fixed target, this may lead to a loss very quickly.
3) Avoid early queen moves. If the queen can be developed to a useful square, it is a piece, just like any other piece, and we should not have special rules for her,
4) Avoid moving the same piece twice in the opening. Black simply ignored this principle in order to place his minors on their ideal squares.
5) Doubled and isolated pawns are weak and should be avoided. You will see that the author deliberately ignored this principle in order to force white to part with bishop for knight in order to defend a weak pawn. Black, at the same time, increased the scope of his bishops. Black also achieved his goal

of increasing his pawn presence opposite the white king so that he could constrain the white king bishop and turn into a bad bishop for the entire game. The entire difference between black's position being a win instead of draw was the respective power of the light-squared bishops.

6) Center pawns are desirable. Not if they are overly committal and deprive the user of other options:

The author defines five kinds of space:
1) Interior space: Region behind a player's pawns
2) Exterior space: Region ahead of a player's pawns
3) Controlled space: Ability to deny access of enemy pieces to key squares
4) Uncontrolled space: Overextended pawns
5) Future space: The unstoppable ability of certain pawns to advance and gain extra interior space.

When computers were first programmed to play chess, they had minimal computing abilities and, thus, were very weak. To draw an analogy: Think of chess programming as a sieve. During the early stages of chess programming, the sieve was very coarse, and there were very few holes. Then the big holes were plugged, and, instead, a whole lot of smaller holes were created. Each one of the smaller holes was then plugged, and this created an exponential increase in yet smaller holes. No matter how sophisticated computers get, they always have the sieve problem.

When computers hit equivalent positions, they are blind. This requires the computer to flip a programming coin. For instance, in Magic, increasing the activity of its rooks caused the computer to "think" that those were the most active moves when, in fact, almost anything else was better. The way to defeat supercomputers of the future, it is necessary to bombard them with equivalent positions and then force the computer to flip a programming coin each time to evaluate the position accurately. Here again I seriously doubt that any computer would evaluate many of the Magic positions with black correctly. In order to do this, the computer would need vast additional programming, which would diminish severely its aggressive nature and make it an inviting target for tactical players. If a computer cannot evaluate the final positions accurately, how is it going to know which moves to make in complex situations?

The sieve analysis has significant application in the odds game. Even with an extremely tight sieve with billions of little holes, tiny drops of water flow through the sieve. They connect downstream as bigger drops. These bigger drops combine with bigger drops to produce a trickle of water. The trickle becomes a stream, the stream becomes a river, and the river becomes a flood.

If we examine the odds game, what you would find would be billions of tiny drops of water (the computer's analytical processes) appearing as a massive flood fifty-three moves later. The "losing" move, 54.bxc3, is the result of billions of drops of water combining downstream to create a flood. The "winning" move, 54...c4, is the flood hidden in the position starting with the first drop of water appearing downstream, the move sequence 2.Kb1 d6. In quiet positions, computer "blunders" will be demonstrated 99 percent of the time to be the end process of twenty-five to fifty positional moves where the computer had to analyze equivalent positions. The other 1 percent will be simple blunders where the computer has major programming problems. In two games that the author played against Fritz 8, it claimed a draw by repetition seven to eight moves ahead but refused to demonstrate the draw by actually moving its pieces, so it ran itself out of time in drawn positions. This is clearly a programming bug that will appear from time to time even in mainframe computers. If memory serves, didn't Hitech walk into a checkmate in two moves that stumped even its programmer, former correspondence world champion Dr. Hans Berliner?

To show how deadly computers will be on the black side of the Sicilian Defense, RM played a Sicilian with competitive intuition against the Fritz 8, got a huge "attack" in an opposite wing attack, where RM castled queenside and Fritz castled kingside. Right at the start of the middle game, when RM had a bishop on g5, the computer put "the question" to the bishop with h6. We were playing the game at game/90.

Without thinking, white knew that the position was a win for black with either an exchange on f6 or a retreat of the bishop. RM instantly played h4 with a passive piece sacrifice. Here is why computers will be so deadly in opposite wing attacks in the Sicilian. For the first two minutes, black decided it had a clear win by accepting the sacrifice, but then something instructive happened: The computer's evaluation of the sacrifice made it realize that the sacrifice was sound, i.e., it started off the evaluation as something like -1.75. Three minutes into its calculation, this evaluation changed to -6.

The next thing that happened is why white can never castle queenside in the Sicilian in the main lines. Suddenly the computer's evaluation of its advantage went from accepting the piece sacrifice (something any grandmaster would avoid doing in seconds) as the best choice based on its evaluation algorithm to a queenside attack having a better evaluation. Just like that, the Fritz 8 ignored the piece, got an overwhelming attack on the c-file, and crushed his king in a few moves. Modern mainframe computers would probably ignore the piece sacrifice in a matter of seconds.

If black maneuvers patiently behind his own lines and gets just enough space to maneuver his pieces to better squares and keep the center fluid (over the long run), it may require deception to win, e.g., pretend to prepare castling and never castle or threaten to open the center and not do so for twenty moves. This will be a very effective strategy: Always lie against computers when playing chess. This will be less successful against human opponents, who will tend to play more aggressively. Only extensive practical results will reveal if this is a good strategy against human opponents.

Sphinx Legend-Moody 1 hour/move: Starting Position
1.e4 Nf6 2.d4 Ng8 3.Nf3 Nf6 4.Nc3 Ng8 5.Bc4 Nf6 6.Bf4 Ng8
7.Qd2 Nf6 8.O-O-O Ng8 9.Rhe1 (see diagram)

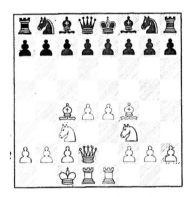

(At this point, black flipped a coin and guessed right; without thinking, he played 1... e6. (see diagram).) The other choice 1...d6 loses instantly. Why?[1]

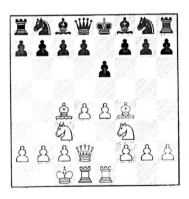

Have white play 1.d3 and then 2.d4 so that black can play 9....e6 10...d6. Why is 10...d6 forced?[2] If we put a pawn on d6 and have black play 1...e6 artificially closing the center. (What is meant by "artificially closing the center"? [3]) Can you guess in the game Fritz 8-Moody 120'/40 (F-M) what Fritz played on its very first "real" move?[4] In response to 1...e6, Sphinx Legend played 2.Kb 1 ?? Why did the computer play this?[5] (see diagram)

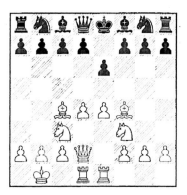

2...d6 (forced — see diagram below). Now white has the best winning "try" in that position. What is meant by "try"[6]?

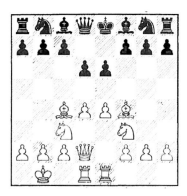

It is now too late for white to see "over the horizon." What is meant by "horizon?"[7]

Now that the computer has squandered its advantage, it decides to "attack" 3.Bg5 (see diagram).

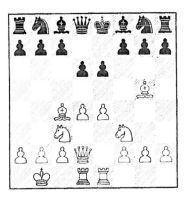

Within the context of "conventional" chess (What does the author mean by "conventional" chess?)[8], GM Lev Alburt suggested 3...Be7 to ease black's cramped position. What is meant by "cramped" position?[9] The author played 3...f6 (see diagram below) because he had a winning plan already, i.e., walk his king to a8 and just attack the cornered king What is meant by a "cornered" king?[10]

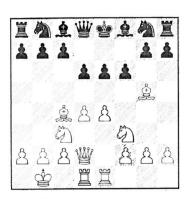

Sphinx has a number of retreat squares. Why doesn't white play 4.Bxf6?[11] Probably a better retreat square than the one chosen by the computer would be 4.Be3 to prevent black's next move. Instead the computer makes the "logical" choice 4.Bh4 (see diagram below) to threaten a disguised attack on the queen. What is meant by a "disguised" attack?[12] Black must defend against the attack. Which is the best way to avoid the disguised attack, 4...Qd7, 4...Ne7 or 4...Be7?[13]

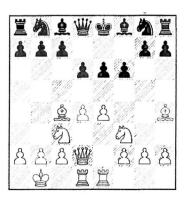

Black, without thinking, immediately played 4...Be7 (see diagram below) just to discourage 5.e5 (see Magic Answers at the end of the book for an explanation.)

One can already sense that the computer is losing the thread of the game. It plays "planlessly." What is meant by the phrase "planlessly"?[14] Lacking any real plan, the Sphinx Legend decided to try 5.Qe3 (see diagram).

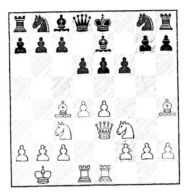

The best plan for white in this position is to play for the f4 break. Thus best is 5.d5 e5 6.Ng1 Nh6 7.f4 Nf7, and white has a tough nut to crack. In some variations, black may even castle kingside, with the idea of b5 offering a pawn to go after the white king. It is clear that it is very dangerous for white to accept the pawn sacrifice because the white king is insecure. But if white avoids accepting the sacrifice by retreating to d3, black follows with Bd7/b4, bumping the knight and a5/Na6 with a powerful attack.

5...Bd7 (see diagram below). Why not knights before bishops, e.g., 5...Nd7 or 5...Nc6?[15] Black plays a "prophylactic" move. What is meant by this?[16]

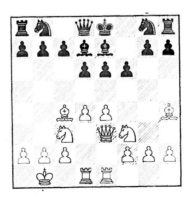

Now the computer embarks on a dubious "plan.. It decides to retreat its king bishop eventually to a2, but it is not a good idea to weaken its queenside. The general rule when facing an impending pawn storm against the castled king is to avoid moving pawns away from in front of the king. The reason is that this makes pawn levers far more effective. From now on, white must be alert to the possibility of b5/b4. 6.a3? (see diagram).

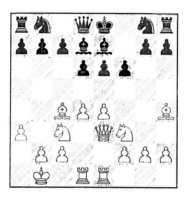

Black immediately takes advantage of this loss of time. Any white advantage has disappeared, and in as few as 6!! moves, black completely repudiates white's chances, at least on a practical level as this game illustrates. What is meant by a practical advantage as opposed to a theoretical advantage?[17] Black now has time for 6...Nh6 (see diagram).

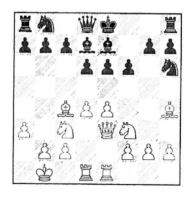

The queen bishop is clearly needed now on the c1/h6 diagonal. Allowing black to get in the maneuver Nh6/Nf7 is very bad for white's chances. 7.Qd2? (see diagram below). It is incredible to the author that after an hour's computation, the Sphinx doesn't at least play 7.d5. What is the computer trying to do?

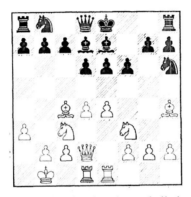

Now black does exactly what he planned all along, reposition the knight to f7. Now we see why he avoided 3...Be7. His combination of king knight, in tandem with the king bishop, is a very powerful offensive and defensive disposition of his pieces. Why was it better to play 3...f6, instead of 3 ...Nf6, defending against the attack on his queen and developing a piece with the "classical" square for the knight?"[18] Now black gets to play the continuation he planned with move 3...f6. The obvious choice now is 7...Nf7 (see diagram).

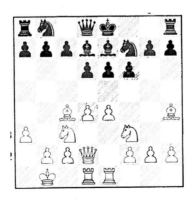

Now at long last, white has an inspiration: 8.d5 (see diagram below). This is about four moves too late but better late than never. It seems highly unlikely that the computer, at long last, sees the value of an early d5/f4.

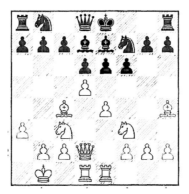

Black now closes the center. (What is meant by closing the center?[19]) And it is clear that the pawn on f6 plays a vital role in black's defense. Now the intended f4/fxe5 can be met with fxe5, recapturing the e-pawn with the f-pawn, without weakening the center with dxe5. Black plays the obvious 8...e5 (see diagram below), a resource he has had ever since move two, 2...d6.

Again after an hour's thought, the Sphinx Legend coughs up 9.Qe3? (see diagram below). This turkey clearly shows now that the computer didn't play d5 with the idea of fixing the e-pawn and then attacking it with f4; otherwise it would have chosen something like Bg3/Nh4/f4. What is going on in its pea brain?

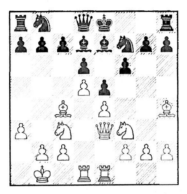

Black now commences a minuet starting with 9...Qc8 (see diagram below). A human competitor might have had an inkling that black was up to no good. Black now begins to assume the initiative. It is entirely possible that black is better here already. A question that may never be answered is, "What was the losing move by white?"

When I described the starting position to the computer programmer NM Eric Schiller, he accused me of trying to "torture" the computer. What will really drive computers bonkers a million years from now is that I predict that white is in zugzwang on the first move!

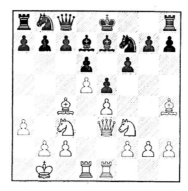

In view of Sphinx's next move, it would be tough to say whether it is being placed on the rack or being drawn and quartered — 10.Rd2? (see diagram below). It is baffling that the Sphinx can think for over an hour and still play something this bad. So far none of black's moves make any sense as far as the Sphinx's programming is concerned. Presumably lacking any long term planning, the Sphinx decides to increase the scope of its rooks (see Magic Answers #5). 10.Rd2 is a typical "computer" move.[20]

Now the author shows his utter contempt for his opponent and plays 10...Nd8 (see diagram below), heading for b7 and c5. Perhaps it is more accurate to play a6/b5 first, but the author was convinced that the Sphinx, by virtue of its play until now, was clueless.

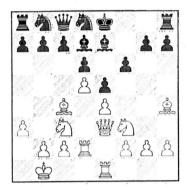

Next white plays the mysterious move, 11.h3 (see diagram below). Apparently the Sphinx decides to redeploy the bishop to g1 (?), but even this is not 100 percent clear. This is as good as anything.

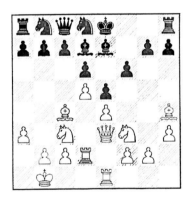

Black just continues to build on his initiative with 11...a6 (see diagram below). This plan, in other circumstances, could be met with 12.a4. Why is 12.a4 bad here?[21] One of the most significant aspects of this game was that black had a plan before he had even played his first move. That plan was never ignored, either for tactical or strategic reasons. The fulfillment of that plan was 0-1:108.

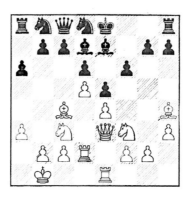

Now black's plan is crystal clear: He intends to follow with 12...b5. White is now left with a difficult choice. White now makes a "mysterious" rook move, 12.R2d1 (see diagram below). One wonders how the computer's analysis and evaluation algorithms could be so screwed up. Once again we see the failure of any long-range planning.

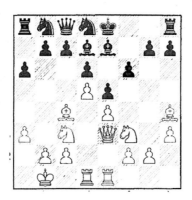

Having said "A", black now says "B" — 12...b5 (see diagram below). Black simply proceeds as if white's plans are meaningless. Using nothing but intuition, he merely places his pawns and pieces on squares where they belong.

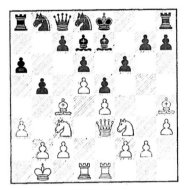

White now makes a decision that will haunt it for the rest of the game: 13.Bb3 (see diagram below) instead of 13.Bd3. This is what is known as a "bad" bishop. Why?[22] Playing against a bad bishop is a fairly refined example of positional play that is easy to understand but much more difficult to implement. Here, for example, white tries to keep black's king bishop "bad" but fails miserably. Black, on the other hand, gives a textbook case of how to play against a bad bishop.

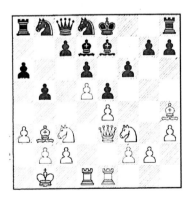

Black now continues to build for the attack with 13...Nb7 (see diagram below) with the "hit" Nc5, going after the bishop on b3 with the very real threat of 14...Nxb3, winning the minor exchange and disrupting white's king pawn shelter. What is meant by a "hit"?[23] What is meant by pawn shelter?[24]

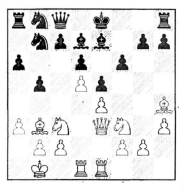

White now, belatedly, plays 14.8a2 (see diagram below), anticipating black's next move. A question might reasonably be asked: "Since the computer knew that black would play Nc5 at some point, why did it play Ba2 in two moves?" This makes absolutely no sense. Again it makes you wonder how the computer's algorithms cause it to make the decisions it makes.

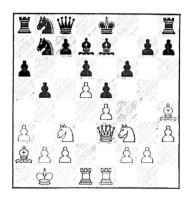

Black now embarks on the plan that he has been angling for since the first move, 14...Kd8! (see diagram below). What would be depressing for the computer (if it had emotions) is that black's king can stay in the center, walk to the queenside, or walk to the kingside, and there is nothing that white can do to stop it. Black, however, intended to place his king on a8.

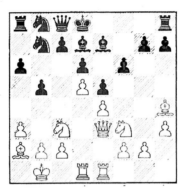

It sure took the Sphinx long enough to realize that it needed h4 for the knight in order to prepare f4. The computer, belatedly, played 15.Bg3 (see diagram).

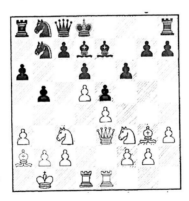

At this point, black plays the most beautiful move of the game, 15...Be8! (see diagram below). This move does everything one could ask of a move. It surveys the entire board; this is a classic example of domination. This bishop dominates the board from now until the end of the game. In fact, the only difference in this game being a win, loss, or draw is due to the respective power of each player's light-squared bishop. The rest of the pieces are in dynamic balance, but the black queen bishop is so much more powerful than white's king bishop, it negates every other potential advantage that white has. At this point, it seems pretty clear that black is better.

At last white finally threatens to play f4! White "decided" that now that the black bishop has abandoned the c8/h3 diagonal, that it is safe to play Nf5. White prepares this with 16.Nh4 (see diagram).

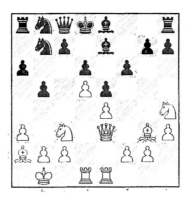

Black continues apace; thus 16...Nc5 (see diagram below) is a logical follow-up. Black seeks to provoke the weakening move b4, bumping the knight. What is meant by "bumping" the knight?[25] Why is b4 a bad move for white?[26] Black is very careful during the following maneuvering to make sure that in the event of b4, the knight has a retreat square on the 7th. Why is this necessary?[27]

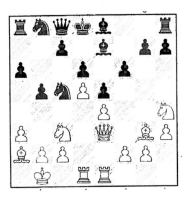

White has the inkling of a plan, beginning with 18.Nf5 (see diagram below) with the idea of 19.f4, 20.fxe5 at last getting counterplay on the kingside. What is meant by counterplay?[28] This natural and obvious move forces the bishop back to f8. What is wrong with the idea of 18...Bd7 19.Nxe7 Kxe7 getting rid of the bad bishop?[29]

Black's next move, 18...Bf8, is forced. What is meant by forced?[30] Although the retreat of the bishop to f8 is forced and obvious, it also stifles white's counterplay on the kingside.

The next move by white, 18.13h2 (see diagram below), is the first hint that white intends to reposition the bishop. If this is the case, here is the minimal depth of search by the computer: 1) Bh2. 2) f4, 3) fxe5, 4) Bg1, 5) Qe2, 6) BxcS. It is difficult to know precisely that the Sphinx Legend came up with this idea.

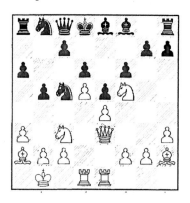

It is amazing how much maneuvering room there is on the 7th and the 8th if the king is treated as a piece like any other piece. Thus black's next move, 18...Qd7 (see diagram below), is a multipurpose move. Black vacates a square for the king and, at the same time, prepares to meet the sham "threat" 19.Qg3. The g7 square is, at that point, doubly attacked and doubly defended. This avoids the potentially weakening move g6. Why would 18...g6 be considered a "weakening" move?[31]

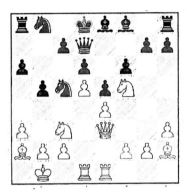

At long last, white plays 19.f4! (see diagram below). This move has been on the computer's brain a long time before it was actually played. White's intent is clear, i.e., to open lines for its rooks. What is meant by opening lines?[32] Why are open lines good for an attacker and bad for a defender?[33]

45

Black prepares for the inevitable opening of the f-file with the move sequence in mind, 19...Kc8 (see diagram below), 20...Qd8, 21...Nbd7, 22...Nf6 to block the soon to be opened f-file. Any plans by white to exploit the f-file are dashed even before they become a gleam in the Sphinx's eye. One of the easiest ways to thwart an opponent's plans is to know what they are. Why is this a critical part of organizing an appropriate defense?[34]

The next move by white, 20.Ng3? (see diagram below), is a mysterious "computer" move. Why is this a mystery move?[34] Regardless of the Sphinx's thinking, 20.fxe5 demands to be played. This just gives black the luxury of being able to close the f-file with a tempo to spare. What is meant by a tempo?[35]

Black continues to rearrange his pieces with 20...Qd8 (see diagram below). Black intends the simple follow-up, 21...Nbd7/22...Nf6, even before the rooks get to the f-file. Why was black concerned about the white "threat" to occupy the open f-file with its rooks?[36]

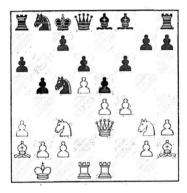

At long last, white plays the move it should have played circa move 7: 21.fxe5 (see diagram below). While desirable from the standpoint that nothing else makes sense, one has to wonder why white didn't play this on the previous move.

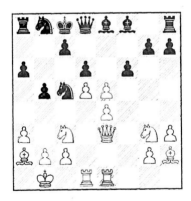

Black has two choices here. There are competing chess principles here. Imagine that you are a computer and have to choose between 21...dxe5 and 21...fxe5 (see diagram below). Which seems better? On the one hand, 21...dxe5 frees the bad bishop, but on the other hand, with 21...fxe5 black maintains symmetry and captures toward the center. This is a no-brainer; black played 21...fxe5 instantly (see note to black's twentieth move).

White now follows an obvious strategy, i.e., rooks belong on open files. Why is this a good idea in general?[37] Why can't white invade on the 7th rank here?[38] White has no better strategy at this point than 22.Rf1 (see diagram).

Black now plays the strategy he planned all along, i.e., 22...Nbd7 (see diagram below). Why didn't black choose 22...Ncd7?[39] One of the things the reader will soon realize is how many of black's moves are "obvious" in hindsight.

White's next move, 23.Rf3 (see diagram below), is consistent with its previous play. This has as an added benefit: the very real need to defend along the third in the subsequent play. Yes, white does indeed need a rook on the third defensively, appearances to the contrary.

Black has already stated his intention to block the f-file with 23...Nf6 (see diagram below). You will note that white is two tempos too slow to do anything with the f-file. First of all, it is blocked, and second of all, there was never any threat to play 24.R1f1/25.Rxf8. Why not?[40]

Now it is abundantly clear that white views the knight on c5 to be a threat. White's next move is 24.Qe2 (see diagram below). This is necessary to free the g1/a7 diagonal, but more consistent is 24.R1f1 immediately and pray.

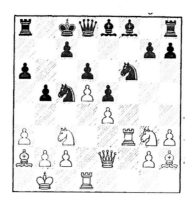

The black king is almost to a8 and plays the obvious, 24...Kb7 (see diagram below). A human player about now would be feeling very ill. He/she would have seen a nine tempo lead in development evaporate and might be prepared to lash out with 24.R1f1/25.Rxf6. Why is this a bad idea?[41]

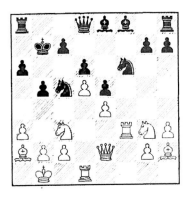

You will note the almost complete lack of any real ability for white to plan anything. Expanding in the center is impossible, gaining counterplay on the queenside with b4 is a chronic disaster, and black blocks the only open file on the kingside. Nevertheless, white's next move, 25.R1f1 (see diagram below), is as good as anything. White waits patiently the whole game for a misstep by black. This is why computers are such dangerous foes. They have no emotions and don't get discouraged. There is a classic story of former world champion Garry Kasparov slamming down a piece and glaring at the monitor when he played Deep Blue, a mainframe computer, in a match. This tactic might have cowed a human opponent. Of course, the computer could have "cared" less.

Now storm clouds begin to gather around the white king. With 25...Rb8 (see diagram below), black's plan is painfully obvious: just occupy the b-file and threaten a pawn storm on the queenside attacking the cornered king (see #10).

At long last, the computer can be demonstrated quite clearly to be on the defensive. It played 26.Bg1 (see diagram below). It can be said with certainty that white has given up any hope of an initiative. At this point, in theory the position is -+; in practice it is -/+ (see # 17).

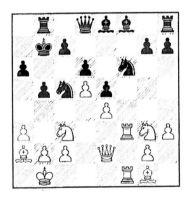

Black now plays the move he intended before he made his first (!!) move, 26... Ka8 (see diagram below). Although black's king is on a8 in a corner, why isn't it a "cornered" king?[42]

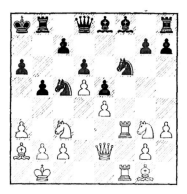

You will now note that white plays a waiting move, 27.Bf2 (see diagram below). What is meant by a waiting move?[43] In a closed position such as this, time has less significance than the possibility that black might mishandle the attack. Actually this is almost a "human" move.

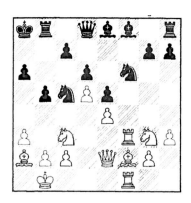

Black calmly proceeds with the attack, i.e., 27...Rb7 below. Why not 27...Rb6?[44] If black meets 28.b4 with 28...Na4, should white play 28.Bxb6, winning the exchange?[45]

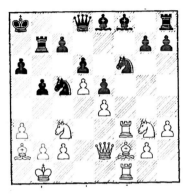

At this point, we again find a situation where white has no useful moves. Perhaps it should entertain the idea of Rg1/Nf5/g4. White thus plays the surprising move (to the author), 28.Rg1 (see diagram below), which is not as mysterious as it originally appeared. My guess is that the Sphinx Legend is seeing at least 10-12 plies ahead at 1 move/hour. What is meant by a ply?[46]

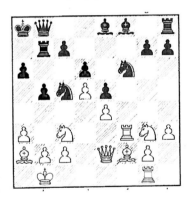

Black now plays a move that is sometimes described as "simple but strong," i.e., 28...Qb8. This sets up a battery. What is meant by a battery?[47] Why is the battery in this position so powerful?[48]

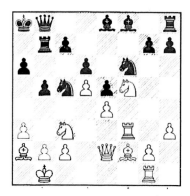

If the author were not playing a computer, he might have stepped into a clever trap, but computers will try to lie but fail miserably at it. With 29.Nf5 (see diagram below), the Sphinx Legend just told me that 29...b4 is not a threat. This is just one of the many positions where tactical shots blossom just below the surface. This is the kind of game common to professionals where all the tactics are in the notes, not actually played over the board. Why isn't 29...b4 a threat?[47]

Black just ignores the tactics and builds for the attack with 29...a5 with a pawn storm. What is meant by a pawn storm?[48] Why is a pawn storm necessary to attack the white king?[49]

At this point, the Sphinx Legend at last sees serious threats of b4 bumping the knight when, is some variations, e4 is hanging and/or the threats along the b-file are real. What is meant by hanging?[50] With 30.Bxc5 (see diagram below), it is clear that white sees bona fide threats against either the e-pawn and/or threats along the b-file. Without actually calculating why this is true, do you believe the computer was justified in "panicking," or are the threats legitimate?[51]

One of the unusual characteristics of this game is the small number of "forced" moves there are in the position, i.e., 30...dxc5 (see diagram below). What is meant by a forced move?[52]

The Sphinx Legend now sees a plan it must have decided several moves earlier. Clearly the Sphinx Legend never regarded 31...b4 in this position as a threat as long as the knight has the retreat square 31.Nd1 (see diagram below). Why isn't b4 a threat in this position?[53]

Black continues to box in the bishop with 31...c4! (see diagram below). Doubled, isolated pawns are to be avoided, yet black never feared them. What was the positional justification in allowing his pawn structure to be dismembered?[54] As a general rule, it is a good idea not to allow doubled pawns (what is meant by doubled pawns?[55]) and/or pawn "islands." What is meant by the phrase pawn island?[56]

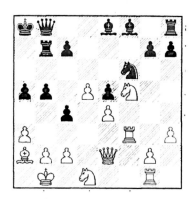

White tries to create threats before black has time to capitalize on his next move. However, after 32.g4 (see diagram below), white makes committal pawn pushes on the kingside, which create other problems.

At this point, black struck at the center with 32...c6 (see diagram below). The point is that white cannot play either 33.dxc6? Why is this good for black?[57] Nor is it desirable to play d6. Why?[58] In the endgame, opposite-colored bishops may give white vague drawing chances, but here in the middle game, the opposite-colored bishops favor the attacker. Why does the presence of opposite-colored bishops favor the attacker in this position?[59]

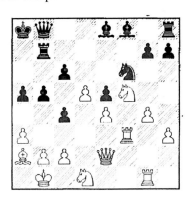

White's position hangs by a thread. Due to the very real threat of 33...cxd5 (why is this a threat?)[59], white stays on message with 33.g5, bumping the knight before black can get in cxd5 (see diagram).

This concession by white, giving up control of the h5 square, allows black's next move, 33...Nh5 (see diagram below). The knight is going to land on f4, where it hits the white queen.

White steps out of the threatened 34...Nf4 with an attack on the a5 pawn without loss of time. What is meant by "loss of time"?[60] White played 34.Qd2 (see diagram below), trying to force black to make the committal pawn move 34...a4. What is wrong with 34...a4 defending the pawn and preparing to attack the white king?[61]

Black releases pressure on the b-file to avoid weakening his pawn levers. However, 34...Ra7 (see diagram below) comes with a price tag (see white's next move).

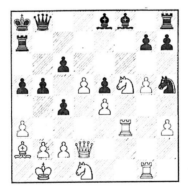

Computers usually will try to tell the truth. Here, for example, white just told me that there are no longer any threats against b2 because it played 35.Nf2 (see diagram). Both sides try to impose their will on the game. What is meant by "will" of the game?[62] For example, black insists on a queenside attack and white kingside counterplay to slow the attack. Whoever gets there first will probably win.

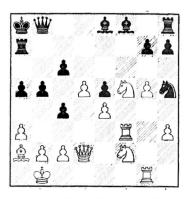

Black prepares to tamp down the kingside threats with the multipurpose move 35...g6 (see diagram).

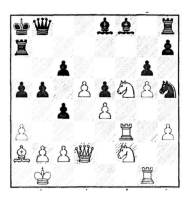

White plays the most desirable retreat, 36.Ne3 (see diagram below). White decided that the knight on f4 is too strong and prepares to greet it when it gets to f4. Why doesn't white want the knight to stay on f4?[63]

Black seeks simplification with 36...Nf4, but this is a double-edged sword. The fewer the number of minor pieces, the greater the likelihood that this will wind up as a heavy piece ending. Why should black avoid this?[64]

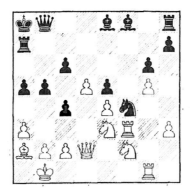

White has been planning its next move for some time, 37.Ng2 (see diagram below). White has managed to simplify the position in order to slow black's increasing positional pressure on the queenside.

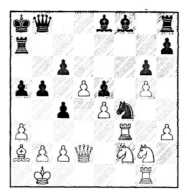

Sometimes during the course of a game in similar situations, black might preserve the piece in order to try to complicate, but to retreat the knight is bad, and allowing Nxf4 is even worse. Thus, black accedes to the exchange of minors with 37...Nxg2 (see diagram).

White makes a move that is desirable from the standpoint of material but makes two major positional concessions in order to achieve it. What are those two major positional concessions that white makes with 38.Rxg2?[65] (See diagram.)

Black makes a surprising redeployment with 38...Bg7 (see diagram below) with the rationale that the queenside attack needs time to mellow, but white's kingside threats must be attended to first. Allowing the knight to sit uncontested on f6 allows too many potential tactical shots.

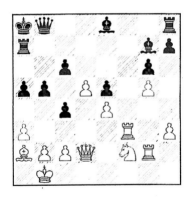

White goes after the f6 square with 39.Ng4 (see below). You will note that as both sides "soften up" the king side by provoking pawn advances, both sides have availed themselves of the squares they get. In the words of former world champion Bobby Fischer, "You have to give squares to get squares."

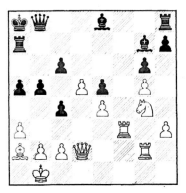

At this point, black makes a surprising move, 39...Qb6 (see diagram below), leaving the e-pawn high and dry. What was the main point of 39...Qb6?[66]

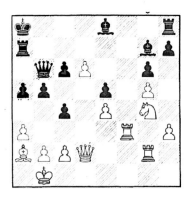

At this point, white decides to relieve the pawn tension. Clearly 40.dxc6 is bad, and white does not have time here for 40.Nf6 Why can't white play 40.Nf6 here?[67] White has not benefited from the pawn tension c6/d5. What is meant by pawn tension?[68] White makes the committal move 40.d6?! (see diagram below). Although a passed pawn on the sixth is usually desirable, why isn't this a good square for the pawn?[69]

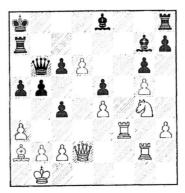

Black needs no invitation, so 40...c5 (see diagram below) was played instantly to preserve the strong bishop.

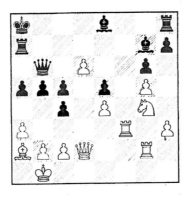

At long last, white begins to create real problems for black with 41.Nf6 (see diagram below). Without this move, white is simply worse. This requires precise play by black.

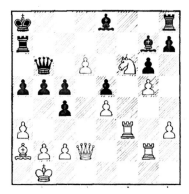

Black now decides to hold off with the immediate Bxf6 to see how white will meet the threat against the e-pawn with 41...Bc6 (see diagram below). Black threatens 42... Bxf6/Bxe4.

The lack of communication between the queen and e5 pawn and the fact that d6 is no longer hanging prompts white's next move, 42.Qc3 (see diagram below).

Black finally is forced to play one of the few tactical shots he has played the entire match, i.e. 42...Rd8 (see below). This was an intuitive sacrifice that was played quickly. What were the variations that black saw with his intuition?[70]

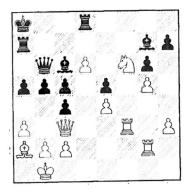

White avoided all the tactics and played the quiet 43.Rd2 (see diagram below), the most tenacious defense. You might be interested to know that the Sphinx Legend, after over an hour, plays the right continuation but that the Fritz 8 plays the wrong continuation after several minutes' computation.

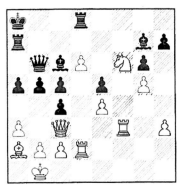

Black has waited to see if the tactics work and now simplifies the center with 43...Bxf6 (see diagram).

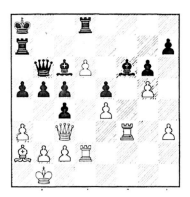

White could play the inferior 44.gxf6, but this leaves it with too many weak pawns, so 44.Rxf6 is better (see diagram below). There is also tactical justification for this, which white never utilized.

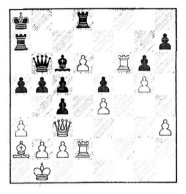

At long last, black clears the center of pawns in anticipation of white's next move. So black continues with 44...Bxe4 (see diagram).

White has to try to keep up with the exchange of pawns. Rxd6 is a threat, so white plays, 45.Qxe5 (see diagram).

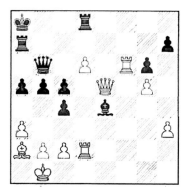

Black now threatens to box in the rook with 45...Bf5 (see diagram below). Hindsight is 20/20. Here, for example, is the right time to pitch the d-pawn with 46.d7 but after 46...Qb7-/+ because of the weak back rank.

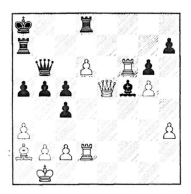

White plays the natural retreat 46.Qg3 (see diagram below) with the idea of defending the h-pawn and defending along the third.

Black pounces on the d7 square with 46...R7d7. At this point, the author knew that black was the only side with winning chances. It is surprising, in one sense, how quickly black makes progress from the position after 46...R7d7 (see diagram below) until one realizes that black is playing actively with four pieces (queen, two rooks, and his king — in this position, the king counts as a piece). Also his bishop stalemates a white rook, so he is playing the middle game as if he were two pieces and the exchange up!

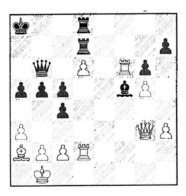

White decides to defend the h-pawn and anchor the pawn on g5; hence white played 47.h4 (see diagram).

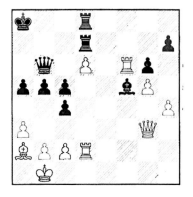

Black, at this point, plays a quiet move that has tactical justification, 47...a4! (see diagram below). What is meant by a "quiet" move?[71] See the note to black's fifty-fourth move to see the tactical justification of this move.

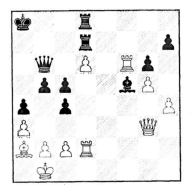

White struggles to keep his only two active pieces posted in the center. Why is it important for white to control the center with 48.Qe5 (see diagram below)?[72]

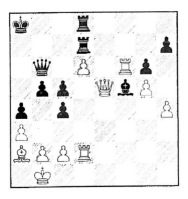

Computers can avoid making forced moves for a very long time, but every so often they come back to haunt it. With 48...Qc6 (see diagram below), black threatens a back rank mate, defends c5, and actively pursues the initiative. This restricts severely white's options. The only problem is this: Where precisely did white waste a tempo that would have allowed it to get luft? It is easy to say at this point that white needs luft, but when?

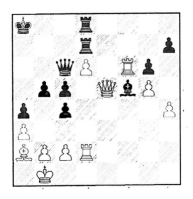

White tries to gum up the center with 49.Rd5 (see diagram below) and hit c5. However, the attack on c5 can be ignored.

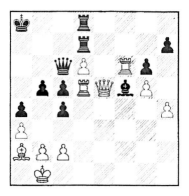

The back rank mate threat allows black to gain a crucial defensive tempo with 49...Kb7 (see diagram below). It is clear that the c5 pawn is defended forever.

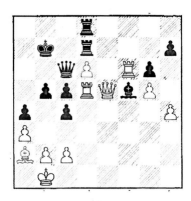

White finally solves his back-rank problem by running to the corner with 50.Ka1 (see diagram below). However, this laborious maneuver repositioning his pieces gives black enough time to convert his positional advantage into a tactical one in a few moves.

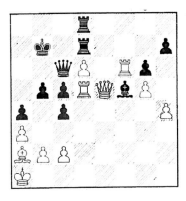

The pawn on c2 is poisoned, i.e., 50...Bxc2?. What does poisoned mean?[73] If 51.Bb1, white frees its rook and bishop with just one move. The correct response is 50...Kb6 (see diagram below) holding the c5 pawn.

White now prepares to get in the critical freeing move, 52.c3, by playing 51.Bb1 (see diagram below). What is meant by a "freeing move"?[74]

Black, at long last, is able to contest the critical e-file with 51...Qc8 (see diagram below). With this move, black prepares to play Re8, driving the queen from the e-file, still defending c5, and gaining access to the a6 square (see note to white's fifty-fourth move).

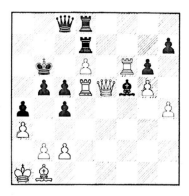

White avoids 52.c3, perhaps not liking the variation 52.c3 Re8 53.Qg3 Bxb1 54.Kxb1 b4. White must never forget that black can bring three majors to the queenside in three moves with all sorts of very real mate threats. You will observe that black controls the critical c4 square, and there is no stopping the pawn roller. While exhaustive analysis will provide a definitive answer, it is significant to the author that the computer chose not to permit its queenside to be compromised with 52.c3. White, instead, decided to hold the first with 52.Rd1 (see diagram).

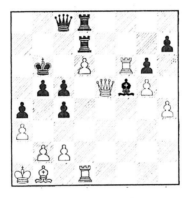

Black proceeds to drive the queen from the center with 52...Re8 (see diagram below). It is surprising just how quickly white's position now collapses.

White has few good options, but it doesn't begin to cause black difficulties. It should have forced black to prove that the pawn roller wins. Instead the Sphinx Legend opts for the retreat square, 53.Qf4 (see diagram below). The only practical try is 53.Qg3 — and pray.

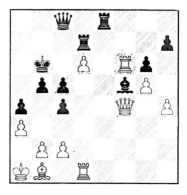

Black, without calculating anything, instantly played 53.c3! (see diagram below). This move has been hanging in the air for the past ten moves and is now played with maximum impact. White is officially busted. The only debate is whether it is a practical -/+ or -+.

White has no good options. If 54.h5, Qc1 or Qf2, 54...cxb2ch emerging with a raging attack, the better pawn structure, and, upon the inevitable gain of the d-pawn, a material plus. The position is -+. On the second variation, 54.b3 or b4, if 54...axb3, do you see a Zwischenzug, or in-between rnove?[75] This variation is also -+. So although the reader might assume the move chosen by the Sphinx Legend is a typical "computer" move, it should be pointed out this choice is no worse than any other option, 54.bxc3 (see diagram).

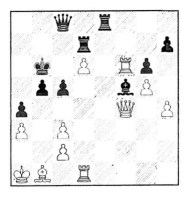

The bad bishop suddenly becomes a dead bishop after black walls in the bishop in a permanent tomb with 54...c4 (see diagram).

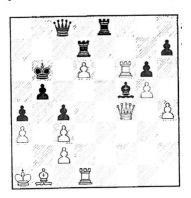

All white can do from now on is shuffle pieces and try to meet each new threat as it appears. So white "passed" with 55.Rd5 (see diagram).

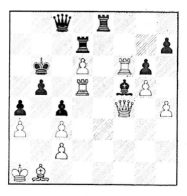

At this point, black's majors, which have lain dormant on the sidelines for most of the game, step into the spotlight: 55...Re4 (see diagram).

White steps out of the hit without "loss of time." The phrase has no meaning here as it would in analogous positions because all the time in the world will not salvage white's position so 56.Qf2ch (see diagram).

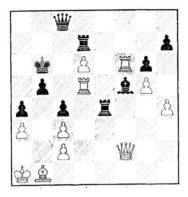

Black just steps out of the attack and "hides" so the big guys can do the heavy lifting. Black played 56...Ka6 (see diagram).

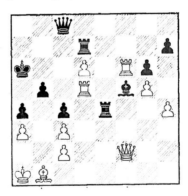

White simply bides its time, waiting to see if the dagger slips from black's hand. There are still swindles in the position. 57.Rd2 (see diagram).

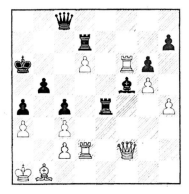

So black decides that the rook should not have all the fun, 57... Qe8 (see diagram).

White tries one of two swindles here with 58.Qc5 (see diagram below), leaving the h4 pawn "en prise," i.e., exposed to capture.

Black ignores the bait and immediately contests the rank with 58...Re5 (see diagram below). Why is the h-pawn poisoned?[76]

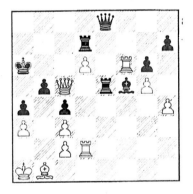

White decides not to try the check on c6 (Obviously it is harmless. Qc6 check is called a "spite" check. What is meant by a spite check?[77]) and plays 59.Rd5 (see diagram below) instead. In theory, it may be acceptable but is tantamount to resignation.

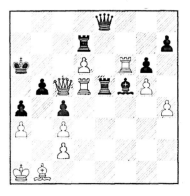

Black is glad to simplify even though the white rook on f6 will have access to the 8th once the queen deserts the 8th. Nevertheless, 59...Rxd5 (see diagram below) is still -+.

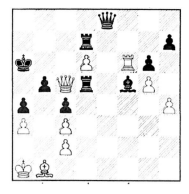

White continues "knowing" it has one more trick up its sleeve it never played! 60.Qxd5 (see diagram).

Black decides on a no-brainer, i.e., he just deprives white of any hope of a swindle (as if computers could hope!) 60...Kb6 (see diagram).

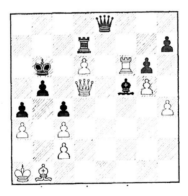

White makes a move: 61.Kb2 (see diagram).

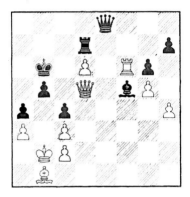

Black finally completes the domination of the white queen with 61...Qe4 (see diagram).

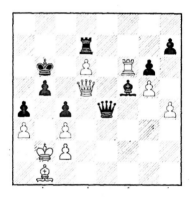

White doesn't even know how to swindle well. A human competitor would try either 62.Qg8 or, even more clever, 62.Qd4ch. (Should black meet 62. Qd4ch with 62....Qxd4, forcing a simple endgame of rook, bishop, and pawns versus rook, bishop, and pawns?[78]) Instead the Sphinx Legend plays its version of resignation, i.e. 62.Qxe4 (see diagram below).

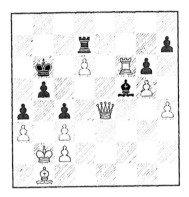

Black's light-squared bishop, which has dominated the board for the entire game, delivers the coup de grace: 62...Bxe4 (see diagram below). The win is now a matter of "technique" for a Class D player and a matter of technique for a grandmaster after 54...c4. What is meant by "technique"?[79] How did black convert a winning position into checkmate, 0-1:108?[80]

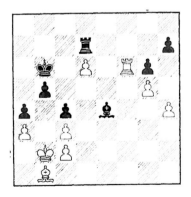

MAGIC ANSWERS

1) ...d6? loses quickly to the tactical shot 2.Bx17ch!! Kxf7 3.Ng5ch, and white has a powerful attack. It is not what comes off the board that matters; it is what stays on the board. Can you find a winning plan for white? In the words of former world champion Bobby Fischer, "Time is life." White's lead in development, which is useless in a closed position, gives white an overpowering attack in an open position. Give black just two moves in a row, i.e., 1 ...d6/2...e6, and black lives for a very long time. It should be pointed out that Fritz 8 did not find 2.Bxf7ch after several minutes of calculation. This concept is over the computer's "horizon" (see seven below).

2) Black has to artificially close the center. A "forced" move means that a player has just one move in the position; everything else is worse. In this situation, if black, with a pawn on e6, plays anything other than d6, white plays 2.e5, 3.d5 with a completely winning attack. Can you see how if, for example, black plays 2...Be7, and white plays 3.e5, how to win the position? Hint: open lines.

3) Artificially closing the center means that if white plays 3.d5, black plays e5, and if white plays 3.e5, black plays 3...d5. You will observe that there is no rapid way now to open the center.

4) After about five minutes of thought, Fritz 8 played 2.Kb1? just like the Sphinx Legend played!

5) Lacking any plan, the Sphinx Legend increases the "scope" of its rooks. What is meant by increasing the "scope" of one's rooks is that the rook has access to one additional square compared to the starting position.

6) A try is an attempt, i.e., a player has an idea that he/she wants to "try" out. In the game F-M, the computer tried a flank attack with g4/h4. It didn't come up with the "ideas" of f4 until much later. The correct plan for white is to play (assuming it plays 2.Kb1 d6) 3.d5 e5 4.Bg3 (black moves) 5.Nh4 black moves, 5.f4 black moves, 6.fxe5. Once the center is closed, this is the fastest way to "open the center." Open the center means trying to get rid of a center pawn in order to increase the scope of your rooks, bishops, and/or queen.

7) What computers "see", they see everything, but if a concept is beyond the computer's "horizon," the computer is completely blind. A human competitor, in a similar situation, might be able to make out vague shapes or patterns beyond what he/she can calculate. This player would know "intuitively and logically" that the sacrifice has to be sound. For example, in the game F-M, when black played 1...d6, Fritz 8 didn't play 2.Bxf7ch because the winning plan was over Fritz's horizon — specifically Fritz 8 "sees" the sacrifice but gives it a lower evaluation than other "quieter" moves. The computer's decisions are driven by evaluation. From the perspective of the computer, if the evaluation is better, then the move is better. Other, more desirable continuations, from the perspective of a human competitor, are simply ignored.

8) "Conventional" just means according to the accepted standards of modern chess theory.

9) A cramped position means that a player has few squares with which to maneuver his/her pieces.

10) Just as the name implies, a "cornered" king is one that is trapped on its first rank (a rank is a row that goes from 1-8 with 1 being the first row of white pieces and 8 being the row of black pieces

next to the edge of the board) and cannot "run" to the sanctuary of the center because its own pieces prevent it from doing this.

11) 4.13xf6 loses a piece to 4...gxf6. It is pointless to sacrifice a piece because white has insufficient "compensation." Compensation means that if you are going to attack in order to gain the advantage, one must have a clear plan to follow up. If there is no effective follow-up, the attack is considered unsound. Here the attacking try 5.e5 loses to 5...fxe5 6.dxe5 d5, and the "attack" fizzles out. Black is much better here because white doesn't even have a check on h5 forcing the king to move. In the game continuation, black simply walked his king to a8 anyway!

12) A disguised attack, for example, in this position would mean, for instance, if black decided to go after white's queen bishop (a good plan, but premature here) in a row, white can now play 5.e5, and the f-pawn is pinned. Pinned means either that the move is illegal, i.e., a move causing the king to be in check, which is called an "absolute" pin, or it leads to the massive loss of material. In this case, if 5...fxe5??, then white plays 6.Bxd8 with a huge gain of material. If the queen is worth 9 points and the bishop is worth 3½, then white gains 5½ points, a winning tactical and positional victory.

Sometimes a pin can seem absolute, e.g., in the following example, black pins a piece protecting the queen, only to realize that the pin is ineffective: 1.e4 e5 2.Nf3 Nc6 3.Bc4 Nf6 4.Ng5 Bc5 (the Wilkes-Barre or Traxler Variation). The author prefers the Wilkes-Barre Variation because the opening was popularized and promoted by the Wilkes-Barre chess club, whereas Traxler only played a few games with it. 5.d4 d5 6.Bxd5 Nxd4 7.Bxf7ch Kf8 8.Bc4 b5 (To avoid the loss of material with the knight fork on f7, black will pick up a bishop and the knight in the corner). 9.Bd3 h6 10.Nf3 Bg4? 11.Nxd4! This pin proved to be harmless, e.g., Bxd1 12.Ne6ch king moves 13.Nxd8 (11...Qxd4 12.Qd2 avoids the mate threat and moves the queen away from the discovered attack). One of the deadliest moves in chess is to play a pin that can be broken by tactical means.

13) The best location for the queen may not be d7 because white may play Qe3 or Qe2 at some point, causing the white queen rook to be directly opposite the black queen, perhaps leading to a discovered attack on the queen. 4...Ne7 is the wrong square for the knight; black wants to play the maneuver 5...Nh6, 6...Nf7, discouraging 7.e5, (This is why e3 may be a better square for the queen bishop so that white can discourage Nh6 due to the threat of Bxh6, forcing gxh6.) Black is busted once his king side is shredded. White is guaranteed to pick up at least one h-pawn. Even though the general rule is "knights before bishops," this only applies to classical chess and, to a lesser degree, hypermodern chess.

Classical chess and hypermodern chess have different approaches to dealing with the center. In classical chess, a player tries immediately to attack and occupy the center. In hypermodern chess, a player allows white to occupy the center with the goal of attacking the center at a later date.

4...Be7 is the best choice for black because of the tactical shot 5.e5? fxe5 6.Bxe7. The bishop on h4 is attacked twice and only defended once. If white wants to maintain material equality, it must play 6.Bxe7 Qxe7 (best). If white follows with 7.dxe5, black may even stand better after 7...d5, counterattacking the white bishop on c4. 8.Bb5ch is harmless, e.g., 8...Bd7 9.Qd3 Nc6/O-O-O, and black, with the prospect of having two center pawns, may even be better here. This just shows how tricky the starting positions are. Once black artificially closes the center, it is a tough slog, although in the game Fritz 8-Moody 120/40, white also blundered with 2.Kb1 after spending a good five minutes on the position.

After over an hour's computation, the computer was able to break through to the kingside due, perhaps, to inaccurate play by black (he used only five minutes for the first twenty moves), but it took the computer over twenty moves and over an hour on the clock to come up with a winning plan. It is clear that the Fritz 8 at 120'/40 plays better chess, in some, but not all situations, than the Sphinx Legend at an hour/move.

14) Planlessly, as the name implies, means playing without a plan. Plan, in the view of many players, can be viewed as positional chess if it leads to a long-term benefit compared to the starting position. A tactical "shot," on the other end, means a move sequence leading to an advantage in an equal position or the ability to "swindle," i.e., gain an advantage through trickery, as opposed to sound chess or to lessen an opponent's advantage. Typically a tactical shot means using a move sequence that is difficult to see, based on a player's "sight" of the board. This leads to the conversion of a favorable position to a winning, or at least a better, position than existed before the tactical shot and/or salvaging a losing position. One of the goals of the tactical player is to cause an opponent to spend valuable time to see if the tactical shot is sound.

15) It is not desirable to play 5...Nb7 because that hems in the bishop, and, of course, 5...Nc6 is bad because this invites 6.Be2/d5. It is clear that once white defends the bishop, the knight has to move, but where? Due to the threat of 7.d5 opening the center, black must beat an ignominious retreat to b8 or try the risky 7...Na5. If 5...Nc6, 6.Be2 Na5 7.b4!, this drives the knight exactly where it doesn't want to go. 7...Nc6 8.d5 with an overpowering attack.

16) A prophylactic move just means sooner or later, it has to be played. A good example would be if white castles kingside. White must

move a pawn in front of the king to avoid any impending back rank mate threats. Computers are notorious for avoiding them until they are absolutely necessary. (A good illustration of what happens when the computer does not give its king "luft," or the ability of the king to avoid back rank mate threats, is seen on move forty-eight... Qc6).

17) A practical advantage may be viewed as a winning advantage white, +-, a big advantage white +/-, a small advantage white, +/=, an unclear or = position, a slight advantage for .black, =/+, a big advantage for black, -/+ or a winning advantage for black, -/+. However, with a theoretical advantage, any advantage by white is checkmate There are no unclear positions, only equal positions or checkmate black. We do not have at the end of a chess game "almost winning for white" at a theoretical level, although it may exist at a practical level.

18) It is not a good idea to play 3...Nf6 because of 4.e5 dxe5 5.Nxe5 Be7, and the open lines give white a crushing attack. How should white win a won position here?

19) Closing the center means blocking the center by creating a pawn link/chain, i.e., two or more pawns on a diagonal that are stymied by a corresponding pawn chain, preventing either side from moving forward in the center. This was one of the themes of the famous theoretician Nimzovich, but, as the game progressed, black simply ignored Nimzovich's hypermodern theories and immediately went after the center. He opened it with advantage even though he gave himself a positional disadvantage in classical chess but an advantage in the author's chess.

20) A computer is programmed by humans, but every so often, the programming goes haywire, presumably because one algorithm takes

precedence over another. In the case of the game, the first move chosen by both the Sphinx Legend and the strong Fritz 8 (after black's 1...e6 with a pawn already on d6) was 2.Kb1. According to the computer, this was the best way to improve its position, i.e., by increasing the scope, or maneuvering room, of its rooks. To put the starting position in perspective, white ordinarily thinks of "climbing" Mt. Everest one step at a time, i.e., the bottom is the starting position, and the top is the most desirable classical position. What the computer never dreamed possible is what would happen if it was placed on the top of Mt. Everest and told to climb uphill? Up has no meaning, so the computer wandered aimlessly at the summit and gradually spiraled downhill toward the base of the mountain.

21) 12.a4 is bad because white cannot afford to risk opening lines opposite his king. 12.a4 does nothing to stop b5 over the long haul, e.g., 12...b6 13.Qe2 Qb7 14.h3 Qa7 15.Bh2 Nb7 with an overwhelming position. Black even has time for castling because the black attack is several tempos faster than the white attack.

22) A bad bishop is one whose mobility is severely restricted by his/her/ pawns. In this case, the pawns on e4 and d5 restrict the mobility of the king bishop. Black now has a sub plan: restrict the mobility of white's king bishop as much as possible.

23) A "hit" just means that a piece or pawn attacks a piece, pawn, or square.

24) Pawn shelter refers to a cluster of pawns around the king that protects the king from an attack. Weakening the pawn shelter means advancing a pawn near the king that increases an opponent's prospects.

25) Bumping just means attacking a piece with a pawn or piece so that it is forced to move.

26) It is usually a bad idea when faced with a pawn storm to weaken the squares around your king. In this case, b4 at any time will provoke a5 at some point, prying open the king position.

27) Black needs a retreat square on the 7th because Na4 is forced in the absence of a safe square on the 7th. This is a very weak move because white has the simple response, Nxa4, which forces bxa4; just like that, the black attack is over. It may seem counterintuitive that the open file favors white. Black can never train enough pieces on the b2 square. White can play Ka1/Rb1 or even maneuver his knight to the d1 square, defending b2 three times.

Black needs his pawn levers here; with doubled pawns on the a-file, a white pawn on a3 (which has now turned into a useful move) and no pawn levers on either the a-file or the b-file, white has unlimited defensive potential, e.g., Ka1, Rd3, Re3 or even eventually, as in the game continuation, Rf3. White also will play Bb1 at some point followed by c3. Just like that, the bad bishop becomes a great bishop, and white is winning. Suddenly the doubled a-pawns are a static liability, and white has the better middle game and endgame.

28) Counterplay means that a player, typically one who is being attacked, can strike back. A classical chess way to do this is to meet a flank attack with an attack in the center, gaining the ability of a player to slow the attack because of actual or threatened ways to favorably improve one's position.

29) The loss of the king bishop is a disaster for black. First of all, black loses a stalwart defender and, as the game progresses, a very powerful attacking piece. After the move couplet Nxe7/Kxe7,

white is better. Aside from the fact that black suffers a positional loss after Kxe7, he incurs a 1/2 pawn disadvantage, i.e., the minor exchange. In addition, it is highly likely that white's bad bishop will become a good bishop.

30) A forced move just means that anything else is much worse.

31) The only reason that g6 would be considered a weakening move is that it might provoke the Sphinx Legend to try h4/h5, breaking up the kingside with some prospects of a wing attack on the kingside.

32) Opening lines means to get rid of pawns that interfere with the scope of yours or your opponent's pieces.

33) Open lines usually means that it increases the attacking side's prospects of an attack, e.g., landing a rook on the 7th (sometimes called a pig because it likes to scarf up pawns on the 7th).

34) Computers are programmed to think logically, so whenever they do something that appears illogical, it can be called a mystery move. Clearly the computer retreating to g3 may be anticipating g6, a move that black, at this stage of the game, has no interest in playing.

35) A tempo can be thought of as a piece of time. In a classical position, time is far more important than it is here because in a closed position, i.e., the absence of open lines, means that the attacking concepts are much slower, and time/tempo, in the conventional sense, is far less meaningful. A three-tempo lead in development in a classical position, according to practical results, is worth a pawn. Here a nine-tempo lead in development is worth, on a practical level, nothing.

36) White now has a "plan," i.e., instead of waiting for black to start playing chess, the computer now has on its radar that black was really playing chess all along; it just didn't look like any kind of chess the computer had ever seen before. Now the computer can begin to play strategically, and this means that black, at long last, has an opponent instead of a mindless machine.

37) Rooks belong on open files because that is where they have the most opportunity to invade your opponent's 7th rank and otherwise be used to conduct an attack. One general rule here with one or more pawns on the 7th is that a rook on the 7th is worth a pawn; this assumes that there are pawns on the 7th. If there are not pawns on the 7th and there are pawns on the 6th, you probably should invade on the 6th (shades of Capablanca?).

38) The multipurpose move, 15...Be8, holds the f7 square. Since the rook is worth more than the bishop, an exchange sacrifice never makes sense here. In fact, there are only one or two sub variations in the entire game that merit consideration of an exchange sacrifice by either side.

39) There is no purpose behind 22...Ncd7. The knight is well-placed on c5, and there is nothing to be gained by retreating it.

40) The reason that doubling rooks on the f-file poses no threat to the bishop on f8 is that on its trek to the f6 square, this knight passes through d7, which incidentally defends f8 as an added benefit. Do the math: f8 is defended twice by the knight. First black defends it with a knight, and then the knight blocks the f-file.

41) Throughout the course of this game, white had a chronic threat of rook X bishop and never played it because it is pointless to give

away material with no ancillary benefits. In other words, the exchange sacrifice makes sense only if it gains an advantage in time or position. Here it gains neither.

42) Although the black king is in a corner, it has mobility. However, black must be careful that white can never play Qa6ch with a queen on b8. For example, if black is forced to play Ra7, white may play Bxa7, winning the exchange.

43) A waiting move can be thought of as, "I have no plans. What does my opponent intend to do?"

44) With 27...Rb6??, black steps into a pin, and now 28.b4, a losing move in almost any other situation, wins for white. White must not have tunnel vision. Even though for the past ten moves b4 is a "bad" idea, white must be alert to the position on the board and not be slavishly devoted to any one concept. Once black plays 28...Ncd7, 29.Bxb6 is +/-, the only other option is to sacrifice the knight and hope for complications. Still it is +/- to +-. (This is, of course, a matter of opinion.)

45) Blindly following a good tactical shot with b4 is no excuse for missing 28.b4 Na4?! with a clever swindle in mind, i.e., 29.Bxb6?? Nxc3ch! 30.Kb2 Nxe2 -+. (This may seem obvious, but sometimes a player forgets a piece or pawn has moved. In this position, with a pawn on b2, Nxc3 check is met with bxc3. White might forget he just played b4, unintentionally leaving the knight "en prise," i.e., exposed to capture, and then walking into the knight fork). However, just 29.Nxa4 is +-. With one careless move, missing a knight fork, white plays a tactical shot only to step into an even bigger tactical shot. Don't be so wrapped up in your own plans that you fail to see the obvious. Most players would see this tactical shot, but in a time scramble, shots similar to this are often missed.

46) In computer lingo, a ply is a 1/2 move, thus each full move is 2 plies. What the author is saying is that the Sphinx Legend appears to be seeing ahead at least six moves, probably on every move. What is critical though is the evaluation algorithms. If they are wrong, it doesn't matter how far ahead computers see; if they can't evaluate the final positions accurately, all the crunching power in the world won't help.

47) It is premature to play 29...b4 due to the following tactical shot: 30.Bxc5 dxc5 (bxc3?? 31.Qxa6ch Ra7 32.Qxa7ch +/-.) 31.Nd1 bxa3 32.Rxa3 +/=. The attack fizzles out. Black is stuck with an overextended pawn position for the rest of the game. Now we see the value of the rook on the third.

48) A pawn storm is the advance of a mass of pawns, usually, but not always, toward your opponent's king position.

49) A pawn storm is necessary here because, in the words of former world champion Garry Kasparov, it is necessary to use pawns to pry open an opponent's pristine king position, a position that has not been seriously compromised in some other fashion.

50) Hanging means that a piece is not connected to another piece or pawn, i.e., it is "hanging" in midair without a net. In most situations, it means that the side with a hanging piece or pawn will lose them without any compensation.

51) To conserve time, it is a useful tool against computers to let them tell you whether or not threats are real. For example, in one game against Fritz 8, the author had a strong attack on the white side of a Sicilian and thought he saw a back rank mate threat. The computer, by not defending against the threat, said it wasn't real. The author persisted in this delusion and, as a result, made

a careless pawn move, squandering his advantage, and had to fight for the draw. When the computer was given the white side of the position, instead of the pawn push, it was able to find the winning continuation for white.

52) As indicated, the Sphinx Legend, in the span of over an hour, has seen ten to twelve plies deep. Clearly it sees material loss staring at it within those five to six moves.

53) The problem with 31...c4/b4 is that there is no effective follow-up, e.g., what happens if white just plays 32.g4 b4? The answer: 33.axb4 axb4 33.Kc1 (running to the center) b3 34.cxb3 cxb3 35.Bb1. This cures a multitude of sins as far as white is concerned. It has shut down the attack, and the bad bishop is no longer bad. The attack is over, and black is stuck with the positional handicap of an exposed king for the duration of the game. In theory this may be acceptable, but as a practical matter, black has squandered his advantage. In fact, white is slightly better here because black has more pawn islands than white (see #56 below).

54) Black allowed his pawn structure to be damaged for several reasons. First of all, the doubled pawns are dynamite in this position (just follow black's next two moves). The c-pawn advances are extremely strong. Black's king bishop is a very powerful addition to the attack now that black has blasted out the d-pawn by exchanging on c5. Finally, even if the pawn on e5 is lost, black gets more than enough compensation by virtue of the enhanced scope of his bishops. For example, white's e4-pawn is very weak over the long run, so black will soon be up the 1/2 pawn with a winning positional edge.

55) Doubled pawns are generally weak. In fact, in the Exchange Ruy (1.e4 e5 2.Nf3 3.Bb5 a6 4.Bxc6 dxc6), white has been known to

give up the minor exchange just to get the advantage of the doubled pawns, which he/she believes is more important than losing the minor exchange + black's greater rook mobility (The author's prejudice is that because of the countervailing factors, black is better in the Exchange Ruy.)

56) The great chess player Capablanca became a world champion even without any appreciable knowledge of "book." He coined the phrase pawn island. Top professionals avoid pawn islands, i.e., individual pawns or clusters of pawns that are not supported by other pawns because pawn islands need constant supervision. Just as a mother can keep track of one unruly child, two become a problem and three a disaster.

This attitude of Capablanca with regard to opening theory would be impossible for a world champion today because opening theory is so sophisticated that ignorance of opening theory can be devastating. GM Sammy Reshevsky walked into the loss of his queen in twelve moves against GM Bobby Fischer, simply because he was unaware of an opening trap that Fischer had uncovered with his massive opening research. Even former world champion Garry Kasparov walked into a known trap played against him in a match with Deep Blue, a computer that defeated Kasparov in the match.

Both Capablanca and Reshevsky, two of the greatest child prodigies of all times, had the same attitude: They would muddle through the openings and get into a balanced middle game, where they "simply" would outplay their opponents in an equal middle game.

57) White should not allow the bishop on e8 to come into the game with tempo. With 33.dxc6 Bxc6, how does white defend e4? Black has managed to blast out a center pawn and, by so doing, increased the scope of his bishops.

58) If white avoids this with an immediate 33.d6, black can now play Bg6/Bxf5/Bxd6, and black has a pawn and the initiative (-/+). Also, the opposite-colored bishops favor the attacker in the middle game, and white will have only a slight possibility of ever reaching an endgame.

59) The very real possibility is that black will win a pawn with cxd5, open the center, and implement a strong attack on the white king position.

60) Loss of time means that a player has to make a move that costs him at least one tempo. One move can cost a whole lot more than one tempo (see Berliner Variation).

61) Black wishes to make sure that b4 is defended with the pawn on a5 with idea of perhaps opening the a-file after b4/axb4 axb4.

62) Will of the game just means that a player tries to steer play into a favorable position. Both sides try to do this; whoever succeeds will usually prevail.

63) Black has annoying pressure against d5 here.

64) Heavy piece endings are notoriously difficult to win even two pawns up. The author is well-aware of this from personal experience. In one WBT, white was up a pawn the entire middle game. Suddenly Fritz 8 allowed a two-move tactical shot, permitting white to win a pawn. Without thinking, white grabbed the pawn, and the computer immediately registered 0000 on its screen, meaning it was a draw. As belatedly white looked at the board, he suddenly realized that he had allowed the computer to build a fortress, so even though two pawns up, the position was a dead draw.

More importantly, though, is that black has the initiative, but his king position is very drafty. Black will have the difficult practical task of keeping the majors out of his position for the rest of the game. Probably black has just enough play to hold the draw.

65) Lurking in white's future (although they are not an immediate threat) are the possibilities of a bank rank threat and a threatened skewer on the h1/a8 diagonal. White eventually has to deal with both threats.

66) The rook on a7 is tied to the a5 pawn. Qb6 relieves the rook of that duty. However, the main threat is cxd5, and if Qxd5ch, Bc6 is extremely strong, and if exd5, e4 is -/+.

67) The reason that 40.Nf6 is bad is because of 40...cxd5. Black fixes his pawn structure and, at the same time, continues to attack. Bad for white at this point is 41.Nxe8 because of 41...dxe4 If 42.Qd5ch Kb8, 43.Qxe4 Rxe8 with a strong passed pawn. Finally on 40...cxd5 41.Nxd5 Qd6/Bf7/Rd8-/+.

68) You will note that for the past several moves that black's c6 pawn was exposed to capture on c6 because of the white pawn on d5, and white's d5 pawn was also exposed to capture because of the black pawn on c6. When pawns can mutually capture one another over the course of several moves but neither side decides to capture, then this is called pawn tension. The primary reason that pawn tension is maintained over several moves is that both sides believe that their capture favors their opponent.

69) The pawn on d6 is devastating as far as white is concerned. The problem is that the capture of the d6 pawn is inevitable so that it is desirable to pitch it at some point to try to get at the black king.

In the meantime, this one pawn shuts down all white's counter-play by blocking the rank, the file, and the diagonals.

70) There was a real need to play 42...Rd8 instead of the obvious 42...Bxf6 43.Rxf6 Bxe4 44.Re2 Qxd6 45.Qe1 and now the rook rather than the queen captures on e5 with a sharp position with chances for both sides. After 42...Rd8, black can meet 43.Nxh7? with 43...Bxe4! skewering a rook, i.e., hitting the rook on g2, which is on the same diagonal as the rook on f3. Bad in this variation is the cheap shot 43...Rxd6 with the threat of a back rank mate threat but throws away the skewer because of the simple interpolation, 44.Rg1 Bxe4 45.Re3 with the threat of Qe1. Now black has thrown away his advantage.

A second try is to pitch the d-pawn immediately with 43.d7 Bxf6 44.Rxf6 R7xd7 -/+. Allowing black to double rooks on the d-file this quickly is not a good idea.

My real concern, though, was the continuation chosen by Fritz 8 in the course of analyzing the game, i.e., 43.Qxe5?! Black has a lot of ways to go wrong here, e.g., 43...Re8 trying to use the pin, but I see no convincing follow-up after 44.Qf4, and it is doubtful black has equality. 43... Qb7 looks dicey, e.g., 44.Rd2 Bxe4 45.Rf4 and again it is tough to believe that black has anything here. The point is that is an important distinction that white already has played Qxe5, protected d6, and prepares, in some variations, to push the passed pawn. Black also gave up control of the e8 square so that 45...Re8 is no longer possible.

The correct reply by black is one of the toughest moves in chess to see, 43...Bf8, giving up the pin but preparing to win the pawn back in all variations. 44.Nd5 Qb8 45.Rd2 R7d7 and black picks up the d-pawn in a variation much worse for white than the game continuation.

71) A quiet move is one that has no immediate tactical implications. Ordinarily it is thought of as a move conferring a slight positional advantage.

72) Occupation of the center is a recurring theme in chess. In classical chess, players try to occupy and control the center from the first move onward, whereas the hypermodern player is only concerned with who occupies it last.

73) A poisoned pawn is one whose capture backfires. Here, for example, if black plays 50...Bxc2?, white simply replies 51.Bb1, and just like that, white turns the table. We are in a heavy piece ending where white has good practical chances to draw.

74) A freeing move can be thought of as escaping a positional bind. Maybe it is converting a bad bishop into a good bishop or a knight with limited mobility escapes into one with great scope. Very commonly it can be thought of as the ability to turn a cramped position into one which is more open but under control.

75) A Zwischengug, or in-between move, occurs in the move sequence: 54.b3 or b4 axb3 55.Rxf5! Qa6! The in-between move compels 56.a4 because of the mate threat. Only then does black play 56... gxf5, white moves, 57...Qxa4ch-+.

76) The pawn is poisoned for the following reason, i.e., 58.Qc5 Rxh4?? 59.Rd5 Qb8 60.Rf8+-.

77) A spite check is often played just prior to resignation. It is hope, annoyance, or despair, depending on your point of view. However, "Always check; it might be mate."

78) The problem with meeting 62.Qd4ch! with 62...Qxd4?? is that it permits white to get back in the game with 63.cxd4 Kc6 64.c3, and black has thrown away the win. The correct reply to 62.Qd4ch is just 62...Kc6-/+.

79) Technique means different things to players of different strengths. The stronger the player, the more subtle an advantage needed to secure a victory. There is one story of GM Korchnoi, in what may have been a World Open, who was asked by an opponent if he would consider a draw. GM Korchnoi's response: "Excuse me, I'm winning."

80) The level of technique that black used to win the position was minimal. First he picked up the d-pawn. (This loss was predictable twenty moves ago yet is over the Sphinx Legend's horizon for most of the game. Even Fritz 8 had a tough time evaluating the final position, calling it "only" -/+ after eight minutes of calculation. Clearly this is a programming bug). Then black walked his king to h5, shielded the h-pawn from being defended by the rook, and ultimately picked up the d-pawn, the h-pawn, and the g-pawn for no compensation. Then black queened two pawns. White sacrificed the rook for one of the pawns. At long last, the Sphinx sacrificed the bishop with Bxc4. Black then checkmated the king on the a-file in 108 moves.

LESSONS OF MAGIC

Purists might argue that odds games have no business in "serious" chess, yet these same players would profess to believe that speed chess is really "chess." Chess without intuition or calculation produces superficial chess where the cheap shot is revered and strength is determined by whoever makes the next-to-last blunder. What is evident here is that the hour he required the computer to calculate, sometimes for seven to eight hours at a time, was enormously beneficial to his intuition. On only one occasion black used calculation and was immediately crushed by the computer. The author retracted one bad concept and, from that point onward, merely placed his pieces and pawns on the squares where they belonged with no calculation more than two or three moves deep. The author used less than one hour total for the first sixty-two moves. Based on the magnitude of the odds and using simul rules as a guide, retracting one bad concept does not detract significantly from the beauty of the game.

It has been said that a master is a player who can see three moves (six plies) ahead in all variations. In incredibly complicated middle games, the author did not miss any tactical shots at least ten to twelve plies deep; otherwise the computer would have seen and played them. Each additional ply is about an order of magnitude greater calculation. If a master can only see six plies ahead in very complicated scenarios and the author was seeing ten to twelve plies ahead in a similar position, it would tend to suggest that the author's intuition was powerful enough to see well beyond the depth of search of even a strong master.

This odds game, as an instructional model, is superb (see text). Probably more basic chess principles are covered in this game than any other game, including any of the classics although some players might regard the starting positions as artificial. How many grandmasters would have seen that 29...a5, forcing white to part with a bishop for a knight with 30.Bxc5, was the correct choice even though it violated two chess principles, i.e., avoid doubled pawns and avoid isolated pawns? This is one of the many opening principles rejected by the author in Magic.

THE NG5 VARIATION: TWO KNIGHTS DEFENSE

Introduction

Opening "theory" is actually a hodgepodge of codified anecdotes; in today's world, computer-generated "perfect" move sequences are believed to be the sterile end result of all-knowing computers. Without proper guidance though, computer generated wisdom has severe limitations. One of the biggest problems is that of the sieve problem (see previous section), i.e., while the computer can see all short and intermediate-level tactics, it will always fall victim to tactics over its horizon. "Tactics" to a computer means the accumulation of small disadvantages caused by the computer flipping too many programming coins that magically show up as blunders ten-plus moves later when the computer "walks" into a tactical shot. As the game Sphinx Legend-Moody established, black gained maybe a twentieth of a pawn positional advantage each move over the course of thirty moves, which caused the computer to play into a losing position.

It is proposed here that the ability to consistently build for a win without resorting to classical chess principles or hypermodern principles, in sensu strictu, means the development of another school of chess, The Slaughter School of Chess, whose motto is "Always make the best move at all times."

Best move is subjective. In over-the-board chess, it can be viewed as a move that compels the most rapid resignation as opposed to the theoretically best move. Even theoretically best is subjective. Once again, using the game Sphinx Legend-Moody as a guide (see previous section), at the bitter end of the game, the computer played into a simple positional loss simply because it didn't know how to lie or to swindle. It missed a diabolical trap for white on the very last move of the game, missing 62.Qd4ch instead of the immediate positional loss with 62.Qxe4?? According to computer "logic," staving off checkmate for as long as possible is desirable, not realizing from a practical standpoint how wrong this is, i.e., assuring the excruciating loss, as opposed to quick death against accurate moves.

Best move in a practical situation may mean doing what former world champion Bobby Fischer used to do all the time: He would set up reasonable positional moves for his opponents, who would then make a simple tactical oversight, e.g., castling into a losing position when the edict, "Castle early and often," is used.

Best move may mean making the sharpest move, the most beautiful move, the most outrageous move, the most complex move in a time scramble, or the most "quiet" move. The final example may not make sense. How can a quiet move be "most quiet"? In a game where the author was outrated by over six hundred rating points in an over-the-board contest, he had held his opponent dead equal in a flurry of tactics in the middle game. He thought he had survived the worst when, to his utter dismay, at the end of the tactical exchange, his opponent made a completely innocuous move. Only then did black realize he was about to be ground down positionally over the rest of the game. While not the best move in "theory," it was a severe psychological blow that ultimately contributed to the quick collapse of a "playable" position.

How does this relate to the Two Knights Defense? Despite hundreds of years of theory and practical play, the entire theory of the opening is all wrong because the best moves in the position very early on have been missed! This may seem like a thoroughly grandiose statement. The author will start out with the Berliner variation of the Fritz, regarded by Dr. Hans Berliner, former correspondence world champion, working in combination with Hitech, the strongest mainframe computer at the time, as the definitive refutation of the Ng5 Variation of the Two Knights Defense.

Here is an alternative to the main line.

1.e4 e5 2.Nf3 Nc6 3.Bc4 Nf6 4.Ng5 d5 5.exd5 Na5 6.Bb5ch c6 7.dxc6 bxc6 8.Bd3 Nxd5 9.h4 Be7 10.Qf3 Nf4 11.Nxf7 Kxf7 12.g3 Bg4 13.Qxg4 Nxd3 14.cxd3 Qxd3 15.Qe2 Rhd8 16.Nc3 c5 17.b3 c4

18.Qxd3 Rxd3 19.bxc4 Rd4 20.Rb1 Rc8 21.Ke2 Rdxc4 22.f3 Ke6
23.Bb2 Nc6 24.Ne4 Ra4 25.Ra1 Nb4 26.a3 Nc2 27.Rhc1 Rac4 28.Kd3
R4c6 29.Rb1 h6 30.a4 a5 31.Ke2 Bb4 32.Kd1 Kd5 33.h5 Rc4 34.Nf2
Bd6 35.g4 Nd4 36.Rxc4 Rxc4 37.Bxd4 exd4 38.Rb5ch Rc5 39.Rxc5 Bxc5
40.Ne4 Bb6 41.d3 Bc7 42.Nd2 Kc5 43.Nb3ch Kb4 44.Nxd4 Kxa4
45.Ne6 Be5 46.f4 Bc3 47.Kc2 Kb4 48.g5 hxg5 49.fxg5 a4 50.Nd8 Ba1
51.d4 Kc4 52.Ne6 Kd5 53.Nxg7 Bd4 54.h6 Be5 55.g6 Kd6 56.Kb1 1-0

From move thirteen to the end of the game Moody-Fritz 8, the
author only provides diagrams. Check books on opening theory if you
think that black can improve. 4...d5 5.exd5 Nd4 6.c3 b5 7.Bf1 Nxd5
8.Ne4 Qh4 9.Ng3 Bg4 10.f3 e4 11.cxd4 Bd6

12.Qe2 (see first diagram)   12...Be6 13.Nc3
                                       (see second diagram).

   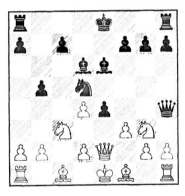

All the analysis of this starting position shows that white is clearly
better, at least by +/-. In order to provide a high-level test of this position, the game Moody (1700)-Fritz (2700+) was played at a rate of
120'/25. White analyzed the position for months before the game and
had extended the analysis out to about 20.O-O-O; he was winning
until the terrible blunder 46.Bxa5?? This is why computers win
games: Humans blunder routinely. If the game had been played in

consultation with a master, it was an easy win. The computer consistently overstated white's advantage at the start of game and had white as only +/= when the position was +- 20 moves later. This game refutes the Berliner Variation. After this game is published, it will never again be played in serious competition.

White's strategy can be summed up as the realization of the author's strategy when accepting a gambit: try to return to a universal position in order to defend tenaciously. A universal position is one where all your pieces are behind your farthest advanced pawn and there is only one or no open files. This strategy is exemplified here.

Here is the game score with the diagrams to follow. 13.Nc3!! This natural developing move has been missed by theoreticians. The only move my computer has in its memory is 13.fxe4. White gains seven!! tempos with this concept. Just count how long it takes for black to connect its rook and add the offside queen, and the fact that black will move a knight three times just to exchange it for a knight whose recapture frees the bishop. White easily gains seven tempos no matter what black plays.

Black has to play 13...Nxc3 (13...Nb4 is met with 14.Kd1 Bxg3 15.Qxb5ch+-). 14.dxc3 (white's ugly duckling becomes a beautiful swan).Bxg3ch 15.hxg3 Qxh1 16.Qxb5ch Kf8. Fritz used a half hour on its first three moves, and it evaluates 17.fxe4 as +- This is reason enough to view the Berliner Variation with skepticism.

What the author finds incredible is that no one is playing the Berliner Variation as what it really is — a gambit. What is standard gambit praxis? Give back just enough material to squelch the attack and use a positional advantage to bring home the point. Here white emerges with a slight material advantage, i.e., bishop and two pawns for a rook, about a 1/2 pawn advantage, and a huge positional plus.

Black now tried 17...Rc8 18.Bf4 c6. (The horizon effect kicks in; white can always win the c-pawn. If I7...Bg4 to stop O-O-O, then white just plays 18.Qg5 Qh5 19.Qxh5 Bxh5 20.Bxc7+-. There is nothing to be gained by defending the c-pawn.) 19.Qc5ch (played instantly in order to gain time on the clock for the impending complications). 19...Kg8 20.O-O-O Qh2 21.Ba6 Rf8 22.d5 (Here is how a Class B player thinks. White gets connected passers with an easy endgame win.) Qh5 23.Qxc6 Bg4 24.Re1 h6 25.Qc7 Kh7 26.Bb7 f6 27.Bc6 Rf7 28.Qd6 Qh2 29.Qc5 Qxg2 30.Qe3 Rd8 31.Qd2 Qh3 32.Qf2 Kg8 33.Ba4 Rc8 34.Bc2 Bh5 35.Bd3 Qd7 36.c4 Qa4 37.b3 Qa3ch (The Fritz says that this is +/=.) 38. Qb2 Qb4 39.Bd2 Qb7 40.Kb1 Bg6 41.Bc3 Qc7 42.Qf2 a5 43.a3 Qb8 44.Ka2 Rb7 45.Qc2 Qxg3?! (All the while, the author was thinking, "Now I'll have a fantastic time going after the kingside in the late middle game." He mindlessly grabbed a pawn, thinking his position was solid. Hence the blunder 46.Bxa5?? gaining four connected passed pawns! White wins easily with 46.Re2 — see second move string.) Now black gets serious counterplay 46...Ra7 (e1 starts to hang). 47.Bc3 Rca8 48.a4 Be8 (The author completely missed this continuation; now black is slightly better.) 49.Ka3 (White thought the endgame of queen and fast h-pawn for black would be playable for white with his strong center pawns, but Fritz quickly shows that this is an illusion. White tried to wriggle out of a poorer position but got ground down in the endgame.) 49...Bxa4 50.bxa4 Rxa4ch 51.Qxa4 Rxa4ch 52.Kxa4 Qxd3 53.Kb4. The concluding moves are given for the record. 53...h5 54.Ra1?! Qxe4 55.Re1 Qg4 56.Kc5 h4 57.d6 h3 58.Bd4 h2 59.Kd5 Qf3ch 60.Ke6 Kf8 61.c5 Qb7 62.Bxf6 gxf6 63.Kxf6 Qf3ch 64.Ke6 Qf7ch Resigns.

While it was true that black won because of a simple tactical oversight, what was the true nature of the innovation? Does white have a winning position by move thirteen? The answer appears to be yes because the author returned to the point of the blunder and put in an obvious alternative. The results were strikingly different. A separate move stream is generated that will follow the parent game given below. In both cases, only white is on move, so each diagram represents, in effect, two plies.

We learn from this game that white, at a minimum, would have a material advantage of bishop and two pawns for the rook for the entire middle game and an overwhelming position but then got greedy. Often against strong computers, the human competitor outplays the computer for over forty moves, only to fall victim to a tactical trick. If human competitors were to play consultation matches against computers, the author predicts that the right combination of players would defeat any combination of computers, primarily because more than 90 percent of all the cheap tactical shots would be seen.

Here is the post-blunder game: 46.Re2 Kh7 47.Rg2 Qd6 48.Bd4 Bf3 49.Rf2 Qg3 50.Qc3 Qg4 51.R.xf3! (This sacrifice underscores a fundamental problem with the evaluation algorithm of computers. It is up the double exchange, but the bishops are boss in this position.) 51...Qxf3 52.c5 (Passed pawns must be pushed!) Rf7 (Notice the disjointed nature of the black army.) 52...Rf7 53.d6 (ditto) Rd8 54.Qc4 Qg3 55.Bb2 Kf8 56.Qd5 Qg5 57.Qd4 Qg4 58.Bc4 Qd7 59.Bd5 a4 60.b4 Qe8 61.Qc4 Rfd7 62.Bc6 Qf7 63.Bd5 Qe8 64.Bd4 Qh5 65.Qc2 Qg4 66.b5 Rc8 67.Qf2 Ke8 68.b6 h5 69.b7 Rb8 70.Qb2 Rbxb7 71.Bxb7 Rxb7 72.Qxb7 Qe2ch 73.Qb2 Qxb2ch 74.Kxb2 Kd7 75.Kc3 Ke6 76.Bg1 g6 77.Kb4 h4 78.Kb5 (Fritz indicated mate in 20 and resigned.)

In each case, white is on move:

12.Qe2

12...Be6 13. Nc3

13...Ncc3

14...Bxg3ch 15.hxg3

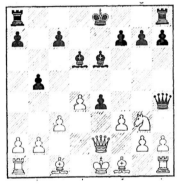

15...Qxh1 16.Qxb5ch

16...Kf8 17.fxe4

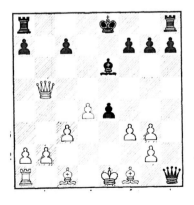

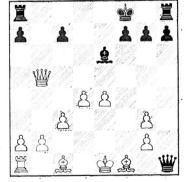

17...Rc8 18.Bf4

18...c6 19.Qc5ch

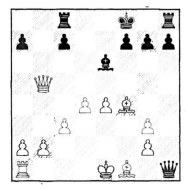

19...Kg8 20.O-O-O

20...Qh2 21.Ba6

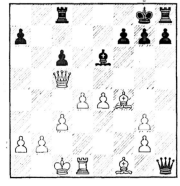

21...Rf8 22.d5

22...Qh5 23.Qxc6

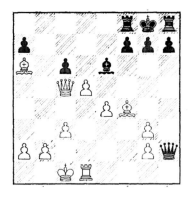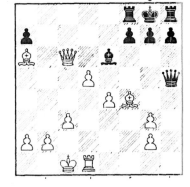

23...Bg4 24.Re1

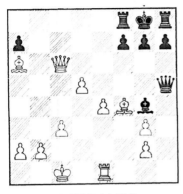

24...h6 25.Qc7

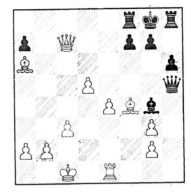

25...Kh7 26.8b7

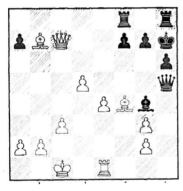

26...f6 27.Bc6

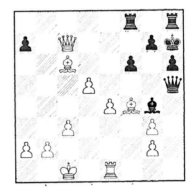

27...Rf7 28.Qd6

28... Qh2 29.Qc5

29... Qxg2 30.Qe3

30...Rd8 31.Qd2

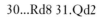
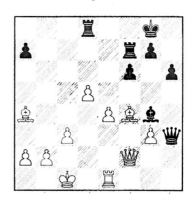

31...Qh3 32.Qf2

32...Kg8 33.Ba4

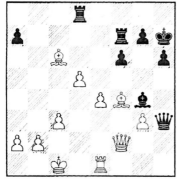
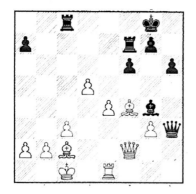

33...Rc8 34.Bc2

34...Bh5 35.Bd3

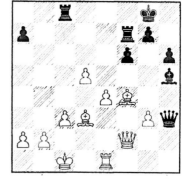

35...Qd7 36.c4

36...Qa4 37.b3

37...Qa3ch 38.Qb2

38...Qb4 39.Bd2

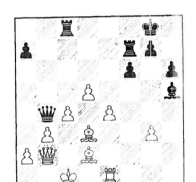

39...Qb7 40.Kb1

40...Bg6 41.Bc3

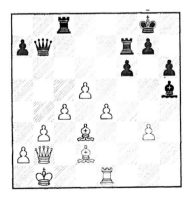

41...Qc7 42.Qf2

42...a5 43.a3

43...Qh8 44.Ka2

44...Rb7 45.Qc2

45...Qxg3 46.Bxa5

46...Ra7 47.Bc3

47...Rca8 48.a4

48...Be8 49.Ka3

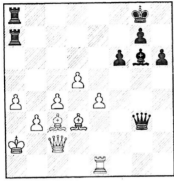

49...Bxa4 50.bxa4

50...Rxa4ch 51.Qxa4

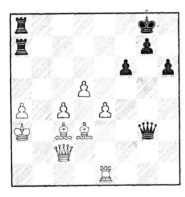

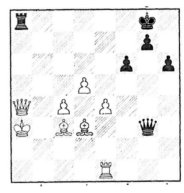

51...Rxa4ch 52.Kxa4

52... Qxd3 53.Kb4

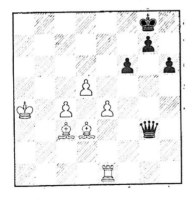

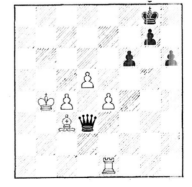

The rest of the game saw black push his h-pawn forward rapidly, where it would queen and cost white his rook.

This is the alternative ending.

45...Qxg3 46.Re2 | 46...Bh5 47.Rg2

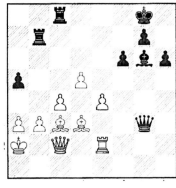 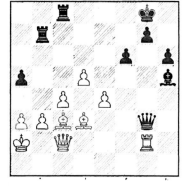

47...Qd6 48.Bd4 | 48...Bf3 49.Rf2

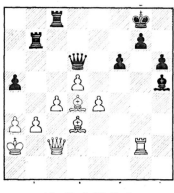 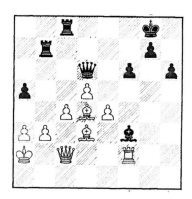

49...Qg3 50.Qc3 | 50...Qg4 51.Rxf3

126

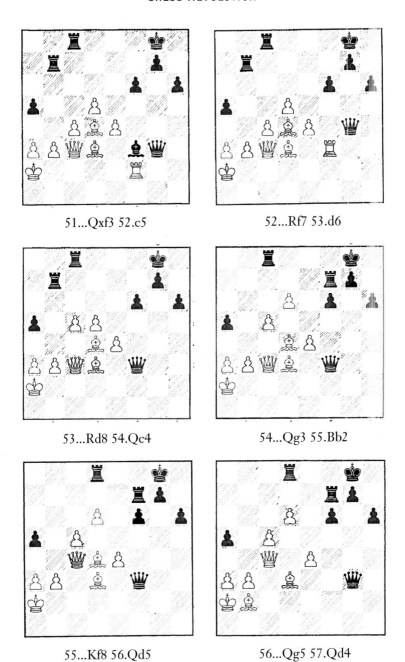

51...Qxf3 52.c5

52...Rf7 53.d6

53...Rd8 54.Qc4

54...Qg3 55.Bb2

55...Kf8 56.Qd5

56...Qg5 57.Qd4

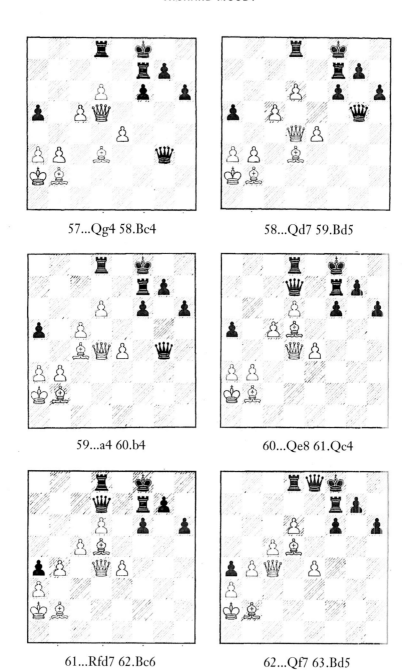

57...Qg4 58.Bc4

58...Qd7 59.Bd5

59...a4 60.b4

60...Qe8 61.Qc4

61...Rfd7 62.Bc6

62...Qf7 63.Bd5

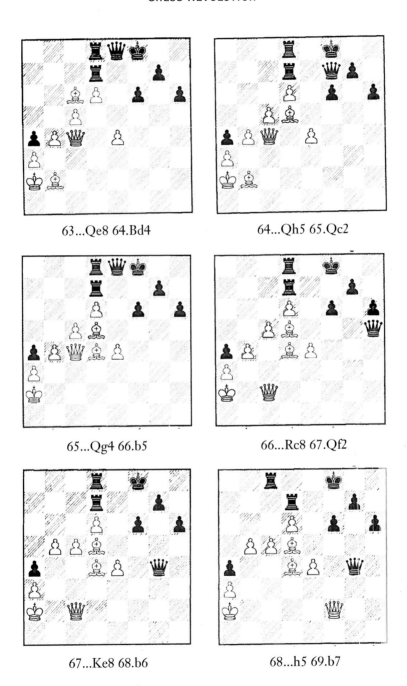

63...Qe8 64.Bd4

64...Qh5 65.Qc2

65...Qg4 66.b5

66...Rc8 67.Qf2

67...Ke8 68.b6

68...h5 69.b7

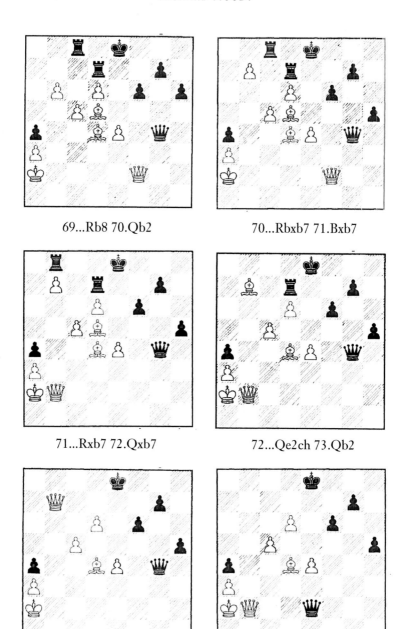

69...Rb8 70.Qb2

70...Rbxb7 71.Bxb7

71...Rxb7 72.Qxb7

72...Qe2ch 73.Qb2

73...Qxb2ch 74.Kxb2

74...Kd7 75.Kc3

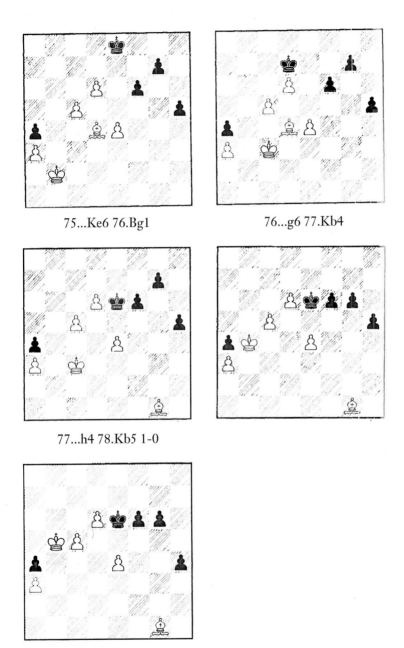

75...Ke6 76.Bg1

76...g6 77.Kb4

77...h4 78.Kb5 1-0

According to Fritz, mate in 20.

ANALYSIS: FRITZ (BERLINER VARIATION)

Quite clearly news of the death of the 4.Ng5 variation is premature. What is astounding is the number of tempos white picks up with 13.Nc3!! — by my count, at least seven when you total up all the tempos that black has to give back just to survive. It is even more astonishing that no one has played the Berliner Gambit like a gambit, instead falling victim to the wild variations (the author was seduced by 12.Qe2 Be6 13.Qf2, holding the piece, but 13...Nb4 14.Na3 yields the grotty Berliner compensation.).

Why no one has looked at 13.Nc3 using standard and rudimentary technique when dealing with a gambit is beyond comprehension. Somewhere the author has heard that the way to defeat a gambit is to give back just enough material to squash the attack (does bishop and two pawns for a rook sound familiar?) and then rely on positional gains to bring home the point. White assumes a raging initiative, putting black through hoops, who stands worse the entire middle game.

The author's journey to this position was long and arduous. GM Lev Alburt and the author looked at competing variations for hours. The move sequence leading up to the Berliner Variation will be filled in so the neophytes who wish to try the 4.Ng5 variation will feel confident if meant with "surprises" when playing the Two Knights Defense. Theory of the remaining variations will be covered elsewhere.

For centuries the Two Knights Defense has been a staple of the attacking player with black. The most brutal attacks, originating from the WBT, 4.Ng5 Bc5?! 5.Nxf7?? are just too sharp for over-the-board play and should be avoided. Should we acknowledge the significance of Traxler, who originated the opening, or the Wilkes-Barre Chess Club, who promoted it?

The Fritz is a different idea. Here black comes up with a different way to defend f7.

The idea is to meet 4.Ng5 d5 5.exd5 Nd4? (the Fritz) 6.c3 (This is good for white, so it is pointless to look for anything stronger.) 6...b5. Using the d4 knight to support this advance is the only choice (Nf5?? 7.d6+-), but this pawn is ultimately lost and costs black the game. White now makes the paradoxical retreat 7.Bf1! (Again, because this is favorable to white, why look for anything stronger?) 7...Nxd5 (Nf5 is relatively best simply sacrificing the pawn and defending a miserable position for the rest of the game, e.g., 8.Bxb5ch Bd7 9.Qa4+/-) 8.Ne4! (Nh3?! was the variation that GM Lev Alburt and the author analyzed exhaustively when the author wrote an unpublished manuscript on the Two Knights Defense. The idea is to meet 8...Bxh3! with 9.cxd4 Bd7 10.dxe5 =.) 8.Ne4 is the toughest variation. It is still not too late to bail with 8...Nf5 9.Bxb5ch Bd7 10.Qa4 Nb6 11.Bxd7ch Nxd7 12.d4 exd4 13.cxd4 Be7 14.Nc3 O-O 15.Be3 Nb6 16.Qd1+/-.

8...Qh4 (There is nothing better, but the anticipated piece sacrifice is unsound.) 9.Ng3

Bg4 10.f3 (Now black is guaranteed of losing a piece — in the words of GM Lev Alburt in analogous situations, "With some, but not full, compensation for the piece.") 10.e4 (The Berliner Variation: The most important thing to realize in this position is that black is making a pawn move in the middle of an attack.) 11.cxd4 Bd6 12.Qe2! (the Muir variation). Once again black should bail with 12...Bxg3ch 13.hxg3 Qxh1 14.Qxb5ch Bd7 15.Qxd5 and white has two minor pieces, a pawn, and an offside queen for the rook +/-. 12...Be6? (book) You will note that black has moved a pawn and retreated a bishop in the middle of the attack. This has to be bad. There again is internal harmony in chess: There has to be a positional refutation of this idea. Again I suppose that 13.Qxh5ch is book. (Once again this is a wrong assumption. The purpose is to meet 12...Be6 with 13.fxe4. Theory also misses 13.Qf2.) Dr. Berliner's mistaken analysis has steered the chess community away from perhaps the most promising opening in chess. It not only kills the Ng5 variation, it indirectly squashes the

Evans because professionals would prefer the dull Ruy Lopez to the sharper Italian game.

White has assiduously avoided the obvious 12.Bxb5ch with the wild Berliner Variations on move 12, and ditto for move 13. Apparently no one has looked at routine development as the thematic way to quell the attack. Hence 13.Nc3!! has been missed by theoreticians. (At least it is not in my Fritz 8's opening library.) Similar improvements for white will be presented in all the main lines.

In "the good old days," i.e., pre-computer days, the author would spend hours shuffling wood only to have GM Lev Alburt point out over and over that there was a tactical shot here or a positional treatment there that needed to be addressed. Little by little, literally concept by concept, it was possible to build an opening from the ground floor up. Like many theoreticians over the past thirty years, the siren call of the sharp Berliner Variation consumed me; it was only after a year's hiatus that one morning, in my mind's eye, the correct way of playing against it became "obvious." The Muir variation, 12.Qe2, seemed like the preferred choice in retrospect, forcing a highly beneficial trade of material and steering toward a simplified position with a clearly winning material plus.

When my Fritz 8 arrived in the mail, it seemed like a good idea to run the Berliner Variation through its silicon brain. In order to get a rating of 2700+, the Fritz 8 has to analyze sharp middle-game positions beyond world-championship level, i.e., the Berliner Variation is an outstanding kind of position to study with a computer. When the 12.Qe2 variation was played over the board, much to my amazement, the retreat. 12...Be6? was Fritz's response. The computer clearly avoided the whole line beginning with 12.Qe2 Bxg3ch etc. +/-. Within a few minutes, two stronger possibilities were "obvious": the quiet 12.Qe2 Be6. 13.Nc3 and the sharp 12.Qe2 Be6 13.Qf2, both of which were not in Fritz's memory. It was obvious at this point that all the analysis of the Berliner Variation was bogus because two out of the three candidate moves had been missed.

Even though a 2700 computer is a great research tool, it has to be steered in the right direction to be effective. Here, for example, when 13.Nc3 was first played, and the computer responded with the forced move 13...Nxc3, when the computer was asked to produce a move, it played 14.bxc3 after several minutes of thought! A human competitor would see instantly that 14.dxc3 straightens out white's pawn structure and turns an ugly duckling into a beautiful swan. More importantly the computer had to be told, "Oh by the way, trapping the queen on the h-file is desirable." (You will note that after the move sequence 13...Nxc3 14.bxc3 Bxg3ch 15.hxg3 Qxh1 16.Qxb5ch Kf8 17.Ba3ch Kg8, now white has blown the opportunity to stop 18...Qh6, and the queen is freed.)

What was instructive about the variations here was the fact that the black queen never got off the h-file or g1 because white controlled all the squares from h3 to h6 and g1 and g3, so the black queen was cornered like a rat throughout the course of much of the middle game. With patient maneuvering, the computer showed me how to exploit its more active pieces and pick up material without allowing counterplay. As a Class B player. it sure seemed like a good idea to go into an endgame with the patzer idea of Qg5/Qh4 forcing the exchange of queens. What a dumb idea! White should have realized his greatest asset was his active queen.

Very early on, based on the computer's evaluation of the 13.Nc3 idea and human/ computer analysis, it was clear that white was winning with 13.Nc3. But following the adage of some dumb chess player, the author started looking for something "stronger." Enter 13.Qf2? holding onto the extra piece due to the fact that 13...Bxg3 is not check. However, black can play more simply with 13...Nb4, more or less forcing 14.Na3 to cover the knight fork on c2. After over eighty games from this starting position, I lost to the Fritz 8 some eighty out of eighty-one games. And then it hit me — 12.Nc3 is a prosaic win. Why, when there is a winning plan for white, look for something stronger?

Here is a different way for a practical player to play the game of chess. When you find a winning plan, never look for anything stronger. Stay on message and don't allow distractions like a pretty tactical shot divert you from the task at hand. This was why the author returned to 13.Nc3 even though for the first ten moves, the computer gave a higher evaluation of the line 13.Qf2. The latter is a red herring, and it took weeks to see through the computer's ruse, i.e., that 13.Qf2 was a "good" idea. Within fifteen moves, despite making no errors, the computer's evaluation of white's position steadily dropped from a high of about 1.75 down to 1.0, down to .75, and eventually, given enough time and a few dubious moves, into negative territory.

The Fritz 8 evaluation algorithms in universal positions are terrible. It considers active pieces always to be more desirable than universal positions; thus when mainframe computers have to evaluate universal positions, they will always assume that the universal player is going to jump quickly into "classical" chess.

The move sequence 4.Ng5 d5 5.exd5 b5 6.Bf1 has no independent significance because the best that black can do is transpose to the Fritz with 6...Nd4 7.c3, and we have reached the Fritz by transposition. The problem facing black here is that the natural move 6...Qxd5 is met with 7.Nc+-. The only independent line is the weak 6...h6, trying to provoke 7.Nxf7, which is met with 7...Kxf7. Here is an analysis game Moody-Fritz (120/40) where the idea 6...h6 was tried: 8.bxc6 Qd5 9.Qf3! Qxf3 10.gxf3 (see diagram).

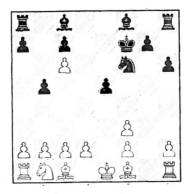

The balance of the analysis is by Fritz 8 in combination with the author: 10...a6 11.a4 b4 12.Bc4ch Be6 13.Bxe6ch Kxe6 14.D3 Nd5 15.Be3 Rb8 16.Nd2 Rb6 17.O-O-O Rxc6 18.Rhe1 Kf5 19.d4 g5 20.Nb3 Nxe3 21.fxe3 Rf6 22.Nd2 Bd6 23.Ne4 Rg6 24.h3 Rf8 25.c4 bxc3 26.bxc3 Ba3ch 27.Kc2 exd4 28.Rxd4 Rb6 29.R1d1 R8b8 30.R1d2 Rb2ch 31.Kd3 Ke6 32.Rxb2 Rxb2 33.Rc4 Kd7 34.h4 gxh4 35.Rxh4+-.

FRIED LIVER ATTACK

The "Fried Liver," or "Fegatello," is one of the oldest openings in chess. Is it sound? Well it depends on who you ask. According to Pincus, "Two Knights Defense Dispute RESOLVED" (see the website under this name for additional variations), the opening is a bust. To test this, the starting position was analyzed below with the Pincus idea, 10.O-O. My apologies to Mr. Pinkus if this game Moody-Fritz 8 (120'/25) mirrors analysis in his book. Fritz 8 pretty much concurs (with prompting) that 10.O-O is +-. 10...Na5 is a bust, but the analysis on line looks pretty good for white too.

Here is plausible play by both sides: 6.d4 (see diagrams below; once again only the white moves are given) 6...Bb4ch 7.c3 Be7 8.Nxf7 Kxf7 9.Qf3ch Ke6 10.O-O!! 10...Na5? (Fritz's book, but it is bad; black must improve here. Two poorer alternatives are: 1) 10...b5 11.Bxb5 Bb7 12.Bxc6 Bxc6 13.c4 Rf8 (Nb4 14.d5ch Nxd5 15.Rd1 +-) 14.cxd5ch Bxd5 15.Qe2 +- or 2) 10...g6 11.Qe4 Rf8 12.f4 Rb8 13.Bb3 a5 14.fxe5 Rxf1ch 15.Kxf1 a4 16.Qg4ch Kf7 17.Qf3ch Kg7 18.Bxd5 +-). Now white just picks up a tempo in a sharp position. This means that this variation is incomparably better than the main line (10.Qe4 b5 11.Bxb5 Bb7 12.f4 Nf6 13.Bc4ch Kd7 14.Qf5ch Ke8 15.fxe5 Nxd4 16.Qf21 Bc5 17.cxd4 Bxd4 18.Qe2 Nd7 19.Nc3 Nxe5 20.Bf4 Qh4ch 21.Bg3 Bxc3ch 22.bxc3 Qxc4 23.Qxe5ch Kf8 24.Rf1 ch Kg8 25.Rf2 Bch 26.O-O-O h5 27.R2d2 Re8 28.Rd8 Qf7 29.Rxe8ch Bxe8 30.Rd8 Kh7 31.Qe4ch Qg6 (g6 Rd5+/-)

32.Qxg6ch Bxg6 33.Rd7 Rf8 34.Rxc7 Rf7 35.Rc5 = to +/=).
Returning to the main line, i.e., 10...Na5 11.Bd3 Bf6 12.Re1 Nc6, this just gives away a tempo. 13.Be4 (You will note that it took black three moves to play Nc6 and white only two moves to play Be4, i.e., white gains a tempo over the main line with 10.Qe4/f4) 13...g5! (As

141

good as anything; black decides to restrain f4) 14.c4 (Black cannot allow simple moves like this. What makes this opening amazing is the ease with which white gets an overpowering position without facing any tough choices, i.e., it is a simple opening to play.) 14...Nxd4 (What else?) 15.cxd5ch Kf7 16.Qd3 Kg7 17.Nc3 (This is a "classical" attack, hence "Knights before bishops is appropriate.") 17...Bd7 18.Be3 Rc8 (desperately trying to get counterplay) 19.Rad1 a6 (to discourage Ne2) 20.Rd2 (Centralization! This is the type example of control of the center.) Two questions: How many players would want to play the black side of this position? How many of the white moves between 10-20 are "tough" to find? This is why this variation is so dangerous. White has too many no-brainers. Amazingly white has equal material to go with an overpowering position. The author concurs with Mr. Pincus: 10.O-O appears to cook 5...Nxd5.

6... Bb4ch 7.c3   7...Be7 8.Nxf7

   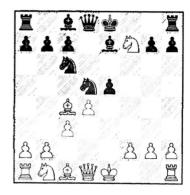

142

8...Kxf7 9.Qf3ch

9...Ke6 10.O-O!

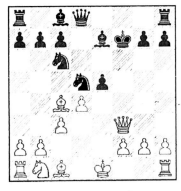

10...Na5 11.Bd3

11...Bf6 12.Re1

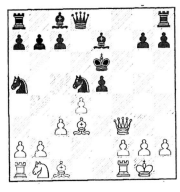

12...Nc6 13.Be4

13...g5 14.c4

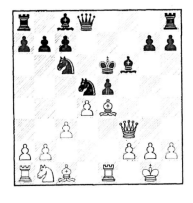

14...Nxd4 15.cxd5ch

15...Kf7 16.Qd3

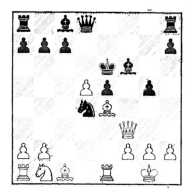

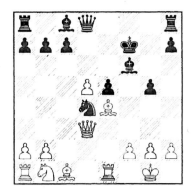

16...Kg7 17.Nc3

17...Bd7 18.Be3

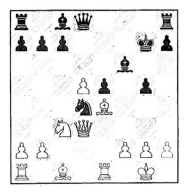

18...Rc8 19.Rad1

19...a6 20.Rd2 +/-

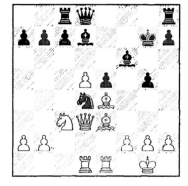

While modern theory has come a long way since *ECO* and *MCO* were published, it would appear that the evaluation of the Fried Liver as not sound for black is incorrect.

Fried Liver

IM Keith Rodriquez and I wrote an article for Yearbook 110, *New In Chess* called, "The Fried Liver Fandango-Reassessment". Our work is an update of Maarten de Zeeuw's article in the Yearbook, 75. This iteration of the opening utilizes superior software, Fritz 15, a 3200 level computer. Our major conclusion is that 5...Nxd5 has not been refuted. The move sequence in question is: **1.e4 e5 2.Nf3 Nc6 3.Bc4 Nf6 4.Ng5 d5 5.exd5 Nxd5 6.Nxf7**

We now look at the four known continuations by White after **6.Nxf7 Kxf7 7.Qf3+ Ke6 8.Nc3 Nb4**. They are ranked from worst to best. **9.a3? 9.Qe4, 9.Bb3, 9.O-O!**

9.a3? Nxc2+ 10.Kd1 Nxa1 11.Nxd5 Qh4! White is busted 12.Nxc7+ Kd7 13.Qf7+ Qe7 14.Qxe7+ Bxe7 15.Nxa8 Kd6! (A key resource; now Black keeps his extra piece; Fritz evaluates this position as -1.24, -/+) **16.d4 Bf5 17.dxe5+ Kc5 18.Bf7 Rxa8 19.Ke2 Nc2 20.Rd1 Rd8 21.b4+ Kb5 22.Rxd8 Bxd8 23.Kd1 Nd4 24.Bb2 Be6! 25.Bxd4 Bxf7 26.Bxa7** (If White cannot play this there is nothing better. I let Fritz think White has three pawns for the piece, but only temporarily. Black, with inexact play, only drew in Canizares-Cuadra-Jimienez, **LSS**, 2006.) **Bd5 27.g3 Bc7 28.Bd4 Bb3+ 29.Ke2 Ka4 30.f4 Kxa3 31.Bc5 Be6 32.Ke3 g6 33.Ke4 Ka4 34.g4 Bxg4 35.Kd5 Kb4 36.Bf8 Bb6 37.e6 Bb3 38.Ke5 Bc7+ 39.Kf6 Bxf4 40.h3 Kc6 41.e7 Kd7 42.Kf7 Bd5+ 0-1**

Here is how the variation should have been played. White did not have enough play for the material and got ground down.

This is much stronger for Black **9.Qe4 c6 10.a3 Na6 11.d4 Nc7 12.Bf4 Kf7 13.Bxe5 Be6 14.O-O Bd6 15.f4 Bxe5 16.fxe5+ Kg8 17.Qf3 g6 18.Bxd5 Nxd5 19.Ne4 Kg7 20.Nc5 Qe7 21.c4 Nc7 22.Qd3 Rhb8** (White has inadequate counterplay for the piece. Fritz

145

calls this - /+) 23.h3 b5 24.b3 Rf8 25.Qc3 Qh4 (Black begins to assume the initiative) 26.Nb7 Kg8 27.Rae1 bxc4 28.bxc4 Rab8 29.Na5 Bd7 30.Kh2 Rxf1 31.Rxf1 Qe4 32.Qf3 Qxf3 33.Rxf3 Ne6 34.d5 cxd5 35.cxd5 Nc7 36.d6 Ne6 37.Nc4 Rb5 38.Re3 Kf7 39.Kg3 Ke8 40.Kf2 Rc5 41.Nd2 Rc2 42.Ke2 Nf4+ 43.Rd1 Rc5 44.Ne4 Ba4+ 45.Ke1 Rxe5 46.Nf6+ Kf7 47.Rxe5 Nd3+ 48.Ke2 Nxe5 49.Nxh7 Bc6 50.g4 Nc4 51.Kd3 Nxd6 52.Ng5 Kf6 53.Nh7+ Ke5 54.Ke2 Nb5 55.h4 Nxa3 56.Kd2 a5 57.Kc3 Bd5 58.Kd2 Nb5 59.Kc1 a4 0-1

To illustrate how opening theory is full of holes, the next developing move has been absent in theory and play.

9.Bb3 c6 10.a3 Na6 11.Nxd5 cxd5 12.d4 Kd6 N 13.Qxd5+ Kc7 14.Qxe5+ Qd6 15.Bf4 Qxe5 16.Bxe5+ Bd6 17.f4 Rf8 18.O-O g6= to +/=.

Here is a centaur game in this variation: 9.O-O c6 10.d4 Qf6 11.Qd1

This is the second centaur game in this variation. 9.O-O c6 10.d4 Qf6 11.Qd1 Ke7! (Keith and I underestimated this key resource and gave best for Black exd4; this rapidly simplifies into an ending where White has two pawns and a Bishop for the Rook with a draw the likely outcome) 12.Re1 Qg6 13.Rxe5+ Kd8 14.Nxd5 Nxd5 15.Qf3 Bd6 16.Bxd5!= Bxe5 17.Be4 Bxh2+ 18.Kxh2 Qg4 19.d5 Re8 20.Qxg4 Bxg4 21.f3 cxd5 22.Bxd5 Bf5 23.Bxb7 Rb8 24.Bd5 Re2 25.c3 (Fritz evaluates this as 0.00, dead equal because the Rook on the second is compensation)

MAIN LINE: TWO KNIGHTS DEFENSE
4.NG5 D5 5.EXD5 NA5 6.BB5CH C6 7.DXC6 BXC6 8.BE2

This is a complex position but, just like the other variations, does not lead to full equality for black. A quick way to lose is 7.dxc6 Nxc6?? 8.Bxc6ch +/= Bc5 9.Nxf7+-. The real choice for black is to drive the knight back with 8.Be2 h6 9.Nf3, not the weird Steinitz 9.Nh3?. Just because GM Fischer made it work doesn't mean it is sound. Black should ignore the knight and just make any ten developing moves in a row, e.g., Bd6/Bc7/Qd6/O-O/Nb7/Nc5/Be6/Rfe8/Re7/R8e8, etc. Black must not dally and hit the knight quickly with 9...e4 10.Ne5 (see diagram).

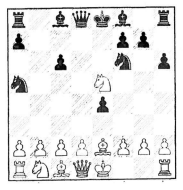

Black has two main choices that will be dealt with here: 10...Bd6 and 10...Bc5. We believe that 10...Bc5 is correct and gives black decent chances in practice to draw (but never equalize). With the Bd6 variation, the best black can hope to do is give up the minor exchange for knight and pawn; this leaves black with a 1/2 pawn disadvantage and a huge positional minus. He faces a three-to-two pawn majority on the queenside and a busted pawn structure. Play here in the Bd6 line will be discussed in a little more detail than some of the other variations because, unlike the Berliner Variation, black has real chances to equalize.

First of all, black has to play something sharp. Thus an alternative such as 10...Be7 should never be considered. More appetizing for black is to try to drive off the centralized knight with 10...Bd6. 11.d4. (When looking at this variation for an unpublished book, 11.f4 seemed better, but Fritz has provided a simple plus for white here in the main line, so there doesn't seem to be any need to look for something stronger.) 11...exd3 e.p. is a forced move.

Black cannot allow white to anchor the knight in the center of the board: 12.Nxd3 Qc7 (with an obvious hit on h2, which may or may not be a threat, depending on which grandmaster is annotating the position. But 13.h3 is natural and good.)

Black now seeks rapid development with 13...O-O. White follows suit. 14.O-O Re8

15.Nd2 (Notice that white has almost a universal position, the most difficult kind of position to attack.) 15...c5 (If this is bad, black has real problems here.) 15...Nb7/Nc5 seems reasonable if there weren't knights on d2 and d3. 16.b3 (The bishop threatens to come into play powerfully with 17.Bb2.) 16...Be5!? (Black seeks to muddy the waters.) 17.Bb2 (Everything comes with tempo; black is just one tempo too slow to really complicate.) 17... Bxb2 18.Nxb2 (White fianchettos the knight!) 18... Bb7 19.Bf3 (White says, "Nope, you are not getting that diagonal.") 19...Rae8 (Black's response, "Okay, I'll just grab the d-file instead.") 20.Bxb7 (Every exchange benefits white. The general rule is this: When you are ahead in material, trade pieces, not pawns.) 20...Nxb7 21.Re1 (Preventing black from doubling anywhere and attempting to force additional simplification.) 21...Rxe1ch 22.Qxe1 Re8 23.Qf1 Qf4 24,Nde4 (Fritz 8 makes an interesting decision; it recognizes that there are no kingside threats, so it just focuses on the queenside.) Fritz's evaluation of the final position: +/-. In the hands of a strong grandmaster, he/she would win at least eight out of ten games against comparably rated players. This is a dismal position for black and a good reason to abandon this variation. There seems little room for improvement. If black can be given the most aggressive attacking concepts and he or she still fails, the opening has to be a bust for black (see diagrams).

10.Ne5

10...Bd6 11.d4

11...exd3 e.p. 12.Nxd3

12...Qc7 13.h3

13...O-O 14.O-O

14Re8 15.Nd2

15...c5 16.b3

16...Be5 17.Bb2

17...Bxb2 18.Nxb2

18...Bb7 19.Bf3

19...Rad8 20.Bxb7

20...Nxb7 21.Re1

21...Rxe1ch 22.Qxe1

22...Re8 23.Qf1

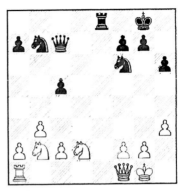

23...Qf4 24.Ndc4+/- to +-

This is a very ambitious try by black, which almost, but not quite, equalizes. White probably has to restrain Qd4 with 11.c3. A residual benefit is that the threat of b4 gains time. Black can best meet that threat with 11...Bd6. Paradoxically, "losing" a tempo here gains in position, compared to an immediate Bd6 (10...Bd6). White should now anchor the knight with 12.f4 and force black to play aggressively with 12...Qc7 13.d4. Threatening to keep the knight on e5 forever has to be met, so 13...exd3 is probably best.

Now comes a critical choice for white: 14.Nxd3? or 14.Qxd3? Theory regards 14.Qxd3 as best (with the vacant square c2, this is possible). 14...O-O 15.O-O Rd8 16. Qc2 (White just lost a tempo; this is why 10...Bc5 is superior to 10...Bd6. In the 10...Bd6 line, white never lost any time during the course of the attack.) Nd5 17.b4 (There doesn't appear any way to relieve the pressure and not allow other possibilities.) 17. -Nb7 18.Na3 (more or less forcing black's hand) 18...Nxf4 19.Bxf4 Bxe5 20.Exe5 Qxe5 21.Ne4 Qg5 22.Qc1 Qxc1 23.Rfxc1+/=. According to GM Lev Alburt (and general principles), white is slightly better, i.e., better pawn structure and a queenside pawn majority. White has retained his/her first move advantage all the way to the endgame. Black has to fight to draw this position. The author invites Ruy Lopez players to take a long, hard look at this position; this is the best that black can do against 4.Ng5.

10...Bc5 11.c3   11...Bd6 12.f4

12...Qc7 13.d4   13...exd3 e.p. 14.Qxd3

14...O-O 15.O-O   15...Rd8 16.Qc2

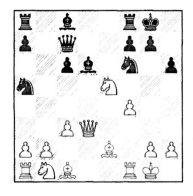 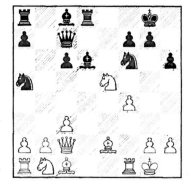

16...Nd5 17.b4

17...Nb7 18.Na3

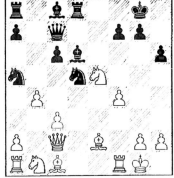

18...Nxf4 19.Bxf4

19...Bxe5 20.Bxe5

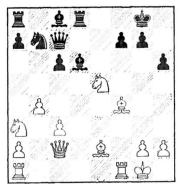

20...Qxe5 21.Nc4

21...Qg5 22.Qc1

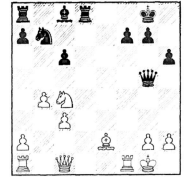

22...Qxc1 23.Rfxc1+/=

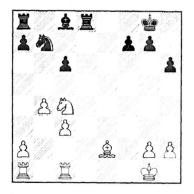

In the event that 8.Be2 allows black to equalize, the sharp 8.Qf3 is very promising. However, the variations are far sharper, far more unclear, and far more difficult to play positionally with white than 8.Be2. The better tactician will win in the sharp 8.Qf3 cxb5 9.Qxa8 variation (see diagram below). It is not what comes off the board that matters. It is what stays on the board. Here the black minors are very powerful. The other variations offer black slight hope of equality.

If 10...Bc5 allows black to equalize, then the author highly recommends 8.Qf3 with this caveat in mind: with a queen on f3, white should always try to retreat his/her bishop to e2. The author has defeated Fritz 8 in this variation and drawn several games in different variations.

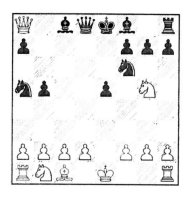

WILKES-BARRE TRAXLER (WBT)
1.E4 E5 2.NF3 NC6 3.BC4 NF6 4.NG5 BC5

The WBT has a fearsome reputation in the sharp variations where the knight captures on f7, but a far less desirable outcome results from the quieter variations. However, it took the author dozens of tries to find the correct move order. Here is how the game score Moody-Fritz 120'/30 occurred after a half dozen false starts. White should hit f7 immediately with 5.Bxf7ch Ke7 6.Bd5 Rf8 (with a nasty hit on f2 in many variations. In such variations as 7.d3, 7...Bxf2ch is possible.). The correct way to proceed is to play 7.Bxc6! to end the possibility of Nd4. This is an idea of Anand-Beliavsky in an article in *Inside Chess* by IM John Donaldson, "Death Knell for the Wilkes-Barre." Black's pawn structure is a static weakness. but before the endgame, God created the middle game.

After 7...dxc6 the author tries to justify the position with 8.Qe2 Ng4 9.f3 Bf2ch 10.Kf1 Bb6 11.Nh3/Nc3/Nd1/Nhf2, but black has enough pressure to equalize. This is the critical position of the WBT, so white must improve: 8.Nf3! Just like that, game over!! (Nxe4 9.Qe2 +/- Fritz 8). There is no attack, and black is struggling to justify both his terrible pawn structure and the missing pawn. This is already at least +/- in a game between super grandmasters and +/= between masters. As is the case for the other variations here, it is white on move. We follow the game Moody-Fritz 8 out to the point that any decent grandmaster could bring home the full point in at least nine of ten tries against comparable opponents.

Black made the first major mistake in this variation, i.e., 8...Kf7 9.d3 Kg8 10.Be3 Bd4?! (Bd6 is better, but it is doubtful that 11...Bxe3 equalizes because white trades in a doubled pawn so that white opposes the open file, making it difficult for black to capitalize on it. The problem facing black over the long run is that he/she is simply a pawn down with no compensation. No matter what, white is going to wind up with a protected passed pawn in the center, a winning position in the hands of, say, GMs Karpov or Korchnoi against any opponent.) The next two moves are easy to find: 11.Nxd4 exd4 (giving white a winning position in the late middle game). 12.Bg5 (When ahead in material, trade pieces, not pawns.) 12...Qd6 13.Bxf6 Rxf6 14.O-O Be6 15.f3 Raf8 (Already black is in sheer react mode with no positive plans.) 16.Rf2 a6 17.a4 (stifling any hope black has on the queenside). 17... Rh6 18.g3 (White has to meet a number of obvious threats, like mate!) Rg6 19.Nd2 c5 20.b3 (To restrain the queenside, white again forces black to come up with some other plan to get counterplay.)

Black now tries a cute tactical trick to improve its position (to no avail): 20...Qf4! (A tactical trick — all sound and fury, signifying nothing.) 21.Kh1 Qh6 22.Qg1 Rf4 (ditto) 23.Re1 a5.

We now enter what can be described as a trial-and-error position. White pokes and prods and tries to force a blunder by the computer. 24.Rg2 Bh3 25.R12 (so much for that idea!) Be6 26.Rfe2 Rf8 27.Rf2 (to see if black repeats the position. If black had repeated the position, white was prepared to try R2e2/Qf2.). Be6 28.f4 Bg4 29.h4 (slowly crawling into black's position). Qh5 30.Qg2 b6 31.Kg1 Qf7 32,Nf1 (unnecessarily cautious — Nf3 immediately is better). Qe6 33.Nd2 Qf7 34.Nf3 Qe6 35.f5 Qe7 36.Ref1 Bxf3 37.Rxf3 c6 38.g4 Rh6 39.g5 Rxh4 40.Qg3 Rh5 41.f6+- (Fritz 8 claims that white is completely winning here.).

White is again on move here.

4...Bc5

5...Ke7 6.Bd5

6...Rf8 7.Bxc6

7...dxc6 8.Nf3

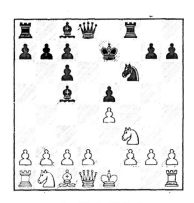

8...Kf7 9.d3

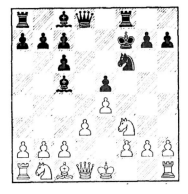

9...Kg8 10.Be3

10... Bd4 11.Nxd4

11 ...exd4 12.Bg5

12…Qd6 13.Bxf6

13…Rxf6 14.O-O

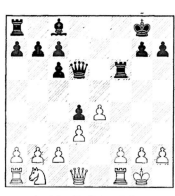

14…Be6 15.f3

15…Raf8 16.Rf2

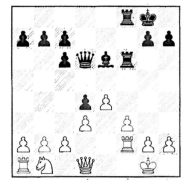

16...a6 17.a4

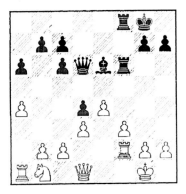

17...Rh6 18.g3

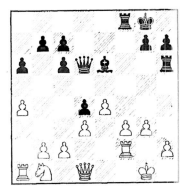

18... Rg6 19.Nd2

19.. c5 20.b3

20...Qf4 21.Kh1

21...Qh6 22.Qg1

22...Rf4 23.Re1

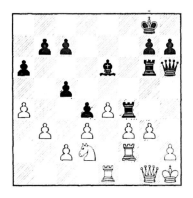

23...a5 24.Rg2

24...Bh3 25.Rf2

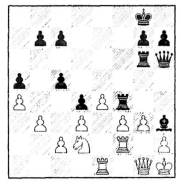

25...Be6 26.Rfe2

26...Rf'8 27.Rf2

27...Rgf6 28.f4

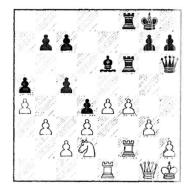

28...Bg4 29.h4

29...Qh5 30.Qg2

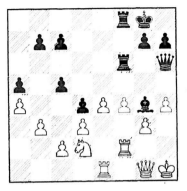

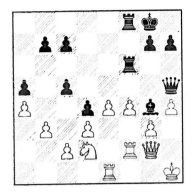

30...b6 31.Kg1

31...Qf7 32.Nf1

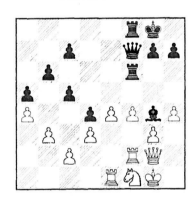

32...Qe6 33.Nd2

33...Qf7 34.Nf3

34...Qe6 35f5

35...Qe7 36.Ref1

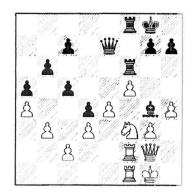

36...Bxf3 37.Rxf3

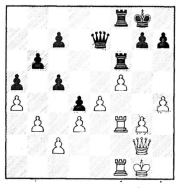

37...c6 38.g4

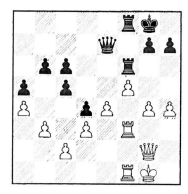

38...Rh6 39.g5

39...Rxh4 40.Qg3

40...Rh5 41.f6 +-

Once again the prickly nature of the universal positions allows white to begin a coordinated advance of his kingside pawns; meanwhile black has little or no counterplay on the queenside. The correct procedure in the WBT is clear: chop on c6 and play Nf3 immediately. This shuts down the attack and forces black to make progress in the middle game. As the subject game shows, this is easier said than done. It will be generally recognized fairly soon that 7.Bxc6/8.Nf3 cooks the WBT.

What should be clear is that black cannot improve here, e.g., 5.Bxd5ch Ke7 6. id5 Qe8?! 7.Bxc6! dxc6 8.d3 Qg6 9.Qe2 h6 10.Nf3 +-. Black has an exposed king and no compensation for the pawn (see below).

PHILIDOR DEFENSE
1.E4 E5 2.NF3 D6 3.D4 EXD4 4.NXD4 NF6 5.QE2

One of the weakest openings in chess, the passive Philidor Defense melds poorly with 1...e5.

After 2.Nf3 d6 3.d4 exd4 4.Nxd4 Nf6 5.Qe2 Be7 6.Nc3 O-O 7.Bg5 Re8 8.h4 h6 9.O-O-O

(Fritz 8 didn't find this shot; now it is either accept the piece or simply stand much worse. Threats of f3/g4 loom in the air.) 9...hxg5 10.hxg5 Ng4 11.f4 g6 (The threat is Nf5 regaining the piece.) 12.Qe1! (a very powerful move threatening both Qc3 and Qh4) Kg7 (to contest the h-file) 13.Nd5! (adding more fuel to the fire) Bxg5 (trying to quell the attack by giving back the piece — black is busted) 14.fxg5 14...c6 15.Qc3! Re5 (to defend against the discovery) 16.Nf6 Nxf6 17.gxf6ch Qxf6 18.Bd3 Kg8 19.Rdf1 Qg7 20.Bc4 (courtesy of 1...e5) 20...d5 21.exd5 b5 22.Bb3 c5 23.Qxc5. (The stronger players can tune out now. This is a train wreck. The game is played out to checkmate so that the class players can see how human/computer tactics are lethal.) Bd7 (Bg4 24.Rh4+-) 24.Qc7 Na6 25.Qxd7 Nc5 26.Qxb5 Nxb3 27.Qxb3 Rf8 28.d6 Rh5 29.Rxh5 gxh5 30.Qd5 Rd8 31.Nf5 Qg5ch 32. Kb1 Rxd6 33.Qxd6 Qxg2 34 Ne7ch Kg7 35.Qf6ch Kh7 36.Qxf7ch Qg7 37.Qxh5ch Qh6 38.Qf7ch Qg7 39.Rh1#.

If black cannot survive with the move sequence Nf6/Be7/ O-O/Re8, he has to be busted. The combination of 1.e5 weakening the f7 square and then following with the passive d6 gives white, effectively, a two tempo lead in development. Add to that the fact that white castles queenside, and we are already talking about a three-tempo lead in development in the early middle game. Black can never recover from his dismal opening (see diagram).

4...Nf6 5.Qe2

5...Be7 6.Nc3

6...O-O 7.Bg5

7...Re8 8.h4

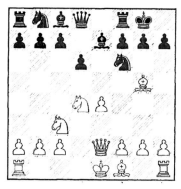
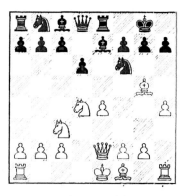

8... h6 9.O-O-O

9...hxg5 10.hxg5

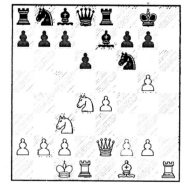

10...Ng4 11.f4

11...g6 12.Qe1

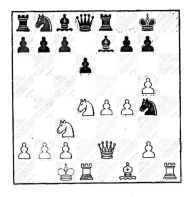

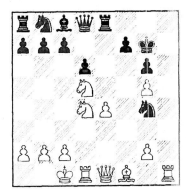

12...Kg7 13.Nd5

13...Bxg5 14.fxg5

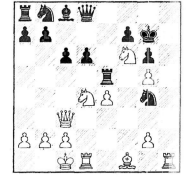

14...c6 15.Qc3

15...Re5 16.Nf6

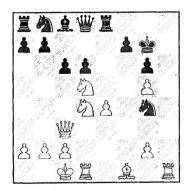

16...Nxf6 17.gxf6ch

17...Qxf6 18.Bd3

18...Kg8 19.Rdf1

18...Qg7 19.Bc4

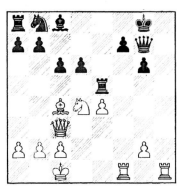

19...d5 20.exd5

20...b5 21.Bb3

21...c5 22.Qxc5+-

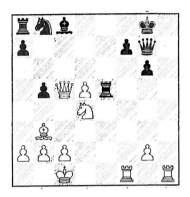

All white has to do to win from the starting position is to play Qe2/Nc3/Bg5/h4/O-O-O, and black is busted. Black must castle kingside quickly or just stand worse.

LATVIAN GAMBIT
1.E4 E5 2.NF3 F5 3.NXE5

The Latvian Gambit has little to recommend it besides shock value. It is inherently unsound, conferring a lasting initiative to white the entire game. Black is never in this game and, slowly but steadily, stands helplessly as white builds for the final assault.

With the move sequence 1.e4 e5 2.Nf3 f5, we reach the Latvian Gambit. Although pattern recognition is helpful, it can also be a hindrance. Here, for example, white noticed that he could transpose to a Falkbeer Countergambit with colors reversed and an extra tempo, i.e., 1.e4 e5 2.Nf3 f5 3.d4? This leads nowhere and is inferior to 3.Nxe5.

> Rule #1: When you find a winning plan, save time
> on the clock and don't look for anything stronger.

To return to the game continuation: 3...Qf6 4.d4 (naturally) d6 (bumping the knight to a good square) 5.Nc4. White is up two tempos in a soon-to-be semi-open position. Many players may not realize that white spent three useful moves with his king knight. Each move is additional development because the knight winds up on a square that it cannot access in less than three moves. White has five tempos here. The knight moved three times, and both bishops are freed. In the author's arithmetic, this counts as five tempos. Black, on the other hand, has gained three tempos. The queen has moved, and black has freed both bishops. Therefore, white has a two-tempo lead in development.

In the internal harmony of chess, if you move pieces to squares that they cannot access in one move, it is additional development. A good example is this: 1.Qd1/Qe2/Qf3 only gains one tempo because the queen can get to f3 from the starting position in one move. The move sequence 1/Qd1/Qe2/Qe3 gains two tempos because the queen

does not have access to e3 in less than two moves. The example here
is even better, i.e., Nf3/Nxe5/Nc4/Ne3/Nxf5. White gives back his
lead in development to win the minor exchange and leave e4 as lunch.
White is already +- here.

> Rule #2: If you have a choice between Qd1/Qe2/Qf3
> or Qd1/Qe2/Qe3, in the overwhelming number of
> situations (barring some cheap tactical trick), it
> usually is better to gain the extra tempo with the
> latter move sequence. This has to do with the inter-
> nal harmony of chess, i.e., gaining time at no cost is
> usually a good idea.

To return to the game continuation: 5.Nc4 fxe4 6.Nc3. White
just gained another tempo. Black spent a pawn move to maintain material equality, which is essential. In addition to the fact that black is
three tempos down, his pawn on e4 is an inviting target. He will have
to spend time to defend it or to decide not to defend it, which would
mean that fxe4 is useless. In a comparable position where a pawn is
lost inevitably, a supercomputer of the future probably would not even
play fxe4 because it would realize that the pawn is lost no matter what,
and, therefore, a reasonable developmental move, as an alternative,
would be desirable.

At this point, we are following the consultation game Moody/
Fritz-Fritz/Moody. 6...Bf5 7.Ne3 Ne7 8.Nxf5 Qxf5 9.Bc4 Nbc6 10.d5
Ne5 11.Bb3 Nd7 12.Nb5 Kd8 13.O-O Qg6 14.c4 Nf5 15.Kh1 Be7
16.Bc2 Rf8 17.Nc3 +-. White picks up a free pawn and prepares the
final breakthrough with the idea of a well-prepared c5 opening the
position (see diagram).

2...f5 3.Nxe5

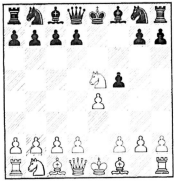

3...Qf6 4.d4

4...d6 5.Nc4

5...fxe4 6.Nc3

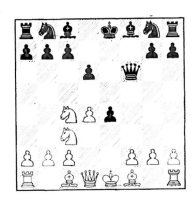

6...Bf5 7.Ne3

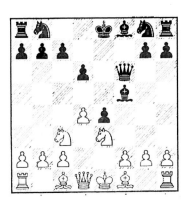

7...Ne7 8.Bc4

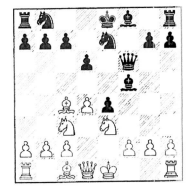

8...Nbc6 9.Nxf5

9...Qxf5 10.d5

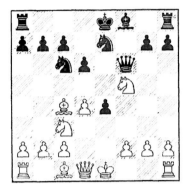

10...Ne5 11.Bb3

11...Nd7 12.Nb5

12...Kd8 13.O-O

13...Qg6 14.c4

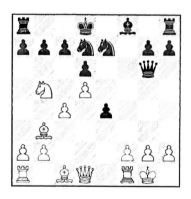

14...Nf5 15.Kh1   15...Be7 16.Bc2

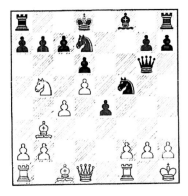 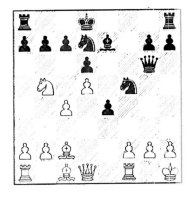

16...Ne5 17.Nc3+-

White picks up the e-pawn at no cost and then just builds for the c5-break, hammering the black king in the center of the board.

ALEKHINE DEFENSE
1.E4 NF6 2.QE2 E5 3.F4

One of the misleading notes in *ECO* is one that treats 1.e4 Nf6 2.Qe2 as equal. Actually after 2...e5, 3.f4 white has transposed to a favorable variation of the King's Gambit. GM Lev Alburt suggested a transposition to a Pirc with 2...d6 (unclear). The move sequence 1.e4 e5 2.f4 exf4 3.Qe2 has been published in *Empire Chess, Rank and File Magazine, Chess Life, Check!*, and *The Universal Attack: The Search For Truth And Beauty* and has appeared in various publications as the Moody Gambit, the Moody-Alburt Gambit, the Heinola-Alburt-Moody (HAM) Gambit, the Heinola-Alburt-Moody-Basman (HAMB) Gambit, and here, the next iteration, the A-T Gambit, i.e., Alburt-Basman-Dlugy-Green-Heinola-Kasparov-Mar-Moody-Resheysky-Rigby-Taylor Gambit! We have four practitioners and eight theoreticians. For 3...Nf6, see below. However, Moody-Green, Postal 1997 saw 3...Nc6!. In order to avoid 4.Nf3 g5! (-/+), white tried 4.c3 Qh4ch! 5.Kd1 d6 6.Nf3 (Kc2 -/+) Qg4! 7.Qf2 Nf6 8.d3 d5! -+ 0-1:27.

We now follow the game Moody-Bullock (Postal, 1994) 1.e4 Nf6 2.Qe2 e5. Here is an interesting alternative seen in Moody-Graham (Postal, 1994). That game saw the move sequence 1.e4 Nf6 2.Qe2 d5!? (TN?). Play continued 3.e5 Ne4 4.d4 (threatening to trap the knight on the open board). 4...h6 5.Nd2 Bf5 6.Qb5ch Nc6 7.c3 Nxd2 8.Bxd2 Qd7 9.Bd3 with a complex game.

The game Moody-Bullock continued 3.f4 (transposing to a favorable variation of the A-T Gambit) 3...exf4 (4...d5!) 4.e5 (now this is better) 4...Nd5 5.Nf3 Be7 6.c4 Nb4 7.d4 Bh4ch 8.Kd1 O-O 9.g3! (threatening to expose the black king to a ferocious attack). 9...Be7 (Black now recognizes that the plan beginning with Bh4ch was not good. According to GM Alburt, white is better here.) 10.gxf3 (favorably regaining the pawn) 10...d6 (nibbling at the center) 11.a3 (bye knight!) Nb4a6 12.Qg2 Bf5 13.Nbd2 Nd7 14.Qg3 (to anchor the Knight on h4) 14...dxe5 15.fxe5 Re8 16.Rg1 Bf8 17.Nh4 Bg6 18.Nxg6 fxg6 (White is still better here.) 19.Bd3 Re6 20.Nf3? (just 20.Kc2 is +/=) 20...Nxe5!! (Ouch! White was blindsided.) 21.Nxe5 Qxd4 (Black has a strong attack.) 22.Re1 Rd8 23.Kc2 Nc5 24.Bf4 Nxd3 25.Qxd3 Qxf4 26.Qxd8 Qf2ch 27.Kb3?? (Kc3 +-) 27...Rd6?? (27...Rb6ch is mate in seven, according to Fritz 8.) 28.Qxc7 Rb6ch 29.Qxb6! (Now white sees the mate.) 29...Qxb6ch +/-. The remaining moves culminate in a post-a-log error in a losing position. The final moves are presented without comment: 30.Ka2 Bd6 31.Rad1 Qc7 32.Rd5 g5 33.Re4 h6 34.Kb3 a6 35.Ka2 Bxe5 36.Rd5xe5 Qxc4?? 37.Rxc4 1:0. Once again it is white on move (see diagrams).

2...e5 3.f4

3...exf4 4.e5

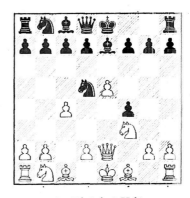

4...Nd5 5.Nf3

5...Be7 6.c4

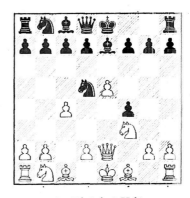

6...Nb4 7.d4

7...Bh4ch 8.Kd1

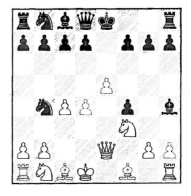

8...O-O 9.g3

9...Be7 10.gxf4

10...d6 11.a3

11...Nb4a6 12.Qg2

12...Bf5 13.Nbd2

13...Nd7 14.Qg3

14...dxe5 15.fxe5

15...Re8 16.Rg1

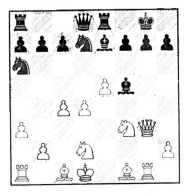

16...Bf8 19.Nh4

17...Bg6 18.Nxg6

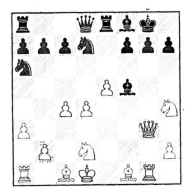

18...fxg6 19.Bd3

19...Re6 20.Nf3

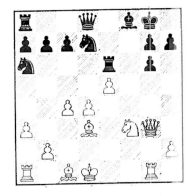

20...Nxe5 21.Nxe5

21...Qxd4 22.Re1

22...Rd8 23.Kc2

23...Nc5 24.Bf4

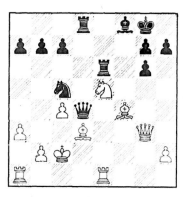

24...Nxd3 25.Qxd3

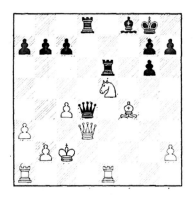

25...Qxf4 26.Qxd8

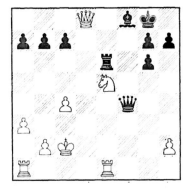

26...Qf2ch 27.Kb3   27....Rd6 28.Qxc7

28...Rb6ch 29.Qxb6   29...Qxb6ch 30.Ka2+/-

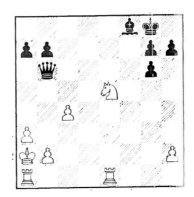

Perhaps instead of the Alekhine Gambit Accepted, he should have tried 3…d5 with a Falkbeer Countergambit.

SUPPLEMENTAL GAMES: ALEKHINE DEFENSE

One of the problems with a new move order is that the practitioner may stray from accurate play, making the practical results useless. Again and again in the supplemental games given here, players blunder at a very high rate, making their play of little use insofar as theory is concerned. For example, in Bodrogi-Krizsani, Budapest, 1995, white made a key error very early, i.e., 1.e4 Nf6 2.Qe2 e5 3.f4 exf4 4.Nf3?. (This is clearly inferior to 4.e5 — see Moody-Bullock in the previous section.) 4...d5 5.e5 Nh5 and black has his extra pawn and threatens the standard ploy of g5. If white tries 6.Qf2 (best), then black is still better after 6...Be7. White is losing his ability to impose his will on the game and has some, but not full, compensation for the pawn.

The next game is Bodrogi-Sziebert, Budapest, 1995, where white could again have improved. 1.e4 Nf6 2.Qe2 e5 3.f4 d5!. (This is a Falkbeer Countergambit and is one of the best tries for black; it is very complex, and the reader is encouraged to look at the analysis of the Falkbeer Countergambit at the end of the supplemental games.)

We get little useful information from the game Bark-Etmans, Enschede Cham. Netherlands, 1996. 1.e4 Nf6 2.Qe2 e5 3.c3? (perhaps to reinforce d4 and keep the knight out of d4, but it is too slow) 3...Nc6? (offsetting errors. Correct is the obvious 3...d5 because c3 is occupied e.g. 4.exd5 Qxd5 5.d4 e4-/+.).

The same dubious plan was utilized by white in Kofidis-Varga, Balatonbereny, 1992; Pace-Perissinotto, Ceriano Laghetto, Italy, 1997; Neri-Nowotny, Wch Sen Bad Liebenze, 1996; and Zorigt-Basman, Lugano, 1968, i.e., 1.e4 Nf6 2.Qe2 d6 3.Nf3? After extensive analysis of the Pirc, the author feels that 3.f4 is best with an Austrian Pirc with a slight pull. Possible play might be 3...c5 4.Nf3 Nc6 5.d3 Bg4 6.c3 with a closed Sicilian that is headed for uncharted waters.

An interesting practical result comes from the game Majdanics-Ponyi, Hungary, 1993. Here white punished black for "castling early and often," forgetting that this is not a classical opening and that other principles apply. 1.e4 Nf6 2.Qe2 d6 3.d3!? g6 4.c3 Bg7 5.Nf3 O-O?! 6.h3! e5 7.Bg5 h6 8.Be3 c5 9.g4+/=. It is clear that 5.O-O was premature. 1-0:50. You will observe how white carved out interior space with d3/c3/h3.

Another way to deal with the Alekhine is to play 1.e4 Nf6 2.Qe2 e5 3.f4 d6? (with a King's Gambit Declined, as in David-Forchert, Berlin, 1993). This cannot be good for black; d6 is too passive. Clearly if the d-pawn is going to move, it should go to d5. 4.Nf3 Nc6 5.c3 Be7 6.d3 O-O 7.g3 d5? (Playing d5 in two moves has to be bad.) 8. Nxe5 dxe4 9.d4+/- 1-0:43

It appears that it is not a good idea to meet 1.e4 Nf6 2.Qe2 with 2...e5 because that invites a favorable transposition to a King's Gambit where black's only hope for equality is 3...d5. Anything else will give white an enduring plus. Very likely 2...d6 transposing to a Pirc is a better choice and will be dealt with elsewhere. The game Moody-Bullock highlighted some of the problems facing black should he venture the black side of the A-T Gambit.

Due to the significance of the Falkbeer Countergambit to opening theory, i.e., it appears in both the King's Gambit and the Alekhine Defense, it will be presented in detail here. First of all, white should avoid the main lines because they offer white little. Here is a plausible alternative to the main line. Once again it is white on move.

3...d5 4.Nc3

3...d4 4.Nd5

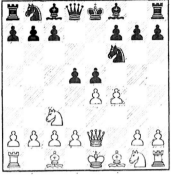

5...Nc6 6.Nf3

6...exf4 7.c3

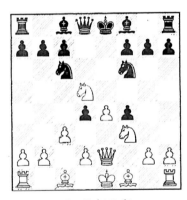

7...Bg4 Nxf4

8...Bd6 9.d3

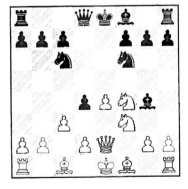

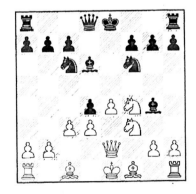

9...Qe7 10.Qc2

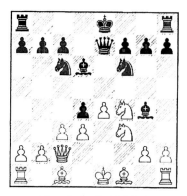

10...Bxf3 11.gxf3

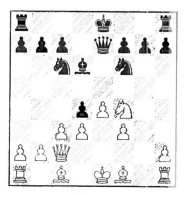

11...O-O-O 12.Ng2

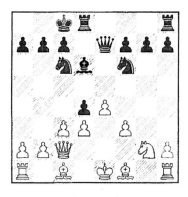

12...Rhe8 13.Bg5

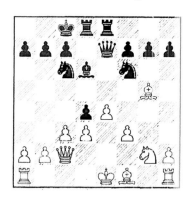

13...Qe6 14.f4+/=

Fritz 8 evaluates the final position as =/+. This, once again, is because the computer cannot evaluate universal positions correctly. In other words, white threatens nothing more complicated than 15.Bh4/16.Bg3 or, even simpler, 15.f5 with a universal position. The problem facing black is that white can retain the pawn tension c3/d4 forever, but if black releases the pawn tension with dxc3, white plays bxc3/O-O-O now that the a2 pawn is defended. More importantly white has the overpowering universal center.

PRINCIPLES OF THE UNIVERSAL ATTACK

The credo presented here is the direct result of scores of games where this system has been honed and refined in correspondence play. It is nothing less than an attempt at a repudiation of hypermodern play. Specifically 1...Nf6 against either 1.d4 or 1.c4 is probably one of the weakest moves any player can make. The reason is remarkably simple: It does nothing to restrain e4. So why play it? Just consider the following move sequence: 1.d4 Nf6 2.c4 g6 3.Nc3 Bg7 4.e4 d6 4.f3. This is one of the strongest openings in chess and clearly refutes the King's Indian. Why? White has a universal position in the opening. White has carved out a vast amount of interior space, black practically none. All white has to do to win is carve out more interior space, shuffle his pieces to better squares behind his lines, push his queenside pawns, and run to the center if black threatens to break through on the kingside. After 5.f3 the position is +/-.

The problems facing black after 1...Nf6 are that it doesn't stop e4, it blocks the diagonal of the king bishop if it should go to g7, it hems in the f-pawn, and it invites a pin with Bg5 in many variations. There appears to be little to recommend 1...Nf6 besides convention.

Here are some of the principles of the universal attack:

1) A side that cannot be attacked cannot lose. The most weakening move by white is 1.e4 because it weakens the f2 square. The most weakening move by black is 1...e5 because it weakens f7. Typically the weakening of f2 is far less significant than the weakening of the f7 square because white has the first move advantage in a potentially open position.

2) Any advantage, no matter how small, can always be converted into a win. If it cannot be converted into a win on a theoretical basis, it is not an advantage.

3) Tactics cannot ensue from the absence of pieces. The most passive openings in chess are those that provoke premature simplification without gaining an advantage. One of the most passive openings in chess is the Panov-Botvinnik Attack because it provokes wholesale simplification.

4) The UA player can always force wide-open tactics by keeping as many pieces on the board as possible and not closing the position. The UA favors the better tactician.

5) In the UA, quality will tell. The better player, rather than the better memorizer, will win.

6) Black should contest a white pawn quickly should white play e5. Even though a theoretical evaluation may favor white, it should not be lost on the reader that black gets the open f-file without sacrificing anything.

7) The right to attack the entire center, not just part of it, is more important than actually occupying it. It is not who occupies the center first that matters, it is who occupies it last.

8) The growth of interior space greatly facilitates a player's attacking prospects by eliminating the need to pass through the center to have wing-to-wing mobility.

9) Always look for ways to transpose favorably to classical chess. Once you acquire an advantage in universal chess, prosecute it with classical chess.

10) Castle on the same wing in the UA, i.e., force white to declare the intentions of his king before announcing your intentions in this regard.

11) Almost all pawn weaknesses can be avoided in the UA.

12) Pawn links occur commonly in the UA, pawn chains never. Thus it is possible to dismiss all of Nimzovich's teachings with respect to pawn chains.

13) Delayed aggression is not passivity; passivity is premature simplification.

14) Superior tactics stem from superior piece placement upon opening the center.

15) Keeping several pawns abreast confers future space to the user, i.e., the unstoppable ability of some of the pawns to advance and gain extra interior space.

16) The UA is not an end unto itself; it is designed to permit the user to transition to favorable classical positions. The most difficult task facing the UA player is when to open the center — too soon and black will be punished, too late and white may catch up in interior space. When to open the center will be the primary test of GMs in the future.

17) The proposed nomenclature: g6/Bg7/d6 can be considered the modern; g6/Bg7/c6/d5 can be considered the modified modern; and any opening where black has knights on d7 and e7 and bishops on g7 and b7 with no pawns on the fifth is a hippopotamus. The diagnostic moves of the UA are g6/Bg7/e6/Ne7, usually followed by the combination of

195

some or all of these moves: d5/Nd7/b6/Bb7/c5. In this sense, it is sort of the cross between the modern and the French.

18) Move order is flexible in the UA, but the diagnostic moves are 1...g6/2...Bg7/3...e6/4...Ne7. Everything else is optional but commonplace.

19) Time is radically different in the UA than in classical chess (see Magic). In classical chess, time means how many pieces have moved from their original squares. In the UA, time is defined as the acquisition of controlled space.

20) Players should always be alert to the possibility of creating advantages with the UA that can be exploited with classical chess, e.g., the acquisition of the bishop pair in a potentially open center. Sometimes black can sacrifice a piece for two center pawns with initiative.

21) One of the most important findings of UA theory is that because a UA position is so powerful defensively (see Magic), the correct procedure for snatching material is to return to a universal position to make the material count.

UNIVERSAL POSITIONS

One of the Holy Grails of the practical player is to learn one opening system with white and black that doesn't require a phenomenal memory. This hypothetical opening goes under the name of the king's Indian Attack and the king's Indian Defense. In the view of the author, the former has little hope of an advantage and the latter is just better for white.

The UA is a good practical choice because it is not passive and permits black to fight for time by acquiring interior space, as opposed to just pushing pieces toward the center. One of the most absurd notions in chess is that knights are more active on f6 and c6 than e7 and d7. What players are confusing is the initial movement of the knights as it applies to classical chess and not how it applies to universal positions. If a knight on f6 has no access to better squares in the center, then it is a passive piece. An active piece such as a knight on e7 can be redeployed to f5, for instance. Which is more active, a knight on f6 or a knight on f5? Just looking at how far away a piece has moved from the 8th is a poor measure of activity.

It bears emphasis as to the newness of the UA that none are present in any of these three books: *A Complete Defensive System Black to Move and Win with I...g6* by GM Andy Soltis; *Winning with the Modern* by GM David Norwood; or *Modern Defense* by FM Ken Smith and NM John Hall. It should also be pointed that UA positions are found extremely rarely in *ECO, BCO, BCO2, MCO 12,* or *MCO 13*.

One time a UA was reached in the game Fancy-Pickering, Luzerne, 1982, but this is a classic example of how not to play the UA. Premature castling is dangerous should white play either Bf4 or Be3/Qd2/Bh6. In the game FM Blumenfeld-Moody, Rudy played the opening very aggressively, i.e., 1.e4 g6 2.d4 Bg7 3.Nc3 e6 4.Nf3

197

Ne7 5.Bf4 b6 6.Qd2 Bb7 7.O-O-O d5 8.Bb5ch c6 9.Bd3 a6? (A critical blunder — black fails to make the transition from the UA to classical chess, i.e., in the UA, time is space followed by maneuvering your pieces to their optimal squares. In classical chess, time is development of pieces. Black should play 9...Nd7 and meet 10.Bh6 with 10...Kf8/Ng8 and try to contest the h-file should white try to open it. Now black tries a risky experiment.) 9...a6 10.Bh6 O-O (Black is curious to test the limits of the system and chooses this instead of 10...Kf8/Ng8). 11.h4 (expected) f6 12.h5 Rf7 13.e5 Bxh6 14.Qxh6 Nf5 15.Bxf5 gxf5 16.g4!! (Oops — black misses this when playing 10...O-O.) 16...Nd7 (It would have been better to play this on move 9.) 17.gxf5 Nf8 18.Rdg1ch Kh8 19.Rg3 20.Rhg1 Ne6 21.Nh4 Ng5 22.exf6 Qxf6 23.Ng6ch Kg8 24.Ne7?! Qxe7 25.Rxg5ch Kh8 26.Ne2 f4 27.Nxf4! Rxf4 28.Rg7 Qe4 29.Rxb7 Rg4 30.Qf6ch 1:0.

To get back to Fancy-Pickering from *Groteske Schachedroffnungen Wagnis mit Methode* by Stefan Bucher, 1.e4 g6 2.d4 Bg7 3.Nc3 e6 4.Be3 Ne7 5.Qd2 O-O (h6) 6.h4 h5 7.O-O-O+-. White has unlimited attacking moves, and black has limited defensive moves. What does black do in response to, say, Bd3/Nge2/Rdg1/g4?

Now that we have defined the attributes of the UA, it is time to address universal positions. UPs are some of the most common positions in all of chess; they are ubiquitous in grandmaster praxis. A UP is defined as a position where there is at most one open file or two or fewer half open files. In addition all of a player's pieces have to be behind the pawn wall and/or no farther advanced than next to the farthest advanced pawn either on an open or half open file.

While it is rare that UPs occur in the opening with white (the exception being the king's Indian Saemisch), they are common with black. Even the greatest players achieve not only UPs but can achieve close to a UA structure. Consider the game Karpov-Kasparov, 1985 World Championship, Game 24. This started out as a routine Najdorf, i.e., 1.e4 c5 2.Nf3 d6 3.d4 cxd4 4.Nxd4 Nf6 5.Nc3 a6 6.Be2 e6 7.O-O Be7 8.f4 O-O 9.Kh1 Qc7 10.a4 Ne6 11.Be3 Re8 12.Bf3 Rb8 13.Qd2 Bd7 (This is a "normal" Sicilian. See diagram.)

Karpov-Kasparov World Cham. Game 24 (after 13...Bd7)

 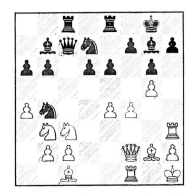

Now compare the diagram on the left to the diagram on the right after the following move sequence: 14.Nb3? What is the point of this? It does nothing to restrain either b5 or d5, and it is useless as far as an attacking move. (Better is simply 14.Nd1, with the idea of Nf2 participating in a kingside attack. White can meet 14...d5 with the plausible move sequence 15.e5 Ne4 16.Qe2 f5 17.g4 g6 18.Qg2, followed by Rg1/c3/Nf2 with pressure.) 14... b6 15.g4 Bc8 16.g5 Nd7 17.Qf2 Bf8 18.Bg2 Bb7 19.Rad1 g6 20.Bc1 Rbc8 21.Rd3 Nb4 22.Rh3 Bg7 (see right-hand diagram above). After the move sequence from move 14 to move 22, why didn't black forego classical chess and just play the UA at the start of the game? Thus we see that the UA is played at all skill levels.

Now it is time to look at UPs in practice. Rather than take a large number of individual games from a variety of sources, we will follow just one issue of *Inside Chess* (v.6. issue 25-26) to illustrate the ubiquitous nature of UPs. We will start with the game Nijboer-Smirin T (T stands for Tilburg, 1993) where the following moves were seen: 1.e4 c5 2.Nf3 d6 3.d4 cxd4 4.Nxd4 Nf6 5.Nc3 Nc6 6.Bc4 Qb6 7.Nb3 e6

8.Bd3 Be7 9.Be3 Qc7 10.f4 a6 11.a4 b6 12.O-O O-O 13.Qf3 Bb7 14.Qg3 Rfe8 15.Rae1 Nd7 (see diagram). Back to the game, 16,e5 Nb4?. (Dubious — it is a bad idea to play when white has a real need to deflect the knight to the wrong side of the board. It was better to just play 16...Nf8, stay in universal mode, grab more controlled space, and crawl out.)

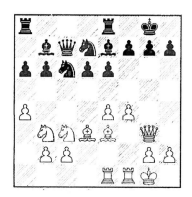 

The second game is Geller-van der Wiel (T): 1.Nf3 Nf6 2.c4 g6 3.Nc3 Bg7 4.e4 d6 5.d4 O-O 6.Be2 e5 7.O-O Nc6 8.d5 Ne7 9.Bd2 Nh5 10.Rc1 b6 11.Re1 Nf4 12.Bf1 g5 13.h4 gxh4 14.Nxh4 f5 15.g3 Nf4g6 (see diagram) UP-/+. (Black can attack with all his pieces over the next fifteen moves.)

The third game is Beliavsky-Boersma (T): 1.e4 c6 2.d4 d5 3.Nc3 dxe4 4.Nxe4 Nf6 5.Nxf6ch exf6. (There is a subtle difference between this and a UP because there is one open file and a half open file. The difference is critical.) 6.c3 Bd6 7.Bd3 O-O 8.Qc2 Re8ch 9.Ne2 g6 10.h4 Nd7 11.h5 Nf8 12.hxg6 fxg6. (This is not a good position because black is losing his pawn shield. 7...O-O was premature.) You will note that prior to white's next move, he is in the piece placement of a UP. 13.Bh6 with a strong attack.

White attained a UP in the game Vaiser-Adianto with 1.d4 d5 2.c4 c6 3.Nc3 Nf6 4.cxd5 cxd5 5.Bf4 Nc6 6.e3 e6 7.Bd3 Bd6 8.Bxd6 Qxd6 9.f4 Bd7 10.Rc1 h6 11.Nf3+/= (see diagram). White has good prospects of converting his UP position into a classical position with the threat of Ne5.

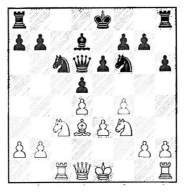

Timman-Peturson (T) also featured a UP in the middle game by white, i.e., 1.c4 e5 2.Nc3 Nf6 3.Nf3 Nc6 4.g3 d5 5.cxd5 Nxd5 6.Bg2 Nb6 7.O-O Be7 8.a3 O-O 9.b4 Re8 10.d3 Bf8 11.Bb2 Bg4 12.h3 Be6 13.Ne4 f6 14.Qc2 Qd7 15.K h2 a5 16.b5 Nd4 17.Nxd4 exd4 18.Nd2. GM Seirawan indicated, "The d4 pawn is the bone in white's throat. If he can clear it, the rest of the game will be a breeze." (However, the backward pawn on c7 has to be at least as bad a positional defect. The d-pawn is artificially isolated and will cause black to distort his position to defend it.) White is better here.

White missed a UP in the middle game that would have conferred a big advantage to white in the game Wely-Morozevich (T): 1.d4 d5 2.Nf3 Nc6 3.Bf4 Bg4 4.c4 e6 5.e3 Bb4ch 6.Nc3 Nge7 7.Rc1 O-O 8.Bd3 Ng6 9.h3 Bh5 10.Bh2 Nh4 11.g4 Nxf3ch 12.Qxf3 Bg6

13.Bxg6 hxg6 14.cxd5 exd5 15.Kf1 Ne7 16.h4 Bxc3 17.Rxc3 c6 18.h5 g5 19.h6? Premature. Better is to drop into almost a UP with 19.Qd1! (see diagram) with the idea of 20.Qd3.

Kaidonov-Piket did feature a fairly typical UP in the King's Indian with white. It transposed into a Saemisch, which the author regards as highly favorable to white. 1.d4 Nf6 2.c4 g6 3.Nc3 Bg7 4.e4 d6 5.Be2 O-O 6.Bg5 Nbd7 7.Qd2 c6 8.Rd1 e5 9.Nf3 exd4 10.Nxd4 Re8 11.f3 a5 12.O-O a4 13.Rfe1 Qa5 14.Bf1 Nh5 15.Be3 +/-. White has more interior space and better piece placement.

In the game Karpov-Vyzmanavin (T), white missed a good chance to play a UP and opted instead for a "classical" position. Here are the moves in that game: 1.d4 Nf6 2.c4 e6 3.Nf3 b6 4.g3 Ba6 5.b3 Bb4ch 6.Bd2 Be7 7.Bg2 c6 8.Bc3 d5 9.Ne5?! (The author prefers

9.Nfd2 (see diagram) meeting 9...O-O with 10.O-O with more interior space and better piece placement, e.g., 10...Nbd7 11.a4! with the threat of 12.Na3/Nc2+/=.) White is better after Nfd2.

Universal theory is well-displayed in Andersson-Rozentalis (T). Both sides achieve UPs in the early middle game. 1.d4 Nf6 2.Nf3 e6 3.g3 b6 4.Bg2 Bb7 5.O-O Be7 6.c4 O-O 7.Nc3 Ne4 8.Qc2 Nxc3 9.Qxc3 f5 10.b3 Bf6 11.Bb2 d6 12.Rad1 Qe7 13.Ne1 Bxg2 14.Nxg2 (see diagram).

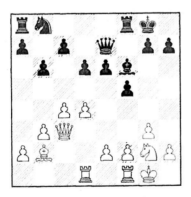

A good illustration of the transposition to a favorable UP in the middle game occurred in the game Bareev-Shirov (T), which saw: 1.d4 d5 2.c4 c6 3.Nf3 Nf6 4.Nc3 a6 5.Qb3 e6 6.cxd5 cxd5 7.Bg5 Nc6 8.e3 Be7 9.Bd3 b5 10.O-O Bb7 1 1.Rfe1 O-O 12.a4 b4 13.Nb1 Nd7 (see diagram). Black is already better and went on to 0-1:46.

The final game illustrating the significance of UPs is the game Karpov-Ivanchuk (T). In this game, white stayed in UP mode, deviating only once with 19.Qa4, to force the exchange of queens. 1.d4 d5 2.c4 e6 3.Nc3 c6 4.e3 f5 5.f4 Nf6 6.Nf3 Be7 7.Be2 O-O 8.O-O b6 9.Qc2 Bb7 10.cxd5 cxd5 11.Bd2 Nc6 12.a3 Ne4 13.Rfc1 Rc8 14.Qd1 Qd7 15.Be1 Rc7 16.Rc2 Nxc3 17.Rxc3 Rfc8 18.Rac1 Bd6 19.Qa4 Nb8 20.Qxd7 Nxd7 21.Rxc7 Rxc7 22.Rxc7 Bxc7 (see diagram). This is about as equal as endgames get, yet they played on another twenty-five moves. To paraphrase GM Larry Evans with respect to the Fischer-Spassky world championship, this is like watching Frank Lloyd Wright playing in a sandbox.

The reader might assume that the theory behind UPs is well-known but consider this statement by GM Seirawan with respect to one of Karpov's games: "Karpov is the most confounding player that I have ever known. Take a good look at this position. All of white's pieces are on the first two ranks, but it is black who has the problem!" Former world champion Karpov is the past master at understanding UPs. This is how he has honed his praxis and is known as a "boa constrictor." Former world champion Kasparov is one of the leading practitioners of UPs on the black side of the Sicilian. Just look at his games with GM Short in the world championship.

The next step in this saga is to ask a simple question: "If UPs are so common and so desirable in the middle game, why not play them in the opening, i.e., why not just ignore most of hypermodern theory?"

This sets the stage for the next section: the Universal Attack. To the best of the author's knowledge, this is the first codification of this new opening system.

UNIVERSAL ATTACK

The basic premise of the UA is that a side that cannot be attacked cannot lose. This basic policy is lacking from existing openings, i.e., no one has viewed the first few moves as having as their primary goal the overprotection of the black king. Instead they look at the center and either its occupation or the right to challenge it in the future. In the UA, the first thing that is done is to secure black's king position. The most efficient way to secure the king position is to play the move sequence 1...g6/2...Bg7/3...e6/ 4...Ne7/5...O-O. You will note that black blocks both diagonals leading to the f7 square, the weakest square in black's position, and, at the same time, black overprotects the f7 square with his rook. As the author's knowledge of this system grew (he used this defense in all thirty games with black he played in the 1994 Golden Knight's correspondence tournament), it became possible to organize the variations that arose from a wide assortment of openings.

What has caused players to avoid this system is that a few practical examples are being used to discourage this promising system. The idea of the UA as opposed to a Hippo is that black always strives to get in d5 in one move, i.e., black secures his king and then immediately contests the center before it gets too formidable.

UNIVERSAL ATTACK: THE EARLY YEARS

A small sampling of the Universal Attack was covered in the previous section on Universal Position. The rediscovery of the UA in the past fifty years is known only by virtue of extensive databases from NM Eric Schiller, IM Colin Leach, and Bill Townsend because, for the most part, it has been ignored by theoreticians. Thus this volume is an attempt to fill a very large void in theory and play.

Universal Attack theory and play were nonexistent in the nineteenth century for all practical purposes. This was the heyday of the Evans Gambit and Romantic, exciting gambit play was the order of the day, and experimentation with French and the Sicilian was just getting underway. In effect, in two remarkable games, the combatants skipped hypermodern chess and went straight to the Universal Attack. The first game most assuredly could have been played by two strong GMs; the second can be viewed as a game between a GM and an IM.

The significance of the first game was pointed out to me by IM Gerard Welling, who indicated that it was surely one of the first games to combine the ideas of g6/Bg7/e6/Ne7. What is highly significant in this game is that when classical chess was the only diet, both sides played universal positions all the way out to move 9!

The first game we will address is a consultation game between Andersson, Kling, and Horwitz versus Staunton, Kipping, and Baden, Manchester, 1857. In today's parlance, this would be considered a consultation game with three grandmasters on either side. This is a very early, very high test of the theory.

The play started out with innocuous moves by white and a universal response by black. 1.e4 e6 2.d4 g6 3.Be3. (This is the first surprise considering the Romantic openings of this era.) 3...Bg7 4.Nd2!? Ne7 (the diagnostic position of the UA). 5.Bd3 b6 6.Ne2. (This has to rank as one of the most daring, pioneering openings of the era.

The author predicts that this sort of opening will be popular in the next century.) 6...Bb7 7.O-O d6? (d5!) 8.c3 Nd7 9.Qb3?. (According to IM Welling, this is how Staunton assessed this move; it is significant that the first move white makes away from universal chess is a strategic blunder.) 9...O-O 10.f4 d5. (Now the classic universal structure appears.)

Watch how black seizes the initiative: 11.e5 Rb8 12.Rac1 c5 13.Qa3? (Bb1: IM Welling) 13...c4 14.Bc2 a6 15.g4 b5. (Due to the resiliency of the black king position, the second player can embark on queenside expansion.) 16.Ng3 Re8 17.b4 cxb3 18.axb3 Rc8 19.Bd3 Qb6 20.Qb2 f6!. (A typical UA strategy — black attacks the head of the pawn chain.) 21.Rce1 Qc6 22.Nb1 fxe5 23.fxe5 Bxe5. (Two of my games feature this same thematic sacrifice. Black gives up a piece for two pawns but "gains" the bishop on b7. Until now the queen bishop has been a bystander; now it's the strongest piece that black has.) 24.dxe5 Nxe5-/+ 0-1:53. Every few games will have diagrams at sporadic intervals. Black is on move in each case as, for example, here (see diagram).

It is unfortunate that we had Morphy-Meek, New York, 1857 (a game pointed out to me by GM Andy Soltis) and not Morphy-Anderssen, New York. The whole course of chess might have been different, but due to this game as much as anything else, the UA practitioners were loath to try it. The problem with Morphy-Meek is not that the opening is unsound so much as the fact that Morphy was a much stronger player. There was nothing wrong with the opening. Play started out auspiciously enough for black: 1.e4 e6 2.d4 g6 3.Bd3 Bg7 4.Be3 Ne7 5.Ne2 b6 6.Nd2 Bb1 7.O-O d5! 8.e5 O-O 9.f4 f5??. (This is a terrible move that throws away a perfectly playable position. The general rule three — that when you are faced with a potential pawn storm, don't weaken your king position. The ensuing attack could be prosecuted successfully by any master; you don't have to be a Morphy to win this one. The next moves need no comment or diagrams: 10.h3 Nd7 11.Kh2 c5 12.c3 c4 13.Bc2 a6 14.Nf3 h6 15.g4 Kh7 16.Rg1 Rg8 17.Qe1 Nc6 18.Nh4 Qf8 19.Nxg6+-.

The next game features, perhaps, the first four pawns attack, a UA in my database. This is Burden-Deacon, London, 1860. 1.e4 g6 2.d4 Bg7 3.c4 e6 4.f4?! (Now this is really extravagant!) 4...Ne7 5.Nf3 c5 6.d5 d6 7.Nc3 Bxc3ch?! 8.bxc3 f5 9.e5 dxe5 10.d6 e4! 11.Ne5 Nec6 12.Be3 b6 13.h4 Qf6 14.Qa4 Bd7 15.Nxd7 Qxc3ch! 16.Kf2 Kxd7-+ 0-1 :65.

In the next game between Mackenzie and Macdonnell, London, 1862, black was a very strong player in the twilight of his career who had conducted a marathon against the Frenchman LaBourdonnais in 1834. Here white meets an unorthodox defense with a calm, well-reasoned attack: 1.e4 g6 2.d4 Bg7 3.Be3 e6 4.Bd3 Ne7 5.Nc3 b6 6.Nge2 Bb7 7.O-O O-O 8.Qd2 d6?. The game loses all theoretical value here; the UA player would play 8...d5 without thinking. Still black is in no danger yet. After just 9.Ng3 Nd7 10.Rae1 c5 11.Nce2 Qc7? (cxd4 12.Bxd4 d5 and I prefer black better minors and a soon to be extra center pawn).

A theoretician new to the author can be credited with two victories at London in 1862. The first game was Burden-Deacon, which was discussed above. The second game, Cremome-Deacon, will be discussed below. 1.e4 g6 2.d4 Bg7 3.f4 e6 4.Nf3 Ne7 5.c3! b6 6.Nbd2 c5! 7.Bd3 Bb7 8.O-O cxd4! 9.cxd4 Nbc6. (This is acceptable here because black has other plans for his d-pawn. Since black has played 6...c5, both sides have UPs.) 10.e5 f6!. (Immediately hitting the head of the pawn chain is good policy.) 11.Ne4 O-O 12.Nd6 Qc7 13.Nxb7?!. (This seems a little too soon.) Qxb7 14.Be4 fxe5 15.fxe5 Nf5 16.g4? Nfe7 17.Bg5 Rae8 18.Qb3 Qb8 19.Bxe7 Rxe7 20.Bxc6 dxc6 21.Ng5 Rfe8 22.Qh3 Bxe5! (again, this thematic sacrifice) 23.dxe5 Qxe5 24.Nf3 Qxb2=/+ 0-1:55.

It is evident that London, 1862, was a tournament of experimentation. Here is the third example of the Universal Attack played at that tournament: Mackenzie-Medley. 1.e4 g6 2.d4 Bg7 3.Nf3 e6 4.Bd3 Ne7 5.O-O O-O 6.Bg5 b6 7.c3 Bb7 8.Nbd2 d6(d5) 9.Qe2 f6 10.Bh4 e5?. (While not losing, this is the wrong idea; you rarely, if ever, play e5 in the UA. Just Nbd7 is better 1-0:31.)

Even the old-time greats can fall victim to positional traps if they are welded to classical chess and at the same time trying out the UA for the first time. Here we see two of the greatest nineteenth century players who try their hand at the UA: Neumann-Schallopp, Altona, 1872. 1.e4 g6 2.d4 Bg7 3.f4 e6 4.Nf3 Ne7 5.Bd3 d5! 6.e5 c5! 7.c3 c4?. (Nuts! It is antithematic to release the pawn tension. Correct is either 7...Nd7 or 7...b6.) 8.Bc2 O-O. (This is why general principles, i.e., castle early and often, will cause you grief because now white just played 14.Kf2!+/= 1-0:52.)

We clearly step out of a period of experimentation in the mid-nineteenth century and get into the orthodoxy of hypermodern and the almost total abandonment of the UA from about 1900-1958. One of the games that has reader interest is the simul game Fischer-Codman, Boston, 1964: 1.e4 e6 2.d4 Ne7 3.Nc3 g6 4.h4 d5! 5.h5 Bg7 6.h6 Bf8 7.Bg5 a6 8.Bf6 Rg8 9.Nf3 Nd7 10.e5 Nxf6 11.exf6 Nf5 12.g4 Qxf6! 13.gxf5 Qxf5 14.Bd3 Qf4 15.Rh4 Qf6 16.Qe2 Bd7 17.Ne5?? Qxh4 18.Qf3 f5 0-1:23.

One of the pioneers who experimented occasionally with the UA was the Slovakian master Maximilian Ujtelky. He generally used openings other than the UA, but here he essays a UA with great flair, Sydor-Ujtelky, Polanica Zdroj. 1965: 1.e4 g6 2.d4 Bg7 3.f4 e6 4.Nf3 Ne7 5.Bd3 d5 6.e5 c5 7.dxc5?. (7.c3 unclear: The move chosen by white is a blunder, so the resulting moves have little theoretical value. Black is better.) Qa5ch! 8.Nbd2 Nd7 9.a3 Nxc5 (and the hit on d3 avoids the fork). Since black is better in classical chess, he plays classical chess from now on. 0-1:40.

The second game by Ujtelky was against Janosevic at Belgrade, 1968. 1.e4 g6 2.d4 Bg7 3.Nf3 e6 4.c4 Ne7 5.Nc3 O-O. (Black does not fear an opposite wing attack. This is the classic move order insofar as overprotecting the black king; black already threatens to break open the center with 6...d5.) 7.O-O h6?! (Why worry about Bg5; the beauty of the UA is that black can meet Bg5 with f6?.) Black should hit immediately with d5. 8.Ne1?! (white goes from classical chess to a UP) d5!, and black seizes the initiative 0-1:35.

Ujtelky tried this system against Pereisipkin at Strbske Bleso in 1978. This led to an interesting draw after the first few moves led to equality: 1.e4 g6 2.d4 Bg7 3.f4 e6 4.Nf3 Ne7 5.Bd3 c5 6.dxc5 Qa5ch 7.Bd2 Qxc5 8.Bc3 Bxc3ch 9.Nxc3 Nbc6 10.Qd2 d5 1/2- 1/2:39.

Michael Basman is known for his unorthodox attempts with both white and black. His UA did not fare so well against Popov, Varna, 1971: 1.c4 e6 2.g3 d5 3.Bg2 g6 4.Nf3 Bg7 5.O-O Ne7 6.Na3 O-O 7.Rb1 a5?!. Black should try something else here. Basman's idea is essentially mixing the UA with premature classical chess. The idea is to prevent b4, but it is poorly motivated. Black needs to grab interior space with 7...c6 e.g. 8.b4 b6 9.b5 Bb7, and it is difficult to see what white has accomplished with this plan.

Not all the UA players are lower-rated players. Former world champion Boris Spassky gives the UA a high-level test against Jan Timman in the TV World Cup, 1982. This is the typical placement of the minors, which is diagnostic of a UA. However, his move order, 4...d6, 10...d5, is not correct in the UA: 1.e4 b6 2.d4 Bb7 3.Bd3 e6 4.Qe2 d6. (Dubious. Black should go directly to the UA with 3...e6 4...Ne7 5....g6 6...Bg7 7...d5=/+.) 5.Nf3 Nd7 6.c4 g6 7.Nc3 Bg7 8.Be3 Ne7 9.Qd2 h6 10.O-O-O d5!. (This is now a full-blown UA where black wasted a critical tempo with 4.d6 and white wasted a tempo with Qe2/Qd2.) 11.exd5 exd5 12.Rhe1 Kf8. (Note the difference it makes not castling. At this point, according to IM Welling, the German master Bernd suggested 12,..dxc4 13.Bxc4 Bxf3.) 13.c5 Kg8 14.Bc2 Nf6 15.Bf4 Nc6=. (Notice how black leaps out of UP configuration to a classical configuration. Since both sides wasted a tempo in the opening, this game is really a superb example of the sharp play of the UA. This led to a hard-fought draw after forty-six moves.)

The second game is Rubinnetti-Spassky, Toluca, Interzonal, 1982. 1.Nf3 b6 2.g3 Bb7

3.d4 e6 4.Bg2 d6 5.O-O Nd7 6.c4 g6 7.Nc3 Bg7 8.e4 Ne7 9.Be3 O-O. (Spassky tacitly offers a different way to transpose to the UA. Should black perhaps play 1...g6 2...Bg7 3...b6 4...Bb7 5...e7 6...Ne7

7...d5 so that d5 can be overprotected and thus the advance of the d-pawn is two squares instead of one?) 10.Qe2 d5 11.Rfd1 dxe4 12.Nxe4 Nf5 13.Bg5 Qc8 14.Bh3 h6 15.Bh3 h6 16.Bf4 Qd8 17.Bxf5 gxf5 18.Nc3 e5 19.Be3 Nf6 20.Nh4 f4 21.Bd2 c6 22.dxc6 Bxc6 23.Bxf4 Qc8 24.Be3 Qh3 25.f3 e4 26.f4 Rad8 27.Rxd8 Rxd8 28.Rd1 Rd3 29.Qg2 Qd7 30.Qe2 Ng4 0-1.

The future world champion plays the UA very strongly here: Makarichev-Kasparov Tbilisi, 1978: 1.c4 g6 2.Nc3 Bg7 3.g3 e6 4.Bg2 Ne7 5.e4 c5! 6.Nge2 Nbc6. (Since black has played c5 here, this can still be considered a UA.) 7.d3 d6? (Nd4! 8.Nxd4 Bxd4=) 8.O-O O-O 9.Rb1 a6 10.a3 b5 (gaining controlled space) 11.cxb5 axb5 12.b4 cxb4 13.axb4 e5 14.Bg5 Qb6 15.Nd5 Nxd5 16.exd5 Nd4 17.Nxd4 exd4 18.Qb3 Bc7 19.Bd2 Rfc8 20.Rfc1 Rxc1ch 21.Rxc1 Rc8 22.Rxc8ch Bxc8 1/2-1/2.

The following UA illustrates how easy it is to go wrong with subtle mistakes. Sirki-Poutiainen, Helsinki, 1974, proceeded with 1.e4 Nf3 2.Nf3 Bg7 3.d3?. (Way too passive. Either white plays hybrid classical chess with the goal of either quickly gaining controlled space and active piece play or white can do neither and just stand worse.) 3...Be7 4.g3 Ne7 5.Bg2 O-O 6.O-O d5 7.Nbd2 c5=/+ 0-1:33.

The Grob is a rare visitor, and the Grob UA is even rarer. Contos-Anderson, Los Angeles, 1972: 1.g4 g6 2.Bg2 Bg7 3.c4 e6 4.Nc3 Ne7 5.d4 d5 6.Bg5 f6 7.Bh4 O-O 8.Nf3 c5? (b6/Bb7/Nd7/c5=/+) 9.cxd5 cxd4 10.Nxd4 exd5 11.h3 a6+/- (weak isolani).

This concludes our peripheral games featuring the UA. Now the thematic continuations will be given in each subvariation.

The Reti UA is defined as any opening where white plays an early Nf3/g3/Bg2 and black plays the typical d5/e6/g6/Ne7/Bg7, either directly or by transposition. At end of the game scores given below, we will follow four thematic games in each case with a diagram after every second move with each of the four games having the same starting position and following four games at a time to illustrate how the variations evolve.

Let's start off with Ryskin-Aleksandrov, Czestochowa, 1992: 1.Nf3 d5 2.g3 e6 3.Bg2 g6 4.d4 Bg7 5.O-O Ne7 6.Nbd2 c5! 7.dxc5 Na6 (temporarily out of a UP) 8.e4 Nxc5 (going back into the UA) 9.exd5 exd5 10.Nb3 Ne4. (Switching to classical mode — black has the initiative.) 11.c3 O-O 12.Bf4 a5 (going after the knight) 13.a4 Nc6. (The knight doesn't interfere with knight on e4; thus Nc6 is acceptable.) 14.Nbd4 Bg4. (This is an excellent way to play UA theory: Acquire an advantage in the UA and then prosecute it with classical chess. Black is better.)

The next is a very thematic UA by black. Busch-Nikcevic, Budapest, 1990: 1.Nf3 d5 2.c4 e6 3.g3 g6 4.Bg2 Bg7 5.d4 Ne7 6.Nbd2 O-O 7.O-O b6 8.Ne5 Bb7 9.cxd5 Bxd5 10.e4 Bb7 11.Ndc4 Ba6 12.Qc2 c5 13.d5 b5 14.d6 Nec6 15.Nxc6 Nxc6 16.Nd2 Qxd6! 17.e5 Nd4 18.Qxg6 Qxe5 19.Qg4 b4 21.Bxa8 Rxa8-+.

Once again we see the player of the black pieces make a successful transition to classical chess. This is a pretty game between Mulder-Vaisser, Montpellier, 1998: 1.Nf3 d5 2.g3 g6 3.Bg2 Bg7 4.d4 e6 5.O-O Ne7 6.c4 O-O 7.Bg5 h6 8.Bxe7? Qxe7 9.cxd5 exd5 10.Nc3 c6 11.a3 a5 12.Na4 Nd7 13.Rc1 Re8 14.e3 Qd6 15.Ne1 b6 16.Nd3 Ba6 17.Re1 Rab8 18.Bf1 Bc4 (going classical!) 19.b3 Bb5 20.b4 Ra8 21.Nab2 Rec8 22.bxa5 Rxa5 23.a4 Ba6 24.Qd2 Bb1 25.Bg2 Ra7 26.Nf4 Nf6 27.Red1 Bf8 28.Qc2 g5 29.Nfd3 c5 30.Qd2 Ne4 31.Bxe4 dxe4 32.Ne5 Qe6 33.Nec4 Rd8 34.Qe2 cxd4 35.exd4 Bg7 36.Qe3 Bd5 37.Rd2 Rc7 38.Rdc2 Bxe4 39.Rxc4 Bxd4-+ 0-1:56.

One of the most common move orders that is inferior was demonstrated in Korchnoi-Short, Skelleftea, 1989; Sherbakov-Rusian, Berdichev, 1990; Litinksaya-Zayec, Azov, 1991: Nogueiras-Arenciba, Capablanca Memorial, 1991; or Wojtkiewicz-Koen, Katerini, 1993. The following position could have been reached directly or by transposition (see below left. For the recommended improvement for black, see diagram to the right.) 1.Nf3 d5 2.c4 e6 3.g3 g6 4.Bg2 Bg7 5.O-O Ne7 6.d4 O-O 7.Nbd2 Nbc6? (lower left) 7.Nbd2 Nd7 (lower right).

 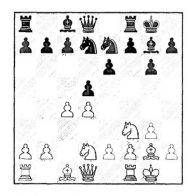

The latter move sequence gives black the chance to seize the initiative with 8...c5. It is argued here and elsewhere that the knight on f3 is misplaced (it blocks the f-pawn) and black should not respond by misplacing his knight on c6, eliminating, in the short term, the option of an early c5 =1+.

The next set of diagrams will be presented in a way that will permit the reader to engage in pattern recognition. In other words, on each page there will be four games in progress with every other move presented as a diagram. The first game is Ryskin-Aleksandrov, the second game is Mulder-Vaisser, the third game is Busch-Nikcevic, and the fourth game is Prosch-Weyrich. The final game demonstrates how easy it is to get a plus with black in the Reti UA. 1.Nf3 d5 2.g3 g6 3.Bg2 Bg7 4.d4 e6 5.O-O Ne7 6.c4 O-O 7.cxd5 exd5 8.Nc3 c6 9.Bf4 h6 10.h4 Be6 11.Qd2 Kh7 12.Rfe1 Nd7 13.Rad1 Rc8 14.b3

Qa5!. (Stepping into classical chess; black is better.) 15.Ne5 Rfd8 16.Qd3 Nxe5 17.dxe5 c5 18.Qd2 c4 19.bxc4 Rxc4 20.Nb1 Qxd2 21.Rxd2 a6 -/+ 0-1:47

For all practical purposes, the Reti UA gives black absolutely no problems whatsoever; in fact black probably is equal already after d5/g6/Bg7/e6/Nxe7. What makes the Reti so dubious in this regard is that the player of the white pieces is looking for fairly calm play in the opening. What happens to that player psychologically when black just starts playing ideas such as Nd7/c5, opening the center favorably? This clearly is not the kind of sharp position the first player wants to defend against when playing this quiet system.

For the diagrams of these four games, see diagrams on the next page.

1.Nf3 d5 2.g3 e6

1.Nf3 d5 2.g3 g6

1.Nf3 d5 2.c4 e6

1.Nf3 d5 2.g3 g6

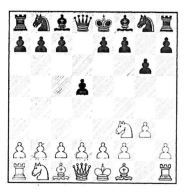

3.Bg2 g6 4.d4 Bg7

3.Bg2 Bg7 4.d4 e6

3.g3 g6 4.Bg2 Bg7

3.Bg2 Bg7 4.d4 e6

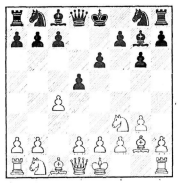

5.O-O Ne7 6.Nbd2 c5

5.O-O Ne7 6.c4 O-O

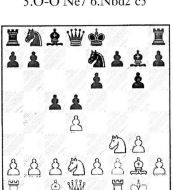

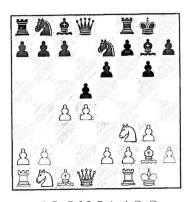

5.d4 Ne7 6.Nbd2 O-O

5.O-O Ne7 6.c4 O-O

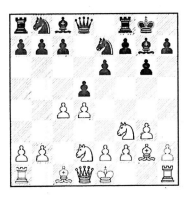

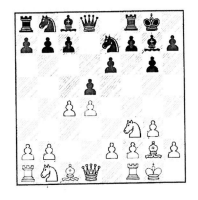

7.dxc5 Na6 8.e4 Nxc5

7.Bg5 h6 8.Bxe7 Qxe7

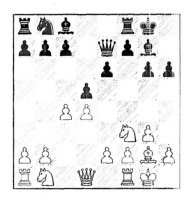

7.O-O b6 8.Ne5 Bb7

7.cxd5 exd5 8.Nc3 c6

9.exd5 exd5 10.Nb3 Ne4

9.cxd5 exd5 10.Ne3 c6

9.cxd5 Bxd5 10.e4 Bb7   9.Bf4 h6 10.h4 Be6

11.c3 O-O 12.Bf4 a5   11.a3 a5 12.Na4 Nd7

11.Ndc4 Ba6 12.Qc2 c5   11.Qd2 Kh7 12.Rfe1 Nd7

13.a4 Nc6 14.Nbd4 Bg4 =/+   13.Rc1 Re8 14.e3 Qd6

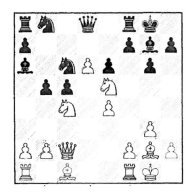

13.d5 b5 14.d6 Nec6   13.Rad1 Rc8 14.b3 Qa5

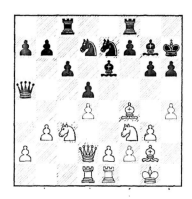

(Game one is finished, so we start with game 2.)

222

15.Ne1 b6 16.Nd3 Ba6

15.Nxc6 Nxc6 16.Nd2 Qxd6

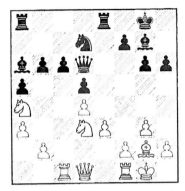

15.Ne5 Rfd8 16.Qd3 Nxe5

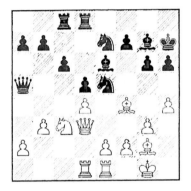

17.Re1 Rab8 18.Bf1 Bc4

17.e5 Nd4 18.Qxg6 Qxe5

17.dxe5 c5 18.Qd2 c4

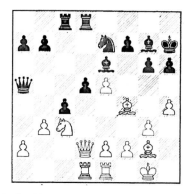

19.b3 Bb5 20.b4 Ra8   19.Qg4 f5 20.Qg5 b4

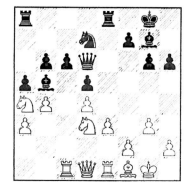

19.bxc4 Rxc4 20.Nb1 Qxd2

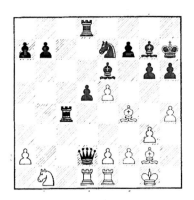

21.Nab2 Rec8 22.bxa5 Rxa5=/+   21.Bxa8 Rxa8 22.Qe3 Qd5 0-1

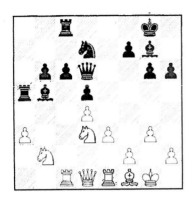

21.Rxd2 a6 -/+

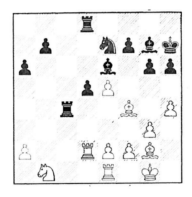

Central UA

The Central UA is different from other UAs because white abstains from the routine development of his/her knights prior to the deployment of one or both bishops. It has little independent significance because a bishop on c4, usually desirable in classical chess, is just a target in the UA because black always plays e6/d5 at some point. The name Central UA is a catchall phrase for any opening where black plays an early g6/Bg7/e6/Ne7 very early in whatever order and then reacts to whatever white plays that does not fit into any of the other categories. Although white often responds 2.d3 in response to 1...e6, we do not present examples of this because black obviously is at least equality with such obvious moves as 1...e6, 2...Ne7, 3...g6, 4...Bg7, 5...d5, 6...c5, etc. Players might wonder why white would ever play something this passive. Perhaps the possibility of a French is feared so that white avoids the main lines of the French, specifically the variation e6/Bb4.

The Central UA tends to evolve into unusual structures, as one might predict. For instance, in Calavia-Klimczak, Postal, 1981, we see 1.e4 g6 2.d4 Bg7 3.Nc3 e6 4.Be3 Ne7 5.Qd2 h5? (h6) 6.O-O-O d5 7.f3 Nd7 8.Bd3 b6 9.Nh3 Bb7 10.Nf2 a6, with the treat of Nd7/c5 =/+ 1-0:29.

Due to the fact that these openings have so little theoretical relevance and that pattern recognition is of no help, we present a few games sans diagrams that illustrate some of the possibilities in the position. The first game is Borik-Petran, Trencin, 1995. 1.e4 g6 2.d4 Bg7 3.Bc4 e6 4.Nc3 Ne7 5.Nf3 d5 6.exd5 exd5 7.Be2 h6 8.Bf4 c6 9.Qd2 Nd7 10.O-O g5!? 11.Nxg5 hxg5 12.Bxg5 Nf6 13.h4 Be6 14.h5 Nh7 15.Be3 Nf5 16.g4 Nxe3 17.Qxe3 Qd6 18.f4 O-O-O -+ 0-1:27.

One of the occasional mistakes by white is an early Bc4, either permitting black to exchange on d5 (e.g., here) or drive the bishop back. Thus in the game Vdovin-Chepukaitis, Moscow, 1999, white got off to a bad start with 1.e4 g6 2.d4 Bg7 3.Bc4? e6 4.Nc3 Ne7 5.Bg5 h6 6.Be3 a6 7.a4 b6 8.Nge2 Bb7 9.Ng3 d5 10.exd5 Nxd5 11.Nxd5 Bxd5 12.Bxd5 Qxd5 13.O-O Nc6 =/+ 0-1:41.

BIRD UA
1.F4/2.E3, 1.F4 2.NF3, 1.E3 2.F4

The Bird UA is fairly rare in my database from Colin Leach, comprising about fifty games, but they are instructive. In the first encounter (Keller-Sosnowska, Naleczow, 1985), one of the more unusual characteristics is how long both sides retain universal positions. If black had played 20...gxf5 instead of 20...exf5, the second player is better because of a potential blockade on the light squares. 1.f4 d5 2.e3 g6 3.d4 Bg7 4.Bd3 e6 5.Nf3 Nd7 6.O-O c5! 7.b3 Ne7 8.Bb2 O-O 9.Nbd2 Qc7 10.Qe1 b6 11.g4 f5 12.h3 Nf6 13.Ne5 Ne4 14.Ndf3 Nc6 15.Nxc6 Qxc6 16.Ne5 Bxe5! 17.fxe5 Bb7 18.Qh4 c4 19.Bxe4 dxe4 20.gxf5 gxf5? (20...exf5 =1+).

Stern-Paulsen, Frankfurt, 1878 allowed black to achieve a mild plus by move 11: 1.e3 d5 2.f4 e6 3.Nf3 g6 4.Be2 Bg7 5.Nc3 Ne7 6.O-O O-O 7.d4 b6 8.e4 dxe4 9.Nxe4 Bb7 10.Nf2 Nd7 11.c3 Nf5= (c5 =/+).

In the next game, Ekenberg-Sverige, 1969, black makes a stellar move: 8...Nbc6: 1.f4 d5 2.Nf3 g6 3.e3 Bg7 4.c4 e6 5.Nc3 Ne7 6.d4 O-O 7.Bd2 c5 8.dxc5 Nbc6! 9.cxd5 exd5 10.Qb3 d4 11.exd4 Nf5 12.O-O-O Nfxd4 13.Nxd4 Nxd4 14.Qd5 Qc7 15.Nb5 Nxb5 16.Bxb5 Bg4 17.Rde1 Rad8 18.Qb3 Qxc5ch 19.Bc3 a6 20.Bc4 Bxc3 21.Qxc3 Rc8 22.b3 b5 23.h3 Bd7 24.Re1 Be6 25.f5 Qxf5 0-1.

Black hits the opening perfectly in Klofac-Krnak, Postal, 1995: 1.f5 d5 2.e3 g6 3.Nf3 Bg7 4.c4 e6 5.Nc3 Ne7 6.d4 c5! 7.dxc5 O-O 8.Bd2 Nbc6 9.cxd5 exd5 10.Na4 Re8 11.Bd3 Nf5 12.Kf2 d4! 13.e4 Ne3 14.Qe1 Bg4 15.h4 Qd7 16.b3 Rad8 17.Nb2 Bh5 18.Nh2 f5! 19.e5 Bxe5 20.fxe5 Nxe5 21.Nf3 f4 22.Bf1 Nxf3 23.gxf3 Bxf3! 24.Rg1 Bc6 25.Rg5 f3 26.Rg3 Ng4ch -+ 0-1:42.

In the next encounter, white faced a backwards pawn on an open file and chose immediate pain as opposed to the dismal defense of the pawn: 1.f4 d5 2.Nf3 g6 3.e3 Bg7 4.Be2 e6 5.c3 Ne7 6.Na3 O-O 7.d3 c5 8.Bd2 Nbc6. (This is justified because white is playing so passively.) 9.Nc2 e5 (ditto) 10.fxe5 Nxe5 11.Nxe5 Bxe5 12.d4 Bd6 13.Bf3 Qc7 14.g3 Bh3 15.Kf2 Rae8 16.Bg2 Qd7 17.Bxh3 Qxh3 18.Qf3 f5 19.Rae1 b6 20.e4?! (b4 -/+) dxe4 -+ 0-1:29.

Once again the Bird fares poorly against the UA. Schauer-Eischner, Dresden, 1993. 1.f4 e6 2.Nf3 d5 3.e3 g6 4.Be2 Bg7 5.d3 Ne7 6.O-O O-O 7.Qe1 c5! 8.e4. (The major drawback to 3.e3 — there is nothing better than to give up a tempo. Black is already better.) 8...Nd7 9.g4 dxe4 10.dxe4 Nf6 11.e5 Nxg4 12.Qh4 Nh6 13.Rd1 Qc7 14.Nc3 Nhf5 15.Qh3 Nd5 16.Nb5 Qc6 17.c4 Nb4 18.Ng5 h6 19.Bf3 Qb6 20.Ne4 a6 21.Nbd6 Nc2 22.Rb1 Ncd4 -/+ 0-1:42.

Black engages in a risky attack on the queenside and pays the price for creating targets. Nemez-Jablecnik, Czechoslovakia, 1995. 1.f4 d5 2.Nf3 g6 3.g3 Bg7 4.Bg2 e6 5.O-O Ne7 6.d3 O-O 7.Qe1 d4 8.c3 c5 9.Kh1 Nbc6 10.Bd2 Rb8 11.a4 b5? 12.axb5 Rxb5 13.Ra2 Rb6 14.Na3 Ra6 15.Ra1 +/= 1-0:29.

It is pretty clear that the Bird offers little hope of success with an early e3 because, sooner or later, white is going to have to play e4, just losing a tempo. Black has the standard piece placement of the UA and can also get in the c5 break effortlessly. Since black has the better minors and more interior space, he/she is just better.

CLASSICAL UA
1.E4 G6 2.C14 BG7 3.NF3 E6 4.NC3 NE7

The classical is a rare visitor because most players like to play 4.c4 with a free pawn move. In this variation, the author played the same sacrifice, once against Hunnings in the 1994 World Open, and once against Vine (Postal, 1994). The sacrifice 17...Nxe5 in the latter game almost resulted in a victory, but white held on in a difficult position to draw. The game Vine-Moody is given below. Due to its rare nature, we will present the game in its entirety with diagrams out to move 26, and then the remaining moves are presented solely as text.

The second game is Fritz 8-Moody to show you how a strong attacker tries to break down the UA with brute force. White may be able to improve, but the resiliency of the UA is evident here. First, Vine-Moody with a diagram after every other move with black on move.

1.e4 g6 2.d4 Bg7 3.Nf3 e6 4.Nc3 Ne7   5.Bd3 O-O 6.O-O d5

7.e5 Nd7 8.Ne2 c5

9.c3 b6 10.Be3 Bb7

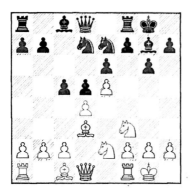

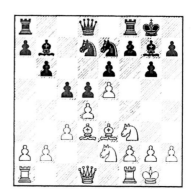

11.Nf4 a6 12.Qd2 h6

13.h3 Kh8 14.Nh2 Nf5

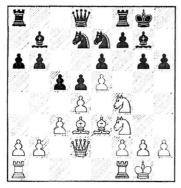

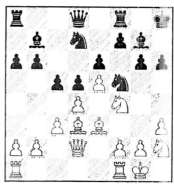

15.13xf5 gxf5 16.f3 Rg8

17.Qf2 Nxe5 18.dxe5 BxeS

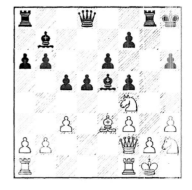

19.Nh5 Qe7 20.f4 d4   21.Nf3 dxe3 22.Qxe3 Bd6

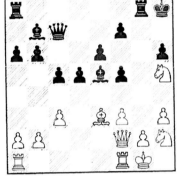 

The second game is Fritz-Moody 120'/40.

1.e4 g6 2.d4 Bg7 3.Nf3 e6 4.Nc3 Ne7   5.Bf4 d5 6.Nb5 Na6

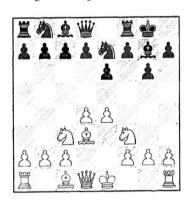 

7.e5 Nb8 8.Be2 a6   9.Na3 Nd7 10.O-O b6

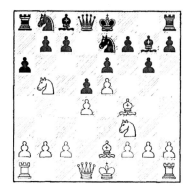

11.c3 h6 12.Nc2 O-O

This is a complex position where white has an advantage in piece development and black an advantage in interior space.

AUSTRIAN UA

The Austrian UA involves the advance of the f-pawn coupled with d4/e4. This is one of the most promising variations for black because white no longer has the resource Bf4/Qd2. We now follow the game Marcuson-Moody, Postal, 1994. My opponent in this game was a postal expert. The game started off in normal channels, and then my opponent got me out of my "book." The first handful of moves were uneventful: 1.d4 g6 2.e4 Bg7 3.Nc3 e6 4.f4 Ne7 5.Nf3 O-O 6.Be3 d5 7.e5 b6 8.Bd3 Bb7 9.Qd2 Nd7 10.O-O c5!. (With initiative. Black's interior space is about to be converted into a classical attack.) 11.Nb5 Nc8! 12.c4?! a6 13.Nc3 Ne7 14.a4 Rc8 15.b3 f6!. (Steering play into extremely sharp tactics. It is clear that this is a doubled-edged position, exactly the kind of position that makes a tactician happy to play either side of this position.) 16.exf6 Bxf6 17.Ne5 Nf5 18.Bxf5 exf5 19.cxd5 cxd4 20.Bxd4 Nxe5 21.Bxe5 Bxe5 22.fxe5 Qc7 23.Rf3 (d6 Qc5ch) Qxe5 24.Re1 Qg7 25.Re6 b5 26.axb5 axb5 27.R3e3 f4 28.R3e5 Qc7 29.Nxb5 Qc5ch 30.Nd4 Bxd5 31.Qf2? (Re7) Qc1ch! 32.Re1 Bxe6! (a petite combination) 33.Nxe6 Rf6 34.Qe2 Qe3ch 35.Qf2 Rxe6 36.Rxe3 fxe3 0-1.

This game illustrates that black has aspirations to share the initiative as early as 10...c5. The reason that the UA may become popular in the future is the ease with which black gains interior space, i.e., future development. This assures that the better player, rather than the better memorizer, will win. An early f4 does not look promising because white needs the resource Bf4/Qd2 to slow down black's initiative on the queenside.

White did not fare well in Courtney-Moody (Postal, 1997). That game saw 1.e4 g6 2.d4 Bg7 3.Nc3 e6 4.f4 Ne7 5.Nf3 b6. (During the preliminaries in the Golden Knights, always played 1....g6/2...Bg7/3 ...e6/4...Ne7/5...O-O, but adopted a more flexible move order in the semifinals). 6.Bd3 Bb7 7.Be3 d5! 8.O-O O-O 9.Qd2?!. (It is hard to say where the queen belongs; with a pawn on f4, it is difficult to see what the queen is doing here.) 9...Nd7 10.e5 c5! 11f5? gxf5-/+. Black has a UP and an extra pawn.

Black missed an obvious and thematic pawn push in Fresen-Crell, Bochum, 1991: 1.e4 g6 2.d4 Bg7 3.f4 e6 4.Nc3 Ne7 5.Nf3 b6 6.Bd3 Bb7 7.Be3 d6?= (d5! 8.e5 Nd7 9.Qd2 c5 10.Nb5 Nc8 =/+). See Marcuson-Moody diagram.

1.d4 g6 2.e4 Bg7 3.Nc3 e6 4.f4 Ne7   5.Nf3 O-O 6.Be3 d5

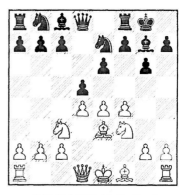

7.e5 b6 8.Bd3 Bb1   9.Qd2 Nd7 10.O-O c5

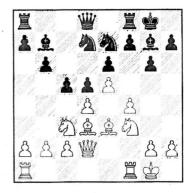

11.Nb5 Nc8 12.c4 a6

13.Nc3 Ne7 14.a4 Rc8

15.b3 f6 16.exf6 Bxf6

17.Ne5 Nf5 18.Bxf5 exf5

19.cxd5 exd4 20.Bxd4 Nxe5

21.Bxe5 Bxe5 22.fxe5 Qc7

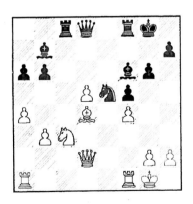

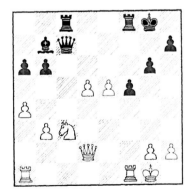

23.Rf3 Qxe5 24.Re1 Qg7

25.Re6 b5 26.axb5 axb5

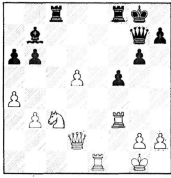
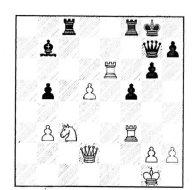

27.R3e3 f4 28.R3e5 Qc7

29.Nxb5 Qc5ch 30.Nd4 Bxd5

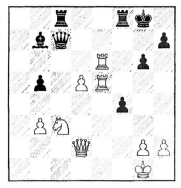

31.Qf2 Qc1ch 32.Re1 Bxe6

33.Nxe6 Rf6 34.Qe2 Qe3ch

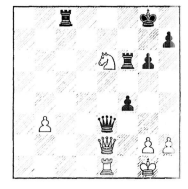

35.Qf2 Rxe6 36.Rxe3 fxe3 0-1

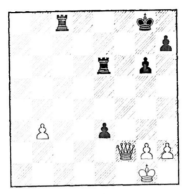

It is pretty clear that black's initiative on the queenside appears more ominous than white's on the kingside, if for no other reason than white has a risky policy of contesting a wide-open center or embarking on unsound sacrificial play on the kingside. What seems pretty clear is that because black has a UP in the opening, a sacrificial attack has little to recommend it.

ENGLISH UA

The English UA can be thought of as any opening where he/she plays any move order that results in his/her having pawns on c4/d4/e4 very early in the game. We will start off this discussion with a brilliancy by Jonas in the game Gabriel-Jonas, Postal, 1991. This game started out with the structure of the King's Indian Saemisch for white and the UA with black. It is an interesting test to see how white fares in this opening and is a valid comparison to the main line of the King's Indian.

The game started out quietly. What cannot be emphasized enough is that players who hope for a quiet positional approach with 1.c4 or 1.d4 are in for a rude awakening. The UA may confer a slight edge for white, i.e., the first move advantage, but how many players hoping for a quiet game would like to be white in Marcuson-Moody (see previous chapter)? The point is this: Black can force his/her will on the game by steering play toward sharp middle games. Compare this to the Panov-Botvinnik Attack; in the eyes of the author, this is one of the most passive openings in chess because it forces premature simplification. You will note that in the UA, the pawn structures are fluid, and few, if any, of the pieces are exchanged in the early middle game, a prerequisite for complications.

Gabriel-Jonas started out quietly enough (see diagram) 1.e4 g6 2.d4 Bg7 3.c4 e6 4.Nc3 Ne7 5.Be3 d5 6.f3 O-O 7.Qd2 c5! 8.cxd5 exd5 9.Nge2 Nbc6!. (Flexibility in the UA is required; black should accept whatever gifts are offered. In this case it is necessary to enforce d4.) 10.Nxd5 Nxd5 11.exd5 cxd4 12.Nxd4 Re8!. (The white king is an embarrassing target!) 13.Nc2 Qb6 (a brilliant shot) 14.Bd3 (dxc6 Bf5 15.cxb7 Rad8 -/+) Nb4 (a brilliant shot) 15.O-O Rxe3 (a stock sacrifice) 16.Nxe3 Nxd5 (piling on) 17.Rae1 Bd4. (This is brute-force chess.) 18.Kf2! Be6 19.a4. (White is reduced to waiting moves.) Rd8

20.a5 Qd6 21.Bb1 Nxe3 22.Rxe3 Qxh2 23.Rfe1 Bf6 24.Rd3 Bh4ch
25.Kf1 Bc4 26.Rec3 Qh1ch 27.Ke2 Qxb1 0-1.

Ostersen-Jensen is a UA where subtle mistakes caused black's un-
doing: 1.d4 g6 2.c4 Bg7 3.Nc3 e6 4.Nf3 Ne7 5.e4 O-O 6.Bg5 c6? (f6!
7.Bh4 b6 8.Be2 Bb1 9.O-O d5 =/+) 7.d5 f6 8.Be3 cxd5. (Black starts
to lose the thread of the game — 8...d6 with an unclear position.)
9.cxd5 Kh8 10.Qd2 Qa5 +/= 1-0:31

Here is Gabriel-Jonas:

1.e4 g6 2.d4 Bg7 3.e4 e6 4.Nc3 Ne7   5.Be3 d5 6.f3 O-O

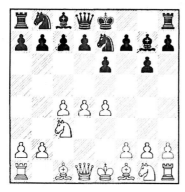

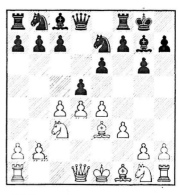

7.Qd2 c5 8.cxd5 exd5   9.Nge2 Nbc6 10.Nxd5 Nxd5

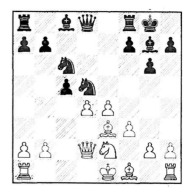

242

11.exd5 cxd4 12.Nxd4 Re8

13.Nc2 Qb6 14.Bd3 Nb4

15.O-O Rxe3 16.Nxe3 Nxd5

17.Rae1 Bd4 18.Kf2 Be6

19.a4 Rd8 20.a5 Qd6

21.Bb1 Nxe3 22.Rxe3 Qxh2

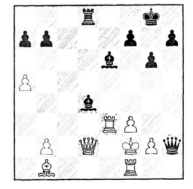

23.Rfe1 Bf6 24.Rd3 Bh4ch   25.Kf1 Bc4 26.Rec3 Qh1ch

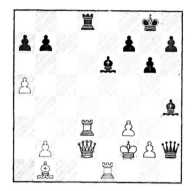 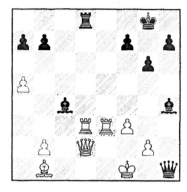

27.Ke2 Qxb1 0-1

Here are some supplemental games.

Santoro-Moody, Postal, 1994: 1.c4 g6 2.Nc3 Bg7 3.d4 e6 4.Nf3
Ne7 5.e4 O-O 6.Bd2? d5 7.b3 b6 8.cxd5 exd5 9.exd5 Bb7 10.Bg5 f6
11.Be3 Nxd5 12.Bc4 Kh8 13.Nxd5 Bxd5 14.O-O Rf7 15.Qc2 Rd7
16.Bxd5 Rxd5=/+ 1/2-1/2:40.

The postal master I faced in the semifinals of the Golden Knights
Tournament, 1997, kept a slight edge out of the opening that he par-
layed into a win: Duliba-Moody: 1.d4 g6 2.c4 Bg7 3.Nf3 e6 4.e4 Ne7
5.Nc3 b6 6.Be2 Bb7 7.O-O O-O. (By the semifinals, I had learned
not to castle prematurely.) 8.Bf4 d5 9.cxd5 exd5 10.e5 c6 11.Rc1 Nd7

12.Bg5 f6 13.exf6 Nxf6 14.Qd2 Rc8 15.Bd3 c5! 16.Rfe1 Nf5?! (a little too aggressive) 17.dxc5 bxc5 18.Na4 c4 19.Bxf5 gxf5 20.Qd4 Qa5 21.Re7 Rf7?. (The critical line is 21...Rc7 22.Bd2 Qxa4 23.Rxc7 Ne8 24.Rxg8ch Nxg8 25.Bc3 Rf7 unclear.) 22.Rxf7 Kxf7 23.Qh4 Qa6. (The knight is too hot.) 24.Nc3 Ne4?? 25.Qxh7 1-0:30.

The next game is Pospishil-Moody, Postal, 1997: 1.d4 g6 2.c4 Bg7 3.e4 e6 4.Nc3 Ne7 5.Nf3 b6 6.Qc2 Bb7 7.Be2 d5 8.Be3 Nd7 9.O-O O-O 10.h4?!. (White needs to resolve the center before going for a wing attack.) 10... c5. (The way to meet a wing attack is to counterattack in the center.) 11.Rad1 Rc8! 12.dxc5 Nxc5 13.g3 Nd7 14.exd5 exd5 15.cxd5 Nxd5 16.Bd4! Nxc3! 17.Bxc3 Bxc3 18.bxc3 =/+ (pawn structure). I knew the "professional" way to win the game was to use black's favorable pawn structure, but black's knowledge of endgames is minimal, and he tried to force a win in the middle game. There was also the additional concern that this might turn into a heavy-piece ending with minimal winning prospects, hence the game continuation 18...Qc7 19.Rc1 Qc6 (with the threat of 20...Ne5) 20.Kh2. (White tries to cover both g2 and h1.) 20...Rfe8 21.Ne1 Rxe2!. (White was so surprised by this move that he requested a diagram to see if we were playing the same position. This is on a par with an opponent in an over-the-board game asking if you really meant to move there!) 22.Qxe2 Ne5 23.f4. (QxeS Re8 queen moves Rxe1, regains the piece with a big attack) 23...Nc4 24.Nf3 Ba6? (critical is Re8) 25.Rf2, and white has survived the worst. 1-0:47.

What can we learn from these games? It appears that black has good practical chances to play aggressively yet safely; thus the English UA should hold a certain appeal for the tacticians out there. Fritz 8 always likes to play e5 in this sort of position, but there is no way of knowing yet whether piece pressure alone can offset black's pawn storm on the queenside.

MODIFIED ENGLISH UA (MEUA)

It would be beating a dead horse to demonstrate how often black falls victim to conventional thinking. Any time the reader sees Nbc6 with a pawn on c7, just think Nd7/c5. The only distinguishing characteristic of a MEUA is that white plays d4 /c4 or c4/d4 but not an early e4. Thus it is somewhat more passive than the English UA. Here is an example of this opening: This MEUA could be titled the dance of the knights. Georgi Orlov would approve. 1.c4 e6 2.g3 d5 3.Bg2 g6 4.d4 Bg7 5.Nc3 Ne7 6.e3 O-O 7.Nge2 dxc4 8.Qa4 c5! 9.dxc5 Nd7 10.O-O Ne5 11.e4 Bd7 12.Qb4 N7c6 13.Qxb7 a5 14.Qb6 Qe7 15.Be3 Nd3 16.Qb5 Rfb8 17.Qa4 Nce5 18.Qd1 Ng4 19.Bd4 Bxd4 20.Nxd4 Ngxf2 21.Rxf2 Qxc5 0-1.

Many of the MEUAs could also transpose to Reti UAs, and just like other Reti UAs, they don't do well against the standard resource, Nd7/c5. It is difficult to believe that white stands better with a pawn on e3 instead of e4 because it is rare in the UA for black to ever play cxd4 where the response exd4 is desirable.

The final Anti-UA is the pawn push variation, i.e., 1.e4 g6 2.d4 Bg7 3.h4 d5! 4.e5 c5 5.c3 Nc6 with a comfortable game.

247

Through theory and practice, the UA (g6/bg7/e6/Ne7) has been molded by the author into an entirely new opening system, as opposed to scattered games where some of the key ideas have been tested but never codified. It is a separate and distinct system from the modern in its insistence on getting in both d5 and c5. In this sense, it can be viewed as a marriage of the French and the modern, with the modern idea of g6/Bg7 and the French idea of e6/d5/c5. It stands in stark contrast to the Indian Defenses that the author believes arc poorly motivated due to the fact that black routinely plays the move sequence Nf6/d6/e5, which is never played in the UA. We believe that the UA will replace the Indian Defenses once it becomes clear how flexible and aggressive the UA can be.

While it is true that former world champion Karpov has made a living from universal positions, e.g., the King's Indian Saemisch, his knowledge is even a mystery to even strong grandmasters. Time is life. Interior space is time. Interior space is life.

PRINCIPLES OF MAGIC:
SUMMARY AND CONCLUSIONS

The single most important lesson that we come away with in this book is that conventional concepts of development sans knowledge of interior space means that opening theory is incomplete. The game "Magic" is the quintessential example of the use and exploitation of the vulnerability of computers and their poor understanding of interior space. The way to defeat supercomputers of the future is to involve them with evaluating piece activity versus interior space, i.e., force them to flip programming "coins" (equivalent positions) based on their algorithms so that they acquire small disadvantages. They will have a tough time reconciling these two variables because they frequently are at odds with one another. Unless it is generally recognized that interior space is time, then tacticians in the future will watch helplessly as their opponents get more interior space, push back the white pieces from their "aggressive" posts, and simply counterattack again and again.

One of the worst responses to 1.e4 is perhaps 1... e5. This response is based on the antiquated notion that the center must be contested immediately. While hypermodern play has rejected this notion, it does so in an inferior way. The teachings of Steinitz and Nirnzovich are, for the most part, rejected by the author, and universal theory is offered in its stead.

One of the concepts missing from chess is that 1...e5 is the single greatest weakening of black's king position and is the cause of immediate misery. Witness the Two Knights Defense. Other attempts to justify 1...e5 fail, for the most part, on first principles.

The Alekhine Defense is sharp in the line 1.e4 Nf6 2.Qe2 e5 3.f4 exf4 4.e5, so black should transpose to the Falkbeer Countergambit with 3...d5 with an unclear position. It is left to other theoreticians to determine if there is any hope here of a white advantage.

In terms of responding to a gambit, it is offered here that any time a player has won material but lost the initiative, it is best to return to a universal position. Examples of UPs illustrate how common they are at the highest levels of play and that they can evolve from almost any opening.

PHILOSOPHY OF ARTIFICIAL INTELLIGENCE

Some have likened the battle between humans and computers in chess to the epic struggle of John Henry versus the machine; in actuality the two contests are radically different. John Henry took on a machine that was abundantly equipped to surpass the physical limitations of the human body. Can we say with certainty what the limitations of the human mind are? How then do we know that computers will eventually become permanent world champion in all forms of chess?

There is only one rule change that is needed for humans to defeat computers in the future: the five-second rule. Under no circumstance should computers be able to make moves in less than five seconds; this applies to the opening and time scrambles at the end of the game. If this is unacceptable, then we should require computers to physically pick up pieces on the board, punch the clock, and physically write the game score on a chess pad. The reason this is important is that most players never realize what a small percentage of the human mind is actually focusing on chess when we play the game. Most of the brain is spent regulating our breathing, causing our hearts to beat, and perceiving the sights, sounds, smells, and touch of the pieces and a general awareness of our physical surroundings. Only a small amount of our CPU time is actually spent analyzing chess. The end result: We spend 10 percent of our brainpower analyzing chess while we are playing it, and the remainder is spent on extraneous activities. The computer, by contrast, can devote 100 percent of its CPU time on chess. No wonder they win!

To many, chess is just a game, but to a student of chess, it is a window into the mind. We devotees believe that chess offers the opportunity to explore strange new worlds (e.g. Zugzwang), to seek out intelligent life (occasionally found at chess clubs and tournaments), and to boldly go where no one has gone before (overlooking checkmate with over an hour on the clock). But when we look at chess objectively, it involves a complexity unknown at even the highest levels of math. The mind must keep track of over one dozen variables: relative king safety; absolute king safety (checkmate); apparent time; actual time; future time; interior space; exterior space; controlled space; uncontrolled space; future space; material; evolving material values; piece coordination; static pawn structure; mobile pawn structure; threats to promote, real or imagined; the role of the minors in the opening, middle game, and endgame; and the role of the majors in the opening, middle game, and endgame, etc. These variables must be integrated from the beginning to the end of the game.

What the mind does is create order out of chaos; what the computer does is to create a different kind of order out of chaos, and this order is unlike anything created by the human mind, except, perhaps, Steinitz. Steinitz was the first human computer.

The impression some have about computers is that they are going to outstrip the human mind in chess and most other mental activities. This seems highly unlikely. (We do not know the limitations of the human mind.) While some may argue that Magic has no practical application, the author merely offers this observation: Given the known rules the computer uses to rely on when it makes its decisions, how many centuries would it take using existing computer programs to be aware of the fact that Magic was playable? How many computers, given existing programming, could discover the starting position, Magic, and know that it would be playable against computers? In other words, simply ask the computer to place on the board from the starting position the maximum lead in development that would be "playable," i.e., produce an evaluation of less than a one pawn advantage with the maximum lead in development.

Some may argue that chess is just a "game," to which the author would respond, "Art is just shapes and colors." Suppose forty years ago computer programmers, instead of focusing on chess, had focused on painting still lifes. In the first five years in the late sixties and early seventies. the computer could draw crude shapes of the outline of an apple. The colors would be all wrong, and the fruit would look bizarre, otherworldly. Art critics would proclaim, "Computers will never produce a work of art." (Does this sound vaguely familiar to chess players?) Within ten years, the computer would get all the shapes 100 percent correct with more accuracy and with greater precision than even the best artists in the world. (Think of it this way: Suppose we took the most complicated mates in three and had a contest in the early 1980s to see who could discover the most mates in three in a set time limit, the chess world champion or Belle?)

Within fifteen years, as an art student in high school, it would get an A+++ on shapes and a D- on perspective, for an average grade of C+. Within twenty years, it would paint still lifes better than most high school students, within twenty-five years, better than most art majors in college, within thirty years, better than all but a handful of the top artists in the world, within thirty-five years, it would be the "world champion" of still lifes. This could have been done with the same cavalier attitude that went into the attempt to destroy beauty in chess and replace it with cold, hard logic.

During World War II, many classes of individuals felt that as long as the Nazis came after someone else, they were okay. What happens when the insane logic of computers causes them to be used in other disciplines to surpass all human accomplishments? First tic-tac-toe, then checkers, then go, then chess, then art, literature, and music. What's left that is human?

Despite the sanguine attitude that computers could destroy creativity in chess, art, and music, perhaps there is way out: We humans must band together against computers. Here is a way for chess professionals to outplay computers for the next several centuries at a minimum. They must see through each other's blind spots.

In an article called "Communal Blind Spot Theory" in the *Mensa Bulletin*, March 1995, 11-12, the author explored a new research methodology he called intuitive iteration II. The steps are remarkably simple. When solving problems, e.g., chess positions, use II in the following manner: 1) Get a gut reaction to the situation; 2) Introduce the facts and logic; 3) Compare your intuition to the facts and logic; 4) If there is a conflict between the two, try to resolve the conflict; 5) If the conflict cannot be resolved, throw out your intuition and the facts and logic; 6) iterate, i.e., start over by getting a gut reaction to the situation. It took the author years to find the move sequence 1.e4 e5 2.Nf3 Nc6 3.Bc4 Nf6 4.Ng5 d5 5.exd5 Nd4 6.c3 b5 7.Bf1 Nxd5 8.Ne4! Qh4 9.Ng3 Bg4 10.f3 e4 11.exd4 Bd6 12,Qe2! in the Two Knights Defense and he explored a logical alternative to the main line, 8.Nh3, with GM Lev Alburt for years that is equal. But this was antipositional and, thus, made the author uneasy. So he returned to the starting position of 8.Ne4 over a thousand times (which, by the way, is Einstein's definition of insanity, i.e., doing the same thing over and over and expecting different results. What he neglected to point out is it is also a great way to create paradigm shifts). He walked away from the position for a year and then woke up one day with the idea of 12.Qe2, which he assumed would be met with 12...Bxg3ch. To his amazement, it was met with 12...Be6?, which is book according to Fritz 8. It took only a matter of seconds to a few minutes to find two alternatives to 13.fxe4, 13.Nc3 and 13.Qf2. The author never even looked at book, 13.fxe4, a non-developing move!

This procedure can be thought of as self-brainwashing, i.e., forcing your mind to look at the same move sequences over and over until the mind rebels and creates new ideas. During a psychology experiment in college, the author was forced to listen to the same nonsense syllables over and over hundreds of times and was then asked to indicate when the nonsense syllables changed. Within a few minutes, the author could detect subtle differences in the sounds, which were dutifully reported to the investigator, a graduate student. Only after the experiment was over did the author learn that there were no changes in the sounds, but that my mind, after listening to the same sounds over and over, simply made up its own sounds! Think of what this means in terms of recovered "memories."

How does this apply to competition between humans and computers? We must begin to play consultation matches with different teams of human professionals going up against any combination of computers that chess programmers wish to array against them. My prediction: Within a year after Magic is published and chess professionals start to play consultation matches against computers (a sub prediction here: The strongest players against computers may not even be top professionals. They may even be below ELO 2200; these anti-computer players must be given the opportunity to crush computers), the average ratings of computers will drop three hundred to five hundred rating points. Do you think a team of world champion Kramnik, former world champion Kasparov, and the strongest female player in the world, GM Judit Polgar, would overlook checkmate in one move the way Kramnik did? The primary result of consultation matches is that human competitors will stop making tactical blunders at least 90 percent of the time; any mistakes they make will be far more subtle.

Hypothesis: Computers will be forced to prove to the mathematics community, chess community, physics community, and other intellectual endeavors that a higher order of logic exists beyond the reach of computers. Like any hypothesis, this one is testable. For chance, randomness, chaos, and entropy to favor abiotic systems over biotic systems, life should be suppressed. Life is predictable, orderly, simple, and anti-entropic, just the opposite of abiotic systems. A predictable consequence is that human imagination will surpass the imagination of computers; thus it is predictable that dozens of teams of top human competitors can defeat the strongest arrays of computers within a year of the publication of Magic.

The purpose of randomness, chance, uncertainty, chaos, entropy, and quantum effects is to achieve higher levels of order in living systems. It is the activation energy of life. This leads to the concept of an intuitive proof, as opposed to a logical proof.

"An intuitive proof is a set of facts capable of being derived by instinct alone that is not accessible to ordinary reasonable logical resolution." An intuitive proof would be that faith, hope, and love are real and that they are eternal.

A general rule of chess in the future is that, as the piece coordination of a player goes down, the depth of tactics of computers increases, i.e., the more the position gets out of hand, the more likely a player will be hit with tactics farther and farther down the road. Then the computer will simply overload pieces or squares five to fifteen moves later. My recommendation: Always maintain good piece coordination when playing against computers. If you can't do this, then you are busted, and the only way out is to out combine the computer with the wildest tactics you can muster.

With the growth of math and law, logic has become more common in the past ten thousand years and there has been an explosion of science in the past century, logic has reached unparalleled heights. Now with the computer revolution, we have a new kind of logic: binary code. With binary code, we have engaged in the most massive, unregulated experiment in the history of the human race. We test steak for its carcinogenic properties with more thoroughness than we test binary code for its impact on the human mind. In a few short years, we will not have any control groups left because every human animal will be infected with binary code. We simply don't have a clue how the mind views binary code. Does it view it as two dimensional, three dimensional or four or more dimensional? Is there a "sub" subconscious that breaks signals down into pixels? Here is a simple observation: On one axis of a graph, plot the growth of binary logic in America over the past fifty years. On the same axis, plot the objective growth of antisocial behavior in America in the past fifty years. Is there a correlation?

We know on earth here that a naturally occurring nuclear reactor created itself in Oklo in Africa. Is it beyond the realm of belief that on some silicon-rich planet thousands of light years away, electricity is created by the photoelectric effect, making the three driving forces of life photosynthesis, chemosynthesis, and the photoelectric effect (or maybe even cold fusion)? Suppose that on quartz crystals metal ions were plated onto the surface of the crystal and a silicon chip spontaneously appeared and replicated.

This purely logical, not spiritual, computer may be destructive to us by the mere act of bombarding us with binary code when our minds work in trinary code, i.e., the computer only sees black and white, on and off. We may have a third option that they don't have, maybe, or gray.

The mere act of observation may be lethal to both of us. This is the classic Schrodinger's cat paradox, i.e., if a cat is in a box in limbo between life and death, it can persist in that state. If an observer opens the box (Pandora's?), it may drive the cat into life or death that would not have occurred if the box had never been opened. Thus our observation of the universe may be highly detrimental to computers and other intelligent life-forms because we introduce causality. Their observation of us may be highly detrimental to us because we don't think in binary code; we think in trinary code. What the Schrodinger paradox tells us is that observation alters the events we observe and may be destructive to other forms of intelligent life.

Bobby Fischer coined the phrase with respect to chess that "time is life." What if he is right, i.e., that time cannot exist in the absence of life? Without time there is no causality, i.e., a past, a present, and a future. Perhaps there is only change in the world of the computer but no causality.

Benko or Fischer random chess has limited appeal to the author because it really doesn't change the dynamics of the position. If we use Magic as the starting position with a pawn on d6 and black on move, it is a very complex, unusual struggle where the better player will win. It quite literally means getting off book and with no opening principles to be found. It is truly an entire game of chess.

There are other options, however. Here is the Hypermodern Advanced variation (see diagram).

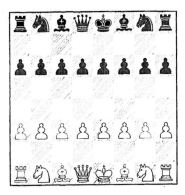

The second is the Classical Advanced Variation (see diagram).

The third starting position is a Hybrid position (see diagram).

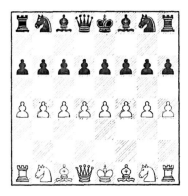

What these starting positions illustrate is the incredible complexity of chess. These additional modifications of the starting position will make chess a viable game for the next thousand years.

ADDENDUM

All analysis and games are vetted with Fritz 15, a 3200-level computer.

Competitive Intuition

Every so often my playing strength jumps from weak B player to strong Grandmaster level for a period of a few hours to a few days. This is based on my performance against strong humans and strong computers. For example I defeated both Fritz 15 and Houdini 3. Before I get to the games where my playing strength increased, I'd like to lay the groundwork for these games. The Ulvestad/Fritz system was studied extensively by world correspondence champion Dr. Hans Berliner.

These two openings typically transpose, so Berliner's choice of the Ulvestad was not a surprise. The key alternative to the Berliner Gambit is a continuation by white that wins a pawn but allows too much counterplay so that white has no realistic winning chances.

This is the definitive refutation of the Berliner Gambit. For those readers who think that this is an obscure variation, I would point out that *BCO 2* first edition devoted a page of analysis to this opening. In the fifth world championship, Berliner won a beautiful game against Estrin. Berliner was so certain of his variation that he said it refuted Ng5 in the Two Knights Defense. Actually it leads to the fastest winning position for white of any major opening in chess. Berliner even offered a thousand-dollar award for anyone who could beat him in his opening. I tried to accept the offer but was unable to contact Berliner.

Here is that game. GM Andy Soltis claimed that this was one of the best one hundred games of the twentieth century.

Estrin-Berliner fifth correspondence world championship: 1.e4 e5 2.Nf3 Nc6 3.Bc4 Nf6 4.Ng5 d5 5.exd5 b5 6.Bf1 Nd4 7.c3 Nxd5 8.Ne4 Qh4 9.Ng3 Bg4 10.f3 e4 11.cxd4 Bd6 12.Bxb5+ Kd8 13.O-O exf3 14.Rxf3 Rb8 15.Be2?. (According to LM A.J. Goldsby, best is 15.a4; Soltis, Nunn, and Huebner also believe that 15.Be2 is a blunder. White must maintain communication between queen and rook so best is 15.Bf1.) Bxf3 16.Bxf3 Qxd4+ 17.Kh1 Bxg3! 18.hxg3 Rb6! 19.d3 Ne3 20.Bxe3 Qxe3 21.Bg4 h5 22.Bh3 g5 23.Nd2 g4 24.Nc4 Qxg3 25.Nxb6 gxh3! 26.Qf3! hxg2+ 27.Qxg2 Qxg2+ 28.Kxg2 cxb6!! (capturing away from the center and awarded two exclamation points by GM Soltis) 29.Rf1 Ke7 30.Re1+ Kd6! 31.Rf1 Rc8! 32.Rxf7 Rc7 33.Rf2 -/+ Ke5! 34.a4?. (According to Soltis, this shortens the game by ten moves.) Kd4 35.a5 Kxd3 36.Rf3 Kc2 37.b4 b5! 38.a6 Rc4 39.Rf7 Rxb4 40.Rb7 Rg4+ 41.Kf3 b4 42.Rxa7 b3 0-1.

I defeated Fritz 8 in the Berliner Gambit when I was able with a rook sacrifice to get bishop and three pawns for a rook with a big initiative. Here is the move sequence: 4.Ng5 d5 5.exd5 Nd4 6.c3 b5 7.Bf1 Nxd5 8.Ne4 Qh4 9.Ng3 Bg4 10.f3 e4 11.cxd4 Bd6 12.Qe2! Be6 13.Nc3!! (Actually Qxb5+ may be better, but I decided to seize the initiative.) Nxc3 14.dxc3 Bxg3+ 15.hxg3! Qxh1 16.Qxb5+ Kf8. Now white proceeded to win the c-pawn, and black consistently overlooked the pawn mass on the queenside. White wound up with connected passed pawns on the fifth, sixth, and seventh, winning two rooks for Bishop and two pawns.

The drawback to 12.Qe2 is that black can play O-O. After 12...O-O 13.fxg4 Bxg3+ 14.Kd1, black clearly has inadequate compensation for the piece, but the position is very sharp. c6 15.Nc3 Bf2 16.Nxe4 Bxd4 17.g3 Qe7 18.Bg2 Rad8 19.Kc2 Rfe8 20.Kb1 Qd7 21.a4 b4 22.g5 a5 23.h4 Qe6 24.Re1. (Black's compensation for the piece is not obvious. Fritz 15 went on to win with white fairly easily but came up with continuations that few humans could find.)

I decided to revisit Estrin's choice and found a key improvement for white.

I was able in the endgame to achieve the advantage of two bishops and knight versus rook, knight, and pawn. Since the two bishops are worth eight and knight three, together they are worth eleven, and the rook, knight and pawn nine. White effectively had a two-pawn advantage, but it is critical to keep his knight on the board. Otherwise black can exchange his g- and h-pawns for white's g-pawn, and white cannot make progress. Once I had a decisive advantage, I relied on Fritz's superior endgame technique to bring home the point.

1.e4 e5 2.Nf3 Nc6 3.Bc4 Nf6 4.Ng5 d5 5.exd5 Nd4 6.c3 b5 7.Bf1 Nxd5 8.Ne4 Qh4 9.Ng3 Bg4 10.f3 e4 11.cxd4 Bd6 12.Bxb5+ Kd8 13.O-O exf3 14.Rxf3 Rb8 15.Bf1! Bxf3 16.Qxf3 Qxd4+ 17.Kh1 Bxg3 18.Nc3! (a key interpolation) Bxh2 19.Kxh2. (Due to the fact that white has two bishops and knight for rook, knight, and pawn, and that black has a weakened pawn structure, the position is +/-.) Nf6 20.Ne2 Qh4+ 21.Kg1 Ng4 22.Qd3+! (driving the king to a vulnerable square) Kc8 23.Qg3 Qxg3 24.Nxg3 Re8 25.b3 Rb6 26.Nf5 Re1 27.Bb2 Rxa1 28.Bxa1 g6 29.Ne3 Nf6 30.Bc4 Ne4 31.Bxf7 Nxd2 32.Kf2. (Nc4 exchanging knights is a positional blunder; if white exchanges knights, black will swap his g- and h-pawns for white's g-pawn, and white cannot break through on the queenside. White will pick up the other g-pawn, and the resulting endgame of three minor pieces for a rook should be a win for the pieces.) White won a rook for a piece, and the resulting endgame of bishop and knight is a theoretical win.

When I imputed a move from Fritz 14 in a game against Fritz 15, I went on to win easily against Fritz 15 in the Berliner gambit. Here are the starting moves: 12.Qe2 O-O 13.fxg4 Bxg3+ 14.Kd1 Re8 15.Nc3 c6 16.Nxd5 cxd5 17.b3 Bf2 18.Bb2 e3? 19.d3 Rad8 20.Rc1 b4 21.Rc5. Now Fritz just punted with a5/a4/a3. I was able to play Kc1/Kb1/Ba1/Rac1. Then I doubled on the fifth. This forced the computer to retreat its queen to defend d5, so I just walked my king to e2, replacing the queen as the blockader. While I was doing this, the computer made waiting moves on the kingside, i.e., f6/g6/Kg7/Kg8, so I played Bf3/Qg2, hitting d5 four times. Next I played Bxd5; two moves later I played Rxb4, and the computer, down a piece and two pawns, resigned.

Against Fritz 8 on the black side of the Sicilian Defense, I came up with an attacking configuration I've never seen before: I tripled on the fifth and picked up a pawn on the fifth. Meanwhile the computer had a passed h-pawn supported by a knight that it was pushing up the board rapidly. I could have blockaded the pawn with my knight but chose instead to attack the computer's king. Fritz queened the h-pawn, and one move later its evaluation went to 0000, meaning it saw a draw by repetition. Then Fritz 8 did something Fritz 10 did as well. It saw a draw by repetition but "froze," burned through three time controls, and lost on time. After the game was over, I forced the computer to move while I tried to play the black position. I blundered three times in a row, which shows just how rapidly I can lose competitive intuition, so I had the computer play both sides of the position. Sure enough, six to seven moves later, the draw by repetition appeared.

To show you why I am a weak B player most of the time, here is a game I played in the recent New York State Open: 1.e4 e5 2.Nf3 Nc6 3.Bc4 Nf6 4.Ng5 d5 5.exd5 Na5 6.Bb5+ c6 7.dxc6 bxc6 8.Qf3 Bb7 (the poorest of three alternatives: Be7, Rb8, and even cxb5 are better) 9.d3?? (transposing moves). My opponent then played 8...cxb5. Game over.

Against Houdini 3, I played the correct move. 9.Ba4 Be7 10.O-O O-O 11.d3 c5 12.Qe2 Nc6 +/=. I eventually retreated my g5 knight behind my pawn wall with all of my pieces in back of my pawns. Houdini probed for weaknesses over the next twenty-five moves, found none, and we soon were up against the first time control. I decided to repeat moves and reached the first time control. Houdini reached the first time control, refused to move, burned through the next two time controls, and lost on time.

There are two ways to defeat strong computers of the future: software glitches and faulty human opening theory the computer fails to vet before playing it.

In the only game I have ever played one-on-one against a grandmaster, I called my chess teacher GM Lev Alburt with an innovation I came up with on the black side of the Blumenfeld Counter Gambit. Lev didn't like it very much, so we began to argue over the phone over my innovation. This evolved into a blitz game over the phone. At a critical juncture, I saw that the only way to increase my attack against Lev's king was by sacrificing the exchange, moving a pinned piece. Lev immediately said, "That loses the exchange." I responded, "I am sacrificing the exchange." He said, "Oh." Clearly Lev had not seen the attacking prospects I got by sacrificing the exchange. I mishandled the attack somewhat so that when Lev offered me a draw, I readily accepted it. Lev then told me that black was better, close to winning in the middle game.

When I have competitive intuition, I never calculate more than two to three moves ahead, just moving my pieces and pawns to the squares where they belong, never taking more than a few seconds/move. Players know this as being in the groove or, as GM Soltis has indicated, the "hand" knows how to play.

HAMB Gambit
1.e4 e5 2.f4 exf4 3.Qe2
1.f4 e5 2.e4 exf4 3.Qe2
One of the difficulties in writing about the HAMB Gambit is that it is so new even nomenclature is very fluid. About the time that Kari Heinola was playing the HAMB Gambit in earnest, I had sponsored a contest in *Chess Life* to test the value of the move sequence above.

Because I spent $100 to promote the opening, NM Alex Dunne as the Correspondence columnist for *Chess Life* decided to call it the Moody Gambit. Because of the large amount of analysis by Grandmaster Lev Alburt contributed to the fundamental new ideas emerging from our joint research, I renamed the opening the Moody-Alburt Gambit in *Empire Chess, Rank and File magazine* and *Check!* Recently with the large data base of games where this opening was played in tournaments, it is clear that IM Basman and Heinola have been the chief practitioners and in recognition of their pioneering work, I have again renamed it the HAMB Gambit.

About 30 years ago GM Alburt even enlisted the help of World Champion Garry Kasparov and Grandmaster Maxim Dlugy to analyze the gambit. Garry suggested that Black could try 3...Be7+ 4.Kd1 Be7 with an unclear position. I was far more concerned that Black would open the center with 3...d5! The reason that computers are so important in chess analysis is they never overlook the obvious. Clearly 4.exd5+ Be7 is good for Black according to extensive analysis by NM Steven Taylor. In about a dozen variations, Black is better, but everyone has overlooked the obvious response to 3...d5 4.d3! Here is some analysis by Fritz 15 of 4.d3 Bd6 5.e5 Bc5 6.Nf3 Nc6 7.Bxf4 Nge7 8.Nbd2 O-O 9.O-O-O with a complicated position with chances for both sides.

Here are some games in the gambit.

The first game is Heinola-Tirkkonen, Uusikaupunki, we, A (3) 3...Be7 4.d4 Bh4+5.Kd1 Nc6 6.Nf3 d6 7.Bxf4 Bg4 8.c3 Qe7 9.Nbd2 O-O-O 10.h3 Bxf3 11.Qxf3 +/- 1-0:41

In this game, Heinola-Mahrlund, Espoo Open Champ. SF, 1985, Black played passively and lost. 1.f4 e5 2.e4 fxe4 3.Qe2 Be7 4.d4 d6 5.Bxf4 Nf6 6.Nc3 O-O 7.O-O-O Bg4 8.Nf3 c6 9.h3 Bh5 10.g4 Bg6 11.Bg2 d5 12.exd5 Nxd5 13.Nxd5 cxd5 14.Bxb8 Rxb8 15.Ne5 Rc8 16.Nxg6 hxg6 17.Qb5 +/- 1-0:27

The best game and winner of the Thematic Tournament, Postal, 1989, sponsored by the author, was Rigby 2271-Green 2015 played the correct continuation on move 4.

1.e4 e5 2.f4 exf4 3.Qe2 Be7 4.Nc3 Nc6 5.Nf3 d6 6.d4 Bg4 7.Bxf4 Bh4+ 8.Bg3 Bxg3+9.hxg3 Nxd4 10.Qf2 Nc6 11.O-O-O Nf6 12.e5 Nxe5 13.Nxe5 Bxd1 14.Bb5+ Kf8 15.Rxd1 Qe7 16.Nf3 c6 17.Bd3 Ng4 18.Qd2 h5 19.Re1 Qc7 +/= 1/2-1/2:39

In the next game White was better but then Black hung a piece. Rigby 2271-Deatherage 2265 Postal Thematic, 1989. 1.e4 e5 2.f4 exf4 3.Qe2 Be7 4.Nc3 Nc6 5.Nf3 d6 6.d4 Bh4+ 7.Kd1 Bg4 8.Qc4 Nf6 9.Be2 Bxf3 10.Bxf3 Bf2 11.Ne2 Be3 12.c3 O-O 13.Nxf4 Bxc1 14.Rxc1

Qd7 15.Rc2 Nxe4? (Black simply drops a piece here. Clearly Black can avoid the loss of the piece temporarily with 17...Nxf4, but then 18.Bxc6 is obviously better for White. The rest is carnage.) 16.Bxe4 Qg4+ 17.Re2 Rfe8 18.Bxc6 Rxe2 19.Nxe2 bxc6 20.Qxc6 Rc8 21.Rf1 h6 22.Qf3 Qe6 23.d5 Qg6 24.Qf5 1-0

Since 3...d6 is so popular in my data base, I decided to play a centaur game in this variation. As I expected Black has minimal chances to win. This just means that Black has at least three superior tries on move 3, 3...Qh4+, 3...Nc6, and 3...d5 Since 3...d6 is so popular in the HAMB Gambit, I decided to play a centaur game in this opening. It was my belief that Black only equalizes with 3...d6. 1.e4 e5 2.f4 exf4 3.Qe2 d6 4.d3 Qh4+ 5.Qf2 Qxf2+ 6.Kxf2 g5 7.h4 f6 8.Nf3 Be7 9.Nc3 Na6 10.Bd2 c6 11.Re1 Nh6 12.g3 fxg3 13.Kxg3 Nf7 14.Nd4 h5 15.Be2 g4 16.Rhf1 (It is clear that White has a lot of compensation for the pawn.) Nh6 17.Nd1! Bd8 18.Ne3 Nc5 19.Ng2 Ng8 20.b4 Ne6 21.Nxe6 Bxe6 22.a3 Bb6 23.c3 Kd7 24.Nf4 Bf7 25.d4 Rf8 26.Bd3 Ne7 27.a4 Bc7 28.c4 c5 29.d5 Ng6 30.Nxg6 Bxg6 31.b5 a5 32.Bc3 Kc8 33.Bxf6 Rh7 34.Rf4 R7f7 35.R1f1 Kd7 36.Bc2 Bd8 37.Bg5 Rxf4 38.Rxf4 Kxf4=

There are two continuations I leave to the reader to analyze—3...Qh4+ and 3...Nc6. White should meet the latter with 4.c3 with the idea of sheltering his King on the c2 square. With 3...Qh4+ 4.Kd1, White has full compensation for the pawn, but the position is very sharp and worthy of additional analysis.

Chess and the Paranormal Realm

About 30 years ago I was analyzing my favorite opening, the Evans Gambit. I ran out of ideas so I asked my 1700 computer, a Par Excellence, what it thought was best. Much to my surprise, it came up with a very good move. A little later I again asked the computer what was best. Again it came up with a very good move. By the third time this happened I just turned the position over to the computer and had it play both sides of the position at blitz speed.

269

What I witnessed was beyond belief. Somehow the Queens were exchanged and to this day I have been unable to find a way to exchange Queens in the opening. Now I was treated to a beyond world champion level play. White was able to achieve enough pressure to force Black to sacrifice the minor exchange to relieve the pressure. Next White with the minor exchange began to maneuver in the center. Black focused on the Queenside so we saw the indirect exchange of pawns. White won a center pawn and Black picked up a Queenside pawn.

At long last I thought the computer blundered. It failed to win a pawn to a two move continuation. So I said to myself, "Aha you stupid computer, at long last you have blundered". What the computer did over the next 15 moves was to sweep through the center and it picked up the pawn. It was clear that the computer wanted the square, not the pawn.

I went back to the point where the computer failed to win the pawn and forced the computer to win the pawn. I fully expected that Black would get an overwhelming attack by sacrificing the pawn. Five moves went by, then six or seven moves, but Black did not regain the pawn. What I noticed, however, was the Black Knights were attacking on the a- and h-files. In other words Black had compensation for the pawn, something that Black did not get when White picked up the pawn when it played thought it was time to do so.

Both sides chopped wood and we entered a simple endgame of Rook and Bishop and connected center pawns for White while Black had a Knight and had an a- and h-pawn. White blockaded the a-pawn with its Bishop and White stepped into the Queening square of the h-pawn with its King. Then it pushed the center pawns to the sixth. When the computer saw it couldn't stop the pawn from Queening, it sacrificed the Rook for a pawn. At this point, I resigned for Black; obviously it knew how to win the position.

So what was going on? Was it a delusion? I believe that a super-computer in the future reached back in time to the 20th century to give me a chess lesson.

Introduction Fritz 15

What is clear in this addendum is that theory has not yet caught up to the state of supercomputers. In the King's Indian Defense, white grabs a huge amount of interior space and wins routinely when Black fails to play actively. I give the HAMB Gambit twice. In the first edition of *Magic* I relied on Fritz 8. Clearly, Fritz 15 is a more accurate assessment of the tactics in the position.

In this book you will see a radical departure from theory and play in the Evans Gambit. I indicated that Black was better after analyzing the positions with Fritz 8. Fritz 15 is a brutal attacker and demonstrated how white had a big plus in the Normal Position with 9.Nc3. In the Compromised Defense, I forced Black to play aggressively and was able to emerge with a complex position where Black may be able to hold. When Black played its "book" move, I was able to get a decisive attack when Fritz tried Nge7 instead of b5.

In the Two Knight's Defense, I was able to get a winning attack in the Berliner Gambit and a winning attack in the Ulvestad variation. I rely on an obscure variation of the Wilkes-Barre Traxler variation to demonstrate a winning plan with white. Fritz 15 keeps the pressure up over the entire board and Black could not defend his position for very long.

In the main line I was able to demonstrate routinely that White had more than enough counterplay against any Black threats. I was able to demonstrate that theory in the ancient Fried Liver Attack is a good middlegame for Black provided he is familiar with theory and play.

In the Latvian Gambit, the Fritz engines have different ways to skin a cat. Fritz 8 simply plays to win a pawn, and, at the same time, trap the black king in the center of the board. Fritz 15 plays an early f3 forcing Black to open the position for the white army while Black is still stuck with a King in the center of the board.

I introduce the reader to the concept of Universal Positions and follow with a variety of move orders by Black that establish the first four moves of the Universal System aka Universal Attack are a new opening system. The reader is referred to the July 2019 issue of *Chess Life*, Grandmaster Lev Alburt's column for a review of Universal Positions and the Universal System.

In the chapter on chess and the paranormal realm, I leave it up to the discerning reader to try to explain to me what was happening.

THE EVANS GAMBIT

History of the Evans Gambit by Ray Kuzanek

The development of chess opening theory, its growth to individual analysis, an evolving understanding of the tactics and strategy inherent in positions through exchanges of ideas, and testing initial conclusions of actual games. Added to these elements is the human penchant for changing fashion, the exercise of imagination, the creation of beauty, and the impact of dominant personalities.

These wellsprings of creativity have affected the development of all chess openings in some degree but can arguably be said to be especially true of the Evans Gambit. A rich past linking historic matches between the towering figures of an era and the gradual refinement of opening ideas gives the student/player a context for his/her own expanded appreciation of the many facets of this opening.

William Davies Evans (1790-1872), the son of a Welsh farmer, went to sea at the age of fourteen and served until the end of the Napoleonic War in 1815. Transferring to the postal service, he reached the rank of captain in 1819 and regularly sailed between Milford Haven, Wales, and Waterford, Ireland. He learned chess from naval lieutenant Harry Wilsen and first conceived of the gambit bearing his name in 1824. Traveling to London in 1827 (or late 1826), he introduced the gambit to Alexander MacDonnell. The opening was analyzed in William Lewis's *First Series of Chess Lessons* (1831-1832) but only became widely known when it was used by MacDonnell in his series of matches with LaBourdonnais in 1834 and 1835.

In Paul Morphy's annotations to the twenty-sixth game of the La-Bourdonnais-MacDonnell match (appearing in the *New York Ledger* of March 3, 1860), Morphy wrote, "The game before us is the first in which that most beautiful of openings, the 'Evans Gambit,' occurs between these distinguished players. MacDonnell had for some time been familiar with attack, having analyzed this debut with its originator, Captain Evans. LaBourdonnais, on the other hand, was comparatively unacquainted with this new style of play, and although unfortunate in the first encounter, deserves great credit for the skill and patience with which he elaborate the defence in subsequent games."

MacDonnell played the gambit six times, winning four and losing one.

LaBourdonnais used the gambit sixteen times, winning eleven and losing three. Many of the lines which were to become the object of intense analysis for decades to come were employed in this match.

Twice black played 5...Bd6, a move employed by Kieseritsky in the 1840s, the subject analysis by Stone and Ware during the nineteenth century used by Pillsbury at Hastings in 1895 and endorsed by Grandmaster Rohde in *The Great Evans Gambit Debate* in one game. Black played 5...Be7, a move which Reuben Fine, writing in *Practical Chess Openings* (1948) commented, "Euwe and some Soviet masters have recently revived." It was also revived by Anand unsuccessfully against Kasparov.

The variation repeatedly revisited during the match was to become known as the "Normal Position". 5...Ba5 or 5...Bc5 6.O-O d6 7.d4 exd4 8.cxd4 Bb6. This position was reached eighteen times with MacDonnell continuing with 9.h3 and LaBourdonnais favoring 9.d5, 9.Bb2 and 9.Nc3.

These games and the tactical themes they represented were featured in the French publication *LaPalamede* (the first magazine totally devoted to chess and edited by LaBourdonnais from 1836-1839 and by St. Amant from 1841-1847), as well as the British periodicals of George Walker and Howard Staunton.

One of the basic issues became whether white should castle before playing d4.

Morphy's view was expressed in his annotations to 6.O-O. "This was considered white's best play until after the death of both these illustrious chess. Later analysis was proved 6.P. to Q fourth followed by seven castles, etc. to be the strongest line of attack at this juncture."

However, Morphy's time of active play was brief, and it fell to Anderssen, Zukertort, and, later, Tchigorin to carry the torch of analytical exploration. An early d4 was thought premature since it allowed the Compromised Defense, which became the focus of extensive analysis.

In the Normal Position, Anderssen and Zukertort explored the fine points of 9.d5 while Tchigorin supported 9.Nc3 (endorsed by Morphy). In the late 1880s, Steinitz's ideas of holding on to the gambit pawn and defending the resulting cramped positions were forcefully advocated but won few converts. The rise of Lasker's Defense in the late 1890s finally took the sting out of the 6.O-O continuation. Morphy's use of 6.d4 was mentioned in articles in *British Chess Magazine* early in the twentieth century, and Tartakower proposed new approaches for white, but fashion had changed, and other openings were contending for the analyst's attention. The strategic ideas of the Ruy Lopez and Queen's Gambit were being established, there was an increased appreciation of closed openings, and the hypermodern school was on the horizon. The era of the ascendency of the Evans Gambit had passed.

The enormous efforts of nineteenth century analysts is apparent by the degree to which it was covered by contemporary texts.

Handbuch des Schachspiels 1843, twelve pages
Handbuch des Schachspiels 1852, fifteen pages
Wormald's *Chess Openings,*1875, fifty pages
Handbuch des Schachspiels, 1880, forty-one pages
Cordel's *Fuhreer durch die Schaetheorie*, 109 pages
Handbuch des Schachspiels, 1902, forty-one pages
Handbuch des Schachspiels, 1916, sixty-one pages

With the passage of time, the old analysis became forgotten. Modern compendiums thought it sufficient to cite a few pages of columns. This circumstance was illustrated by Bernard Zuckerman's (an acknowledged expert on chess openings) comment in the 1982 issue of

Chess Life regarding the Normal Position, that "no one mentions
14...Nge7 after 10...Bd7" This move was, in fact, mentioned in *MCO*
2nd edition, 1913.

Bobby Fischer's adoption of the Evans in informal play during
the 1960s sets him apart from most current players in the serious approach he took toward the gambit. His 1963 victory over Reuben Fine
in an obscure variation of the Compromised Defense and his subsequent reworking of a 1893 analysis by Freeborough and Ranken re-
flect an appreciation for chess ideas irrespective of the era in which
they initially surfaced. A remarkable exception to this modern neglect
was the 1976 and 1997 publication of *Play the Evans Gambit* by Cafferty and Harding, which pulled together analysis from numerous
nineteenth century sources. Harding's subsequent publications, Bot-
terill's serious treatment of the opening in *Open Gambits*, and the recent contributions of world champion Kasparov and GM Shirov mark
a minor renaissance for the Evans.

Evans Gambit Accepted 5...Be7
This variation was popularized by GM Anand in his game against
Garry Kasparov. Here is that game. 1.e4 e5 2.Nf3 Nc6 3.Bc4 Bc5 4.b4
Bxb4 5.c3 Be7 6.d4 Na5 7.Be2 (7.Be2 d6 8.Qa4+ c6 9.dxe5 dxe5
10.Nxe5 Nf6 11.O-O b5 12.Qc2 O-O 13.a4 Qc7 14.Nf3 a6 15.Bg5=)
exd4 8.Qxd4 Nf6 9.e5 Nc6 10.Qh4 Nd5 11.Qg3 g6 12.O-O Nb6.
(This strikes me as dubious; the obvious 12...O-O seems better.) 13.c4
d6 14.Rd1 Nd7 15.Bh6 Ncxe5 16.Nxe5 Nxe5 17.Nc3 f6 18.c5 Nf7
19.cxd6 cxd6 20.Qe3 Nxh6 21.Qxh6 Bf8 22.Qe3+ Kf7 23.Nd5 Be6
24.Nf4 Qe7 25.Re1 1-0.

Modern Chess Openings, Eighth Edition gives the more aggressive
response to 7.Be2, 7...d5 8.dxe5 dxe4 9.Qa4+ Nc6 10.Qxe4 Be6 11.O-
O Qd5 12.Qa4 O-O-O with about an equal position.

Although Walter Muir played several games with this system, I
feel that after 7...exd4, 8.O-O is inaccurate. A fairly standard idea in
this position is to play 8...d3.

Clearly neither the queen nor the bishop wants to occupy the d3 square. Black has the better pawn structure. Play might continue 9.Bxd3 d6 10.Qc2 Nf6=.

Another game with 5...Be7 was seen in Shirov-Timman, Biel, Biel (7), 1995. 7.Be2 cxd4 8.Qxd4 d6 9.Qxg7 Bf6 10.Qg3 Qe7 11.O-O Bd7 (Qxe4 12.Nd2 Qg6=) 12.Nd4 O-O-O. (Once again 12...Qxe4 is equal; white won this game but clearly black had to blunder for the win to occur.)

In Winants-Kremer, Amsterdam Donner Open, Amsterdam (7), 1996: 7.Be2 exd4 8.Qxd4 d5 9.exd5 Nf6 10.c4 c6 11.Nc3 O-O 12.O-O Re8 13.Bb2 Bf8 14.Rfd1 cxd5 15.cxd5 Bg4 16.Bb5 Bxf3? (Bd7=)+/- 17.gxf3 Re7 18.Ne4 Nh5 19.Kh1 a6 20.Be2 Re8 21.Rg1 f5 22.Ng3? (d6+-) Nc6 23.Qd2 Nxg3+ 24.Rxg3 Ne5 25.Rag1 Ng6? (Qd6+/-) 26.d6 Bxd6 27.Bc4+ 1-0.

To test the variation, I played a centaur game in this line. 5...Be7 6.d4 Na5 7.Be2 d6 8.Qa4+ c6 9.dxe5 dxe5 10.Nxe5 Nf6 11.O-O Qc7 12.f4 O-O 13.Nd2 Bd6 14.Nd3 b5 15.Qc2 Re8 16.e5 Bf5 17.Kh1 Rad8 18.Nf3 Bc5 19.Nd4 Bxd4 20.cxd4 Nd5 =/+ 21.Bd2 Nc4 22.Qc1 Ndb6 23.Bc3 Na4 24.Nc5 Nxc5 25.dxc5 Bd3 26.Re1 Bxe2 27.Rxe2 Rd3 28.a4 a5 29.Re1 Qd8 30.axb5 cxb5 31.f5 h6 32.c6 Qd5 -/+.

The above game cannot feature best play by white, so I started looking for improvements for white at an earlier stage of the game.

5...Be7 6.d4 Na5 7.Be2 d6 8.dxe5 (I reject as unsound, Qa4+) dxe5 9.Qxd8+ Bxd8 10.Nxe5 Nf6 11.f3 O-O 12.Kf2=. The thicket of variations will soon appear as the number of forced move sequences goes down.

I played another centaur game with the belief that the variation below favors white.

5...Be7 6.d4 d6 7.Qb3 Na5 8.Bxf7+ Kf8 9.Qa4 Kxf7 10.Qxa5. (Black's plan seems dubious; white has already regained his gambit pawn, and the black king is somewhat exposed.) exd4 11.cxd4 (white repairs his pawn structure) Nf6 12.Nc3 c6 13.Qa4 Rf8 14.Qb3+ d5 15.O-O Qb6 16.Qc2 dxe4 17.Nxe4 Kg8 18.Bg5 Kh8. (White has failed to exploit the awkward initial position of the black king position, so black just castles by hand.) 19.Ng3 Bd6 20.Bxf6 gxf6 21.Rfe1 Bg4 22.Qe4 Bxf3 23.Qxf3 Bxg3 24.hxg3 Qxe5=. (A heavy piece ending like this is tough to win; when I played this phase at blitz speed, white got a big advantage.)

Here is an attack straight out of the nineteenth century. Brady-Puttiera, Yerevan, Armenia Ol 32 (2) 1996. Obviously Fritz improves on white's attack, but that does not detract from this game. 5...Be7 6.d4 d6 7.Qb3 Na5 8.Bxf7+ Kf8 9.Qa4 Kxf7 10.Qxa5 b6 11.Qb5 Bd7 12.Qe2 exd4 13.cxd4 h6 14.O-O Nf6 15.e5 (Nc3+/-) Nd5 16.Re1 Qc8 17.Na3 Re8 18.Qe4 Be6 19.Nc4 (exd6 cxd6 20.Bxh6+/-) Kg8 (the losing move — just Nb4 is equal) 20.Bxh6 Nc3 21.Qg6 Bf8 22.Ng5 +- 1-0:46

Here is a another centaur game in this variation. 5...Be7 6.d4 d6 7.Qb3 Na5 8.Bxf7 Kf8 9.Qa4 Kxf7 10.Qxa5 b6 11.Qb5 Bf6 12.O-O Bd7 13.Qe2 Ne7 14.Nf6+ Bxf6 15.Bxf6 h6 16.Be3 Rf8 17.f4 exf4 18.Qc4+ Kg6 19.Bxf4 Qc8 20.Na3 Qb7 21.Qd3 Kh7=.

Stone-Ware Defense 5...Bd6

This anti-positional concept is surprisingly sound. Black will attempt to play Be7 at a later date; meanwhile it is clear that white should avoid dxe5 temporarily. Here are some book moves with the final few moves the suggestions of Fritz 15. What is somewhat surprising is that, in an age of romantic play, Bd6 was so popular in the early days of the Evans. 1.e4 e5 2.Nf3 Nc6 3.Bc4 Bc5 4.b4 Bxb4 5.c3 Bd6 6.d4 Nf6 7.O-O O-O 8.Nbd2 h6 9.Re1 Re8 10.Qb3 Qe7 11.Bd3 Na5 12.Qc2 b6 13.Bb2 Nc6 14.Nc4 Bb7 15.Rad1 Nh5 16.Bf1 Rad8 17.Nxd6 Qxd6 18.Qa4 exd4 19.cxd4 Qb4 20.Qc2 d5 21.a3 Qf8 22.e5 Nf4=.

Even though the position is equal, there is a lot of play in the position, so 5...Bd6 suggests it is playable for both sides.

The next several practical tests give some strategies both sides can attempt. The first game is LaBourdonnais-Macdonell, match, 1834. 5...Bd6 6.O-O h6 7.d4 Nf6 8.dxe5 Bxe5 9.Nxe5 Nxe5 10.Bb3 Qe7

11.f4 Qc5+ 12.Kh1 Neg4 (a tactical oversight based on a faulty assessment of the position) 13.Qe2 Qh5 14.h3 O-O 15.e5 Re8 16.Qf3 Qh4 17.exf6 d6 18.Na3 (fxg7+-) Re1 19.Bd2 Nf2+ 20.Kh2 Bxh3 21.Qxf2 Qxf2 22.Rxf2 Rxa1 23.gxh3 g6 24.Rg2 Kf8 25.f5 g5 26.h4 1-0. The next game is Kemeny-Pillsbury, Hastings, 1895. 5...Bd6 6.d4 Nf6 7.O-O O-O 8.Nbd2 Qe7? (Ne8=/+) 9.Bd3 Ne8 10.Nc4 f6 11.Ne3 g6 12.Nd5 Qd8 13.Be3 Be7 14.Nd2 d6 15.f4 Ng7 16.f5 g5 17.h4 gxh4 (h6) 18.Qg4 Kh8 19.Qxh4 Qd7 20.Kf2 Bd8 21.Rh1 Ne8 22.Rh3 Na5 23.Rah1 Rf7 24.Be2 Rg7 25.Bh5 Kg8 26.Bxe8 Qxe8 27.Qxh7+ Rxh7 28.Rxh7 Bxf5 29.exf5 Qf8 30.Rh8+ Kf7 31.R1h7+ Qg7 33.Bh6 1-0.

The next game sparked a theoretical debate. Markosian-Mukhaev, Moscow Open, Moscow (6) 1995. On the one hand, white essayed a very effective strategy in the opening, engaged in an interesting sacrifice that black declined, and then went on to win.

According to Harding and Cafferty's *Play the Evans Gambit* p.209, white could improve.

5...Bd6 6.d4 Nf6 7.O-O O-O 8.Re1 h6 9.Nbd2 Re8 10.Bd3 Bf8 11.Nxe5 Nxe5 12.dxe5 Rxe5 13.f4 Re8 14.e5 Nd5 15.Qf3 c6!16.Qe4 Nf6 17.Qf3 c6-/+. (If black tries 15...Nxc3, white has 16.Bc2 with a winning attack. This continuation takes away any compensation for the material.) Getting back to the above game, play continued 15.Qf3 c6 16.Qe4 Nf6 17.Qf3 d5 18.Rf1 Ng4? (Bc5+; =/+) 19.Nb3 c5 20.Bc2 d4 21.h3 dxc3? (Ne3=) 22.hxg4 c4 23.Qe4 f5 24.Qxc4+ Be6 25.Qe2 fxg4 26.Qe4 Qh4 27.Qh7+ Kf7 28.Bg6+ Ke7 29.Rd1 Red8 30.Ba3+ Rd6 31.Rxd6 1-0.

The tactical nature of the Evans is well-displayed in this miniature. Neumann-Mayet, Berlin, 1895. 5...Bd6 7.O-O f6 8.a4 b6 9.Na3 Bxa3? 10.Bxa3 d6 11.dxe5 dxe5 12.Bxg8! 1-0.

While a final verdict on the Stone-Ware Defense is still in the future, it remains certain that the opening is a matter of taste. As is customary, here is a centaur game with Fritz 15 in this variation. 5...Bd6 6.d4 Nf6 7.O-O O-O 8.Nbd2 Rb8 9.Rb1 b6 10.Re1 Bb7 11.Bd3 exd4. (Since white is better after this move, black must improve here.) 12.e5 dxc3 13.Nc4 Nxe5 14.Ncxe5 Bxe5 15.Rxe5 d5 16.Bg5 h6 17.Bh4 Qd6 18.Bg3 Qd8 19.Nd4 Ne4 20.Nf5 Qf6 (+/-)21.Ne7+ Kh8 22.Nxd5 Bxd5 23.Bxe4 Bxe4 24.Rxe4. (Black has compensation for the piece; unfortunately black's army is disjointed, and he can't hold his extra pawns. There is also the danger of a mate in some variations.) Rad8 25.Qb3 Rfe8 26.Rc4 c5 27.h3 c2 28.Qxc2 Qc6 29.Qb3 g5? 30.a4 Re6 31.a5 f5 32.f3+- f4 33.Be1 Qd5 34.Qa4 Kh7 35.axb6 axb6 36.Re4 Rxe4 37.fxe4 Qd4+ 38.Qxd4 cxd4 39.e5 1-0.

"Normal Position" Evans Gambit

There is so much theory and practical play in the normal position, so named because of its ubiquitous appearance in nineteenth-century chess, that I thought centaur games would be especially useful. The win by white can be readily known from general Evans Gambit principles. Black never got his queenside untracked. 4...Bxb4 5.c3 Ba5 6.d4 exd4 7.O-O Bb6 8.cxd4 d6 9.Nc3 Na5 10.Bg5 f6 11.Bf4 Ne7 12.Bd3 O-O 13.h3 f5 14.Re1 h6 15.Bh2 fxe4 16.Bxe4 Bf5 17.d5 Qd7 18.Rc1 Rae8 19.Qd3 Bxe4 20.Rxe4 Nf5 21.Rf4 a6 22.Rb1 Ne7 23.Ra4. (It is readily apparent that black's position on the queenside gives white more than adequate compensation for the pawn. 17.d5 was especially important.) Kh8 24.Bf4 Qf5 25.Qd2 Qh5 26.Kh2 Qg6. (Now we get to see a beautiful combination by Fritz playing both sides of the position.) 27.Bxh6! gxh6 28.Rg4 Qf7 29.Qxh6+ Qh7 30.Qc1 Ng6 31.Ne4 Ne5 32.Nxe5 dxe5 33.Rb4 +7.10

I decided to see if white stood better in other variations of the Normal Position, so this is another centaur game. 9.Bb2 Nf6 10.Nbd2 O-O 11.e5 Nh5 12.g3 d5 13.Bb5 Bd7 14.Nb3 g6 15.Re1 a6 16.Bf1 Ng7 17.Bg2 Ne6 18.a4 a5 19.Qd2 Qe7 20.Reb1 Rfb8 21.Bc3 Rd8 22.h3 Ng7 23.Qh6 Nf5 24.Qd2 Ng7 25.Qh6 Nf5 1/2-1/2.

Here is another crushing win by white in the Normal Position. 9...Nce7 (9...Na5 =) 10.e5 Ng6 11.e6 fxe6 12.dxe6 N8e7 13.Nc3 O-O 14.Nd5 Nxd5 15.Qxd5 Ne7 16.Qd3 Qe8 17.Bg5 d5 18.Bb3 c6 19.Bc2 Nf5 20.e7 Rf7 21.Ne5 Rxe7 22.Bxe7. (White regains his sacrificed material; now comes the attack.) Qxe7 23.Rae1 Qg5 24.Nf3 Qd8 25.h4 g6 26.h5 Qf8 27.hxg6 hxg6 28.Re2 Bd7 29.R1e1 Qg7 30.g4 Ba5 31.Rb1 Nd6 32.Ne5 Re8 33.Nxd7 Rxe2 34.Qxe2 Qxd7 35.Bxg6 Bc3 36.Kg2 Bd4 37.Rh1 Bg7 38.g5 Nf7 39.f4 b6 40.Qh5 Qe7 41.Bxf7+ Qxf7 42.Qxf7+ Kxf7 43.Kf3 +7.32.

Here is another centaur game in a main variation.

4...Bxb4 5.c3 Ba5 6.d4 d6 7.O-O Bb6 8.dxe5 dxe5 9.Qb3 Qf6 10.Bb5 h6 11.Bxc6+ bxc6 12.c4 Qd6 13.Rd1 Qe7 14.Ba3 Bc5 15.Bb2 Nf6 16.Nxe5 O-O 17.Nd2 Ng4 18.Nd3=. In this game, black avoids the Compromised Defense. 5...Ba5 6.d4 exd4 7.O-O d6 8.Qb3 Qf6 9.e5 dxe5 10.Re1 Nh6 11.Bxh6 gxh6 12.Bxf7 Qxf7 13.Nxe5 Qxb3 14.axb3 Bxc3 15.Nxc3 dxc3 16.Nxc6+ Kf7 17.Ne5 Kf6 18.Rac1 Re8 19.f4 Re7 20.Rxc3 Be6 21.R3e3 Rg7 22.b4 h5 23.Nf3 Bd5 24.Nh4 Rd7 25.Re5 Bf7=.

This is a key centaur test of an alternative move order. This appears to be the most important improvement on move order. By castling before playing d4, black has d6, allowing the Normal Position. 5...Ba5 6.O-O d6 7.d4 exd4 8.cxd4 (Bb6 is a Normal Position) Nge7 9.Ng5 d5 10.exd5 Nxd5 11.Nxf7 Kxf7 12.Qf3+ Qf6 13.Bxd5+ +-.

This centaur game is a key test of the Compromised Defense. In the previous century, it was considered to be highly important, but other lines won out. In the first centaur, we will explore the key moves that are difficult to find with unlimited time and impossible to find over-the-board.

5...Ba5 6.d4 exd4 7.Qb3 Qf6 8.O-O dxc3 9.e5 Qg6 10.Nxc3 Nge7 11.Ba3 Bxc3 12.Qxc3 O-O 13.Rad1 Re8 14.Rfe1. (The entire white army is ready and primed to attack.) Nd8. (An act of desperation; already black announced he is not happy with black's position.) 15.Nd4 Ne6 16.Nxe6 +/- fxe6 17.Bd3 Qg5 18.Qxc7 Nc6 19.Qd6 g6 20.Rc1 a5 21.g3 Qd8 22.h4 Ne7 23.Be4 Nf5 24.Qd2 Kg7 25.Rc3 Ra6 26.Rb1 Kg8 27.R1c1 Rc6 28.Bxc6 +- bxc6 29.Bc5 Qc7 30.Qg5 Ba6 31.g4 Ng7 32.Rf3 Be2 33.Re3 Bxg4 34.Qxg4 Qb8 35.Rd3 Qxe5 36.Rxd7 Qf5 37.Qxf5 Nxf5 38.Bb6 Nxh4 39.Rd8 Kf7 40.Rxe8 Kxe8 41.Rxc6 a4 42.Rxe6+ 1-0.

This is the second test of the Compromised Defense.
7.Qb3 Qf6 8.O-O dxc3 9.e5 Qg6 10.Nxc3 b5!! (This sacrifice is
much better than 10.Nge7.) 11.Nxb5 Rb8 12.Qa3 Nge7 13.Bd3 Qg4
14.Rb1 O-O 15.h3 Qh5 16.Nxa7 Bb4 17.Qa4 Ra8 18.Rxb4 Rxa7
19.Qxa7 Nxa7 20.Rh4 Qxh4 21.Nxh4 Nac6 22.Nf3 Re8 23.Bd2 Ng6
24.Bc3 Kf8 25.Re1 Nf4 26.Bc4 Bb7 27.Rd1+/=.

Evans Gambit 5...Bc5 Variation

Here is a centaur game in the 5...Bc5 variation. 4...Bxb4 5.c3 Bc5 6.d4
exd4 7.cxd4.
Bb4+ 8.Nd2 Bc3? 9.Bxf7+ Kf8 10.Ba3+ d6 11.Bb3 Bxa1 12.Qxa1.
(White has a powerful position with an edge of +/-, which is reason
enough not to play Bc3.) Na5 13.Bc2 Nf6 14.O-O g6 15.Qc3 b6
16.Nb3 Kg7 17.Nxa5 bxa5 18.Qxa5. (White has a big lead in development. If I was not playing against a 3200 computer, the win should
be routine.) d5 19.e5. (Now I have a protected passed pawn and a bind
on the c5 square so that black cannot isolate my passed pawn.) Ne4
20.Bxe4 fxe4 21.Ng5!. (Fritz finds the refutation of Qxg5.) c6 22.Qc5
h6 23.Nxe4 Qd5 24.Qe7+ Qf7 25.Qh4 g5 26.Qg3 +- Qg6 27.Qe3
Bf5 28.f3 Rhd8 29.Bd6 a5 30.Ng3 Kh7 31.f4 g4 32.Re1 Rac8 33.Qb3
Rg8 34.e6 Rce8 35.Qb7+ Rg7 36.e7 Bc8 37.Qc7 a4 38.Bc5 Rf7
39.Ne4 g3 40.Nxg3 Bf5 41.Qd8 Qg8 42.Qd6 Qg6 43.Nxf5 Qxf5
44.g3 Rf6 45.Qe5 Kg6 46.Kg2 Qc2+ 47.Re2 Qd3 48.h3 Qc4 49.g4
Qd5+ 50.Qxd5 cxd5 51.f5+ Kh7 52.Kf3 Rf7 53.Kf4 1-0.

Here is the second centaur game in the 5...Bc5 variation. 5...Bc5
6.O-O d6 7.d4 Bb6 8.dxe5 dxe5 9.Qb3 Qf6 10.Bg5 Qg6 11.a4 Nh6
12.Bxh6 gxh6 13.a5 Bxa5 14.Bb5 Bb6 15.Nxe5 Qf6 16.Qd5 O-O
17.Nxc6 bxc6 18.Qxc6 Qg5 19.Kh1. (White has two pawn islands
while black has five pawn islands. White has unlimited time to play
against all those weak pawns. In this kind of position, the knight is
the better minor piece.) 5...Bc5 6.d4 Bb6 7.O-O d6 8.Qb3 Qd7
9.Nbd2 Na5 10.Qc2 exd4 11.cxd4 Ne7 12.Re1 O-O 13.a4. (With
compensation, white does better in this move order.) 5...Bc5 6.d4 Bb6

7.Nxe5 Nxe5 8.dxe5 Ne7 9.Ba3 O-O 10.O-O Nc6. (According to Fritz, the exchange sac is the best of several bad choices. Black is too close to the position to realize that the power of the extra rook is beyond the computer's horizon.) 11.Bxf8 Qxf8 12.Kh1 Nxe5 13.Be2 Qc5 14.f4 Nc4 15.Bxc4 Qxc4 16.Nd2 Qc6 17.a4 Qxc3 18.Rc1 Qd4 19.Nc4 Qxd1 20.Rfxd1 Bc5 21.Ne5 Bd6 22.Nd3 c6 23.e5 Be7 24.Nc5 Bxc5 25.Rxc5 Kf8 26.Kg1 Ke7 27.f5! Ke8 28.g4 h6 29.Rc3 b6 30.f6 gxf6 31.exf6 d5 32.Rxc6 Bxg4 33.Rxd5 Bf3 34.Re5+ Kd7 35.Rc1 Rg8+ 36.Kf2 Kd6 37.Re7 Bd5 38.Rg1 Rxg1 39.Kxg1 a5 40.Kf2 Bb3 41.Ke3 Bc4 42.Kd4 Bb3 43.Kc3 Bd5 44.h4 h5 45.Kd4 Bb3 46.Ke4 Kc6 47.Ra7 Kc5 48.Kf5 b5 49.Rxa5 Bxa4 50.Kg5 1-0.

Here is an interesting try for equality by black. 1.e4 e5 2.Nf3 Nc6 3.Bc4 Bc5 4.b4 Bxb4 5.c3 Ba5 6.d4 exd4 7.O-O Nge7 8.cxd4 d5 9.exd5 Nxd5 10.Ba3 Be6 11.Nbd2 Bxd2 12.Qxd2 Qf6 13.Bb5 Ne7 14.Bxc6 Nxc6 = to +/=. This move order suggests that white should play Qb3 before castling.

The tactical nature of the Evans Gambit makes it ideal for computer analysis. While improvements will be found for black, I believe the Evans is +/- in many variations except 5...Be7, which is =. In other variations where white does not have a plus, he can achieve variations with compensation for the gambit pawn.

Wilkes-Barre Traxler, Two Knights Defense

The WBT has a rich history that is available from many sources, but I will spare the reader the need to buy entire books on the opening. This one line will allow the reader to play 4.Ng5 without being blown away by the tactics. 1.e4 e5 2.Nf3 Nc6 3.Bc4 Nf6 4.Ng5 Bc5 5.Bxf7+ Ke7 (Kf8 6.O-O) 6.Bc4!. (There are reams of analysis online dedicated to 6.Bb3, but from my experience with Fritz 15, the white advantage drops to +/= fairly quickly where the better player will win.) d6 7.Nc3 Na5. (Time has less meaning in the WBT than most wild openings; black is too concerned that Nf7 is a threat. The immediate 8.Nf7 is not a threat if white hasn't castled. For example 8.Nf7 leads to about an equal position.) 8.Be2 h6 9.Nf3 Re8. (This blew me away. What is Fritz thinking? The obvious move is Rf8 with no hope of an attack. Fritz realizes the attack on the file is ephemeral and believes that white must play c3/d4, undermining support of the e-pawn, hence Re8.) 10.d3 a6 11.O-O. (In the Bb3 line, white castles queenside, but then black plays ideas like g5/Nh5 with the threat of Nf4; white is forced to play the awkward Qf1.) Kf7 12.Nd5 Kg8 13.Nxf6+ Qxf6 14.c3 Nc6 15.Be3 Ba7. (Black has to hope that the doubled pawns that white gets after Bxe3 16.fxe3 slow the queenside pawn mass.) 16.Bxa7 Rxa7 17.Nd2 Be6 18.Nc4 Rf8 19.Ne3 Raa8 20.Bg4 Bf7 21.g3 Qe7 22.Qe2 (white builds for f4) Rae8 23.a3 g6 24.Nd5 Bxd5 25.exd5 Nd8 26.Qd2 Kg7 27.Rae1 h5 28.Bh3 Qf6 29.Re4 Nf7 30.Bg2 Nh6 31.Rfe1 Re7 32.Bh3 Nf5 33.d4 Rfe8 34.Kg2 Kf7 35.dxe5 Rxe5 36.Qd3 (forcing simplification) Kg7 37.a4 R8e7 38.a5 Re8 39.Rxe5 dxe5 40.Bxf5. (White will create threats on both wings and pick up decisive material.) gxf5 41.c4 Re7 42.Qf3 Kg6 43.Qb3 f4 44.Qxb7 f3+ 45.Kg1 e4 46.Qc6 (forcing the exchange of queens with a winning rook and pawn ending) Kg7 47.Qxf6+ Kxf6 48.b4 Re8 49.b5 Ke5 50.Kf1 Kd4 51.bxa6 Kc5 52.h4. (Now h5 is a static weakness.) Kxc4 53.Rd1 Ra8 54.d6 cxd6 55.Rd6 Ra7 56.Ke1 Kc3. (Almost human; there are mate threats by black.) 57.Rh6 Ra8 58.Rxh5. (The connected passers are decisive.) Rxa6 59.Rd5 Kc4 60.Rf5 Kd3 61.h5 Ra8 62.Rd5+ Kc4 63.Rg5 Ra6 64.g4 Kd4 65.Rf5 Rh6 66.Kd2 1-0.

Universal System, a.k.a. Universal Attack

In the 1994 Golden Knights, I played the same first five moves against my thirty opponents: g6/Bg7/e6/Ne7/O-O. The goal of the Universal System is to get into a playable middle game. The US differs from the Rat, Modern and Hippo because black always tries to get in an early d5, not d6. The one move order that black cannot play is 1.e4 g6 2.Nf3 Bg7 3.d4 e6 because of the response 4.Nc3! Ne7, and Fritz 15 earned its 3200 rating by playing a continuation no human oppo- nent has played, h4!, and white has a comfortable plus. If black faces the move order e4/Nf3/d4, he must avoid the US and transpose to a

Pirc with g6/Bg7/d6/Nf6. Although black seems to weaken his dark squares, Fritz was never able to exploit them. If white hasn't played c4 by move three, black should play d6/Nf6. The only exception is if white plays g3/Bg2.

I decided to play centaur games against Fritz 15 to see if white could find a refutation of the US. Here are those games. Here is what happened when I played Fritz 15 without help from the computer.

1.c4 g6 2.d4 Bg7 3.e4 e6 4.Nc3 Ne7 5.Nf3 d5. (The hallmark of the US player; d5 is always played, except for those variations where white fails to play c4 on the first three moves of the game.) 6.Be2. (This is book for the computer.) O-O 7.cxd5 exd5 8.e5 f6! 9.exf6 Bxf6. (Black gets an open file at no cost.) 10.O-O c6? (Nf5=) 11.Bf4 b6 12.Re1 Na6 13.Rc1 Nc7 14.Ne5 Ne6 15.Bh6 Bg7 16.Bxg7 Kxg7 17.Bg4 Qd6 18.Bxe6 Bxe6 19.Ne2 Rac8 20.Qd2 c5?! 21.Nc3 Nf5 22.Nb5 (+/-) Qe7 23.Nd3 Rf6 24.dxc5 bxc5 25.Qa5 g5 26.Re5 c4 27.Nb4 Qc5 28.Na6 Qb6 29.Qxb6 axb6 30.Nac7 Bf7 31.Nxd5 Bxd5 32.Rxd5 Kg6 33.Re1 h6 34.Rd7 +-.

There is no point playing out this endgame, as Fritz has it as +-.

The remaining games are centaur games.

1.f4 d5!. (I played about a dozen US games against Fritz 15, but once it got pawns on f4/e5/d4, it gradually increased its advantage from +.35 to +.5 to +.7 to +/- to +- with an eventual breakthrough on the king side, so black should play 1...d5 to prevent e4.) 2.Nf3 g6 3.g3 Bg7 4.Bg2 e6 5.d4 Ne7. (This is the correct move order to reach the US.) 6.O-O O-O 7.Be3. (Players seeing this would immediately recognize this as a computer move.) Nd7 8.Bf2 c5 9.Nc3 cxd4 10.Nxd4 e5 11.fxe5 Nxe5 12.Qe1 Ng4 13.Rd1 Nxf2 14.Qxf2 Qb6 15.Rd3 Be6 16.Nxe6 Qxf2+ 17.Rxf2 fxe6 18.e4 Rxf2 19.Kxf2 Rc8 20.Bh3 Rc6 21.exd5 exd5 22.Ke2=.

I predicted the King's Indian Attack would pose no problems for black. 1.Nf3 g6 2.g3 Bg7 3.Bg2 e6 4.d4 Ne7 5.e4 d5 6.Nc3 b6 7.O-O O-O 8.Re1 Nbc6 9.e5 h6 10.b3 Bb7 11.Rb1 a5 12.a4 Na7 13.h4 c5 14.h5 g5 15.dxc5 bxc5 16.Nxg5?. (It's amazing that a 3200

285

computer could get lost in the tactics, but that is the case here.) hxg5 17.Bxg5 Nac6 18.f4 f6 19.exf6 Bxf6 20.Rxe6 Bxc3 21.Qg4 Bg7 22.Bxe7 Nxe7 23.R1e1 Bc8 24.h6 Rf7 25.hxg7 Rxg7 26.Qh5 Bxe6 27.Rxe6 Rh7 28.Qg5+ Rg7 1/2-1/2 (see the July 2019 column "Back to Basics" by Grandmaster Alburt.)

This game was played without computer assistance. Note the complete absence of tactical shots. 1.c4 g6 2.g3 Bg7 3.Bg2 e6 4.Nc3 Ne7 5.e4 c6 6.d4 d5 7.exd5 cxd5 8.cxd5 Nxd5 9.Nxd5 exd5 10.Ne2 Nc6 11.O-O O-O 12.Be3 Bg4 13.Qd2 (book) Bxe2 14.Qxe2 Nxd4 15.Bxd4 Bxd4 16.Rad1 Qb6 17.b3 Rad8 18.Rd3 Rfe8 19.Qc2 Re7 20.R1d1 Bf6 21.Bxd5 Kg7=. (Material is equal, neither side has pawn weaknesses or a lead in development, and the Bishops of Opposite Color is an easy ending to hold.)

Here is another game with easy equality for black. White cannot afford to play quietly with 3.g3.

1.c4 g6 2.Nc3 Bg7 3.g3 e6 4.Bg2 Ne7 5.e4 d5 (c5) 6.cxd5 exd5 7.exd5 O-O 8.Nge2 Re8 9.O-O c6 10.dxc6 Nbxc6. (White has an extra weak pawn.) 11.d3 Nf5 12.Nf4 Bd7 13.Re1 Rxe1+ 14.Rxe1 Ncd4 15.Qd1 Bc6 16.Bd2 Qb6 17.Bxc6 bxc6 18.Rb1 h6 19.Kg2 Qb7 20.Ne4 c5 21.f3 Qa6 22.a3 Rc8 23.Kh1 g5 24.Nh5 Bh8 25.Rc1 Qxd3 26.Nhf6+ Bxf6 27.Nxf6+ Kg7 28.Ne4 Qxf3+ 29.Nxf3 Nxf3=.

Black stood well in the opening and the middle game and was eventually dead equal.

1.d4 g6 2.c4 Bg7 3.e4 e6 4.Nc3 Ne7 5.Nf3 d5. (Black's first five moves are diagnostic of the Universal System.) 6.Be2 Nbc6 7.e5 O-O 8.O-O dxc4 9.Bxc4 h6 10.Be3 Nf5 11.Rc1 Rb8! 12.Bb5 Bd7 13.Bd3 Nce7 14.Ne4 Bc6 15.Re1 Bxe4 16.Bxe4 Qd7 17.Qe2 c6 18.Red1 Nxe3 19.fxe3 Nd5 20.a3 Rfd8 21.Nd2 h5 22.Nc4 Bh6 23.b4 b5 24.Bxd5 cxd5 25.Nd6 a6=.

White went into a queen-less middle game with an exposed king. Black was able to use a couple of tactical shots two moves deep to secure equality.

1.c4 g6 2.d4 Bg7 3.g3 e6 4.Nc3 d5 5.Nf3 dxc4 6.e4 c5 7.dxc5 Qxd1+ 8.Kxd1 Nf6 9.Bxc4 Nbd7 10.c6 bxc6 11.Kc2 Bb7 12.Bf4 Ng4

13.Rhf1 c5 14.Rad1 h6 15.Bb5 O- O-O 16.Rxd7 Rxd7 17.Bxd7+ Kxd7 18.h3 Nf6 19.Rd1+ Ke8 20.Be5 Rg8 21.Kd3 Bc6 22.Rb1 a5 23.Rd1 h5 24.Bd6 Nd7 25.Nd2 a4 26.Nc4 Bxc3 27.Kxc3 Bxe4=.

The tactics in this game are so simple, I didn't have to use the computer to equalize.

1.e4 g6 2.c4 Bg7 3.d4 e6 4.Nc3 Ne7 5.Nge2 d5 6.Bg5 c6!. (Fritz released the pawn tension with dxc4.) 7.cxd5 cxd5 8.exd5 exd5 9.g3 Nbc6 10.Bg2 Be6 11.O-O O-O 12.Re1 Qd7 13.Nf4 Rfe8 14.Qd2 Nxd4 15.Bxe7 Rxe7 16.Ncxd5 Bxd5 17.Rxe7 Qxe7 18.Nxd5 Qd7 19.Qa5 Nc6 20.Qb5 Rd8 21.Rd1 Nd4 22.Qxd7 Rxd7 23.f4 f5 =.

This is one of the sharpest move orders I've seen in the US, but most of the tactics are only two to three moves deep.

1.c4 g6 2.d4 Bg7 3.c4 e6 4.Nc3 Ne7 5.Nf3 d5 6.Be2 O-O 7.cxd5 exd5 8.e5 Nbc6 9.O-O f6 10.Re1 fxe5 11.dxe5 a6 12.h3 h6 13.Be3 Be6 14.Qc2 Qd7 15.Rad1 Kh7 16.h4 Bg4 17.Bc5 b6 18.Ba3 Rad8 19.Nxd5 Nxd5 20.Bxf8 Rxf8 21.Qe4 Nce7 22.Ng5+ hxg5 23.Bxg4 Qb5 24.hxg5 Rf4 25.Qe2 Qxe2 26.Bxe2 Bxe5 27.g3 Rf5 28.f4 Bxb2 29.Bf3 Bc3 30.Re6 Bb4 31.Be4 Bc5+ 32.Kh2 Nc3 33.Rd7 Nxe4 34.Rxe4 Rf7 35.Rxc7 Kg7 36.Kg2 Nf5 37.Rxf7+ Kxf7 38.Re5=.

White played the highly committal 12.h6. It may have been better to exchange on g6, but there is no immediate way to attack the black king. The series of exchanges that took place between moves 14 to 28 left a sterile position with no winning prospects.

1.c4 g6 2.d4 Bg7 3.e4 e6 4.Nc3 Ne7 5.Nf3 d5 6.Be2 Nbc6 7.e5 dxc4 8.Qa4 O-O 9.Qxa4 b6 10.h4 a5 11.h5 Nb4 12.h6 Bh8 13.O-O Ba6 14.Qb3 Bxe2 15.Nxe2 Qd5 16.Qa4 c5 17.Bg5 Qc6 18.Nc3 Nd5 19.Qxc6 Nxc6 20.Nxd5 exd5 21.dxc5 bxc5 22.Rac1 Nxe5 23.Nxe5 Bxe5 24.Rxc5 a4 25.Rxd5 Bb2 26.Rd7 f5 27.R1d1 Rf7 28.Rxf7 Kxf7 29.Rd7+ Kg8 30.g3 Rc8 31.Ra7 a3 32.Kf1 Rc2 33.Be3 Rc8 34.Ke2 Rc2+ 35.Kf3 Rc3 36.Rg7+ Kh8 37.Rd7 Kg8 38.Ke2 Rc2+ 39.Kd1 Rc4 40.Ra7 Rc8=.

King's Indian Defense

According to my theory of Universal Positions, the King's Indian Defense should favor White. In all the games listed below, I achieved a vast amount of space that permitted me to maneuver behind my pawn wall. This patient maneuvering will be usable against computers which will try to use a piece attack against the pawn wall. In one game I made only one piece move in the first ten moves of the game!

Moody (1600) Fritz 15 (3170) Games were played at 40/1 and 40/2. **1.d4 Nf6 2.c4 g6 3.Nc3 Bg7 4.e4 d6 (Black discourages an early e5) 5.f3 O-O 6.Bg5** (This is more active than Be3) **c5 7.d5 (** If White allows cxd4 we have a Marcozy Bind) **a6 8.Qd2 Qa5 9.Be2 Re8** (Now Black can play Nfd7/f5)**10.Bd1** (White decides to try to get in Nge2; Nfd7; This is a sucker move) **b5 11.Be2 bxc4? 12.Bxc4** (Fritz is completely wrong here. Now that White can play Nge2/O-O, I prefer White) **Nfd7** (Thematic, but doubtful; Black never gets in f5) 13.**Bb3** White temporarily shields the b-file) **Ne5** (Leaping into the center)**14.Nge2** (I disagree with Fritz, I prefer White) **Nbd7 15.O-O Rb8** (Putting pressure on b2)**16.Rab1** (White knows that Black's only hope is to pressure the Queenside) **Nb6 17.Qd1 Bd7 18.Kh1 Bb5** (Doubtful; this Bishop is a target) **19.Bc1 Ned7 20.Nxb5 axb5 21.a3 Nc4 22.f4! Qa6 23.Rf3!** (We begin to see an attack; Fritz routinely fails

To see pieces in the King's field) **Rb7 24.Qf1 Ra8 25.Nc3 Ncb6 26.Qe1! Rbb8** (Plan less) **27.h4** (White begins his attack) **Nc4? 28.Bxc4!** (White now has a protected passed pawn) **bxc4 29.h5! Rb3 30.hxg6** (White softens up the Black King position) **fxg6 31.Qh4 Qb7 32.Ra1 Bd4 33.f5 gxf5 34.Rg3+!** (Storm clouds are gathering around the Black King. The computer has no feel for the attack and doesn't fully appreciate what is meant by having pieces in the "King's Field") **Kh8 35.Bh6 Bf6 36.Qh5 f4** (Desperation; Fritz just gave up a pawn essentially for nothing) **37.Bxf4 Qc8** (Better late than never; Black realizes his Queen is needed on the Kingside to blunt White's attack) **38.Rf1** (Fritz missed this move) **Qe8 39.Qh6 Qf7**

40.Qh3! (For most Grandmasters this is a trial and error position; this is +/-) **Rb7 41.e5** (Black seems to think that the attack magically appears with 40.Qh3) **dxe5 42.Bg5 Rf8 43.d6 Qe8 44.Ne4** (The Knight joins the party) **c3 45.Bh6 Rg8 46.Rxg8+ Qxg8 47.bxc3 Qg6** (A residual benefit of the attack+2.33) **48.Nxf6 exf6 49.Rf3 Qe8 50.Kh2 e4 51.Rg3 Ne5 52.Qf5 Rf7 53.a4 Qd7 54.Qxe4 Qb7 55.Qe2 Qc6 56.Qb5 Qxb5 57.axb5** (The passed pawns are deadly;+3.02 The rest of the game was played without comment simply because the computer is in a dead lost position refused to resign) **Rd7 58.b6 Rb7 59.Kh3 c4 60.Be3 h6 61.Bd4 Kh7 62.Kh4 Rd7 63.Re3 Nc6 64.Bc5 Ne5 65.Re1 Kg6 66.Ra1 Rd8 67.b7 (+6.80)**

This is the second King's Indian Defense win with White against Fritz 15. My play against Fritz is based on the fact that Fritz has vastly superior ability compared to me in winning a won game. Whenever I reached an advantage of +/- I would combine forces with the Fritz engine to rely on its superior ability to convert a winning position into a won game.

1.d4 Nf6 2.c4 g6 3.f3 Bg7 4.e4 d6 5.Ne2 O-O 6.Nbc3 e5 7.d5 a5 8.Be3 Nfd7 9.h4 Nb6 (The Black Knights have horrible squares and will need much time to place them on better squares) **10.Nc1** (The best way to defend c4; it is a developing move) **Na6 11.g4 Bf6 12.g5 Be7 13.b3 Bd7 14.Qd2 f5 15.a4 f4 16.Bf2 Be8 17.N3a2 Nb8** (Black belatedly realizes his Knights had horrible squares) **18.Nd3 N6d7 19.O-O-O** (I thought that the opposite wing attack favored White; Fritz has this as +.56) **c6 20.Bh3 Na6 21.Nc3 Qc7 22.Bg4 Kh8 23.Kb2 Rd8 24.Ne2 Ndc5 25.Nxc5 Nxc5 26.h5!** **Bxg5 27.hxg6 Bxg6 28.Bxc5!** (Fritz didn't see the attack) **dxc5 29.d6 Qb8 30.d7** (White has a winning attack) **b6 31.Kc2 Be7 32.Nc1 Kg7 33.Qg2 Kf7 34.Nd3 Rg8 35.Qh3** (Black now must deal with every new attack as they occur; Fritz evaluates this position as +-) **Rg7 36.Be6+ Kf8 37.Bf5 Kf7 38.Qg4 Bf6 39.Rh6 Qc7 40.Nf2 Ke7 41.Bxg6 Rxd7 42.Rxd7 Qxd7 43.Qxd7 Kxd7 44.Bf5c Kc7 45.Rxf6**

Rg2 46.Rf7+ Kb8 47.Bg4 Rxf2+ 48.Kc3 h6 49.Re7 Re2 50.Rxe5 Kc7 51.Re7+

Here is the third win: **1.d4 Nf6 2.c4 g6 3.f3 Bg7 4.e4 d6 5.Nc3 O-O 6.Bd3 e5 7.d5 Nh5 8.Nge2 Qh4+ 9.g3 Qe7** (In another game Fritz tried Qh3, but after **10.Kf2** White has a clear advantage)**10.h4 Qf6 11.Rf1 Qd8 12.Bg5 Bf6 13.Be3 Na6 14.Qd2 Nb4 15.Bb1 c6 16.Rh1** (To avoid any tactical shots on the Kingside) **Be7 17.a3 Na6 18.Bc2 Nf6** (Now it is clear that the Black excursion on the Kingside fails dismally.) **19.Kf2** (It is too dangerous to castle Queenside.) **h5 20.Kg2** (White evaluates this as +.7) **Bd7 21.b4 Nc7 22.Nc1** (White begins to gain time by maneuvering in a Universal Position) **b5 23.dxc6 Bxc6 24.Nb3 Rc8 25.Na5 Ba8 26.Rad1 bxc4 27.Nxc4 d5 28.Nxe5 Bd6 29.Nc4** (Starting a flurry of tactics) **dxc4 30.Qxd6 Ncd5 31.Qxd8 Nxe3ch 32.Kf2 Nfg4ch 33.fxg4 Nxg4ch 34.Ke2 Rcxd8 35.Rxd8 Rxd8 36.Rd1 Rxd1 37.Bxd1** (Fritz has this as close to winning with White) **Kg7 38.Kd2 Kf6 39.Be2 Ke5 40.Bxc4 Nh6 41.Kd3 Bb7 42.a4 f5 43.Bd5 fxe4 44.Bxe4 Bxe4 45.Nxe4 Nf5 46.a5 Kd5 47.Nc3+ Kc6 48.b5+ Kc5 49.b6 axb6 50.a6 +-**

In this game number, Fritz plays a dubious incursion into White's camp only to be driven back with tempo. The tactical shot on move 45 is worth the price of admission.

1.d4 Nf6 2.c4 g6 3.f3 Bg7 4.e4 d6 5.Bd3 O-O 6.Nc3 e5 7.d5 Nh5 8.Ne2 Qh4+ 9.g3 Qh3 10.Kf2 (There is no Queen invasion) **a5 11.a3 Na6 12.Bc2** (In anticipation of Nc5) **Nf6 13.Bg5 Nc5 14.Qf1 Qd7 (Qxf1 is +/= to +/-) 15.b4** (Using his superior wing to wing mobility, White now launches a powerful Queenside attack) **Na6 16.Qc1 Qh3 17.Rb1 Kh8 18.Qd2 axb4 19.axb4 Ng8 20.Ng1 Qd7 21.Kg2** (+.68) **Nf6 22.h4 Nb8 23.Nge2** (+/-) **Kg8 24.c5!** (The winning breakthrough) **Qe7 25.Na4 Bd7 26.Nec3 Rc8 27.h5! h6 28.Bxh6 Nxh5 29.Bg5 Bf6 30.Be3 Bg7 31.cxd6 Qxd6 32.Nc5 b6 33.Nxd7 Qxd7 34.Bb3 b5 35.Qe2 c6 36.Bc5 Qd8 37.Qe3 Nd7 38.dxc6 Nxc5 39.bxc5 b4 40.Nd5 Rxc6 41.Rbd1**

Qe8 42.Nxb4 Rf6 43.Nd5 Rc6 44.Qg5 Nf6 45.Qxg6! (This shot ends the game; +3.49)

In this King's Indian Defense White carves out a vast amount of interior space and just pushes Fritz off the board. As is customary, once I achieved an advantage of +/-, I had Fritz play both sides of the position. The tactics by Fritz with White are especially pleasing. This game illustrates that uncontested space can be punished. Look at the number of moves Black made with his Knights including the "win" of the King Bishop on its original square. You will observe that once the tactics are over, the position is +-.

1.d4 Nf6 2.c4 g6 3.f3 c5 4.d5 d6 5.e4 Bg7 6.h4 Nbd7 7.g4 Ne5 8.Nh3 h5 9.g5 Nfd7 10.f4 (You will note that in the past ten moves by White, only one was a piece move!) **Ng4** (If things don't go well for Black, the advanced piece will be a liability **11.Qc2 Bd4 12.Nc3 Ne3 13.Qd3 Nxf1 14.Kxf1** (Black suffers from a lack of interior space so White just "churns" his pieces to gain time) **O-O 15.Kg2 Nb6 16.a4 Nd7 17.Bd2 Nb8 18.Rhf1 Bg7 19.f5 Nd7 20.Qc2** (Look at the board now. White will soon have a won game because he has no weaknesses and Black will soon run out of any useful moves; look how easily White improves his position while Black spins his wheels) **Ne5 21.Nd1 a6 22.Nf4 +/= Rb8 23.Bc3 b5 24.cxb5 axb5 25.Ne3 bxa4 26.Rxa4 Qc7 27.Ra2 Qb7 28.R1a1 Qb5 29.Ra7 Rb7 30.R7a2 Rb8 31.Ra4 Re8 32.Ra7 Rb7 33.Qa4+/- Qxa4 34.R1xa4 Rb3 35.Rc7 Rb7 36.Rxb7 Bxb7 37.Ra7 Bc8 38.Kf2 Kh7 39.Bxe5 Bxe5 40. Fxg6ch Fxg6 41. Ne6 +-**

King's Indian Six pawn attack

Black tried to get counterplay with 11...h5 but after 12.g5 Nh7, the Knight is out of action so Black is playing a piece down. White tried to contest the center with 19.e6, but this is too little too late. Then Black tried the desperate 15...f5 which allows 16.f4 Ng4 17.Nxg4 hxg4 18.Qc2 Bxc3 19.Qxc3. White's advantage is +/- and the win is a matter of technique. In this game Black plays a dubious incursion into White's position only to be driven back with tempo. White steadily makes progress over the entire board demonstrating great wing to wing mobility due to his possession of vast amounts of interior space. **1.d4 Nf6 2.c4 g6 3.Nc3 Bg7 4.e4 d6 5.f3 O-O 6.Bd3 e5 7.d5 Nh5 8.Nge2 Qh4ch 9.g3 Qh3 10.Kf2 a5 11.Qf1 Qd7 12.g4 Nf6 13.Ng3 Qe7 14.h4 Na6 15.Be2 Nd7 16.h5** (White has a plus because the pawn shelter around the Black King is compromised)**Ndc5 17.Be3 b6 18.Kg2 Nd7? +/- 19.Qd1 Bb7 20.Qd2 Rfd8 21.Rh2** (White is rapidly getting a significant plus) **Nac5 22.R1h1 Nf8 23.Bd1** (Now we see the advantage of interior space; White just gains time by churning his pieces) **Re8 Nc5 24.a3 Ba6 25.b4 Ncd7 26.Bb3 Rec8 27.hxg6** (This has been on White's screen for 10 moves) **hxg6 28.Bh6 f6 29. Red8 30.Nd1 Bc8 31.Bxg7+- Qxg7 32.Rh8+ Kf7 33.Bc6 Ra7 34.Nc3 Ba6 35.Qa2 Ke7 36.bxa5 Rb8 37.axb6 cxb6 38.Nf1** (White has unlimited time to attack his opponent's King) **Rc7 39.Nb5 Bxb5 40.cxd5 Ra7 41.Ne3 Nc5 42.Nc4 Ra4 43.R1h6 Nd3 44.Kg3 Nc5 45.Qe2 Qf7 46.Qc2 Qg7 47.Qc1 Rxc4 48.Qxc4 f5 49. Qe2 +-**

White makes nine pawn moves in a row and stands better! **1.d4 Nf6 2.c4 g6 3.f3 Bg7 4.e4 d6 5.h4 Nbd7 6.g4 c5 7.d5 Ne5 8.a4 h5 9.g5 Nfd7 10.Be2 Nb8 11.Ra3 Na6 12.Nh3 Bd7 13.Nf2 Nb4 14.f4 Ng4** (Possibly the losing move; White sticks his opponent with a weak g-pawn and wins it. Even though the White King is on the Kingside, White pried open the position leading to massive simplification and a winning position) **15.Nxg4 Bxg4 16.Bxg4 hxg4 17.Rg3 a6 18.Kf2 Qd7 19.Nc3 O-O-O 20.Kg2 Kb8 21.Qxg4 e6 22.Bd2 Qe8 23.f5! exf5 24.exf5 Be5 25.Bf4 Bxf4 26.Qxf4 Nc2 27.fxg6 fxg6 28.Qe4** (+/-) **Nd4 29.Qxe8 Rdxe8 30.Rg4 Re5 31.Rf4** (White is relentless in his pursuit of the Black King) **Nf5 32.Kf2 Kc7 33.a5 Rh7 34.Ne2 Rxe2** (Depth 27; it is amazing to me that Black would simplify into a dead lost position) **35.Kxe2 Ng3+ 36.Kf3 Nxh1 37.Kg2 b6 38.axb6ch Kxb6 39.Kxh1 Rh8 40.Kg2 Ka5 41.Kg3 Kb4 42.Kg4 a5 43. Rf6 Kxc4 44.Rxg6 Kd4 45.Rxd6 Rb8 46.g6 1-0**

In this game Black plays the correct c5, not e5, but he could not neutralize the White initiative on the Kingside. **5.f3 O-O 6.Be3 c5 7.d5 e6 8.Qd2 exd5 9.cxd5 a6 10.a4 Nbd7 11.Nh3 Ne5 12.Nf2 Bd7 13.Be2 b5 14.O-O b4 15.Ncd1 Qa5 16.Qc1 Rfe8 17.b3 Ra7 18.Nb2 Qc7 19.Bh6** (White seeks to exploit the drafty nature of the Black King in a future attack.)**Bh8 20.Re1 Bc8 21.Qc2 Qb8** (Black has no useful moves) **22.Rad1 a5 23.Bc1 Ned7 24.Nc4** (White's advantage is +.61) **Nb6 25.Bb2 Bg7 26.f4 Nfd7 27.Nxb6 Qxb6 28.Bb5 f6** (Fritz has this as +/-)**29.Ng4 Rf8** (White clamps down on the position) **30.Ne3 Qd8 31.h4 Nb6 32.h5 Re7 33.hxg6 hxg6 34.e5!** (White pries open the position even though that is where his King is hanging out; I suspect that many Grandmasters would not be aware that this is the winning plan) **fxe5 35.fxe5 Bf5 36.Bd3 Bxd3 37.Qxd3 Qe8 38.exd6 Re4 39.Nc2 Rff4 40.Bxg7 Kxg7 41.g3 Rg4 42.Qf3 Qf7 43.Kg2 Ref4 44.Qxg4 Rxg4 45.Re7 Kf8 46.Rxf7ch Kxf7 47.Kf3 Rg5 48.Ne3 Rh5 49.Rc1 Nd7 50.Re1 Ne5+ 51.Ke4 Nd7 52.Rf1+ Kg7 53.Rf4 Rh3 54.Kf3 Ne5+ 55.Kg2 Rh8 56.Re4 Nf7 57.Re6 Kh6 58.Nc4 Rd8 59.Kf3 Kg7 60.Kf4 Rh8 61.Nxa5 Ra8 62.Nc4 Nh8 63.a5 1-0**

This game underscores the importance of controlled space; White has unlimited time to build for the attack over the span of 20 moves. Black has a deficit of space and that restricts his ability to counterattack. Look at the large number of Black moves seems almost like the actions of a drunken opponent!

5.f3 O-O 6.Be3 c5 7.d5 e6 8.Qd2 exd5 9.cxd5 a6 10.a4 Nbd7 11.Nh3 (White uses the fact that Black has lost communication with the h3 square) **Ne5 12.Nf2 Bd7 13.Be2 b5 14.O-O b4 15.Ncd1** (This retreat is a developing move.) **Bc8 16.Re1 Re8 17.Bg5 (+/=) Rb8 18.b3 Ra8** (Clearly Black is confused by my stellar play!) **19.Rc1 Bb7 20.Bh6 Bxh6 21.Qxh6 Ned7 22.Ne3 Rb8 23.Nc4 Ne5 24.Nd2 Ned7 25.f4 (+/-) c4** (This just loses a pawn for nothing) **26.Bxc4 Qb6 27.Qh4 Rbc8 28.Rcd1 Kg7 29.Kh1 Nc5 30.f5** (The fury of the White attack will soon become evident) **Qd8 31.Qf4 h6**

32.fxg6 fxg6 (The Black King position is getting drafty; White closes in for the kill) **33.Nd3 (+-) g5 34.Qf5 Nfd7 35.Nxb4 Ne5 36.Rf1** (The final moves need no comment; White wins a won game) **Rf8 37.Qxf8ch Qxf8 38.Rxf8 Rxf8 39.a5 Nxc4 40.bxc4 Rf4 41.Kg1 Nxe4 42.Nd3 Nc3 43.Nxf4 Nxd1 44.Nd3 Kf6 45.Ne4ch Ke7 46.c5 Bxd5 47.cxd6ch Ke6 48.Nd5ch Kf7 49.d7 Ke7 50.Nf6 Bc6 51.Ng8ch Kd8 52.Nxh6 Bxd7 53.Nxa6 Be6 54.g3 Nc3 55.Kf2 Bc8 56.Nc5 Kc7 57.Nf7 g4 58.Ke3 Nd5ch 59.Kd4 Nb4 60.Ne5 Nc2ch 61.Ke4 Kd6 62.Ncd3 Na3 63.Nf2 Bb7ch 64.Kf4 Nc2 65.Nexg4 Nd4 66.Ne4ch Ke7 67. Nc5 +-**

5.f3 O-O 6.Be3 c5 7.d5 e6 8.Qd2 exd5 9.cxd5 a6 10.a4 Nbd7 11.Nh3 (White takes advantage of the lack of communication with the h3 square) **Ne5 12.Nf2 Bd7 13.Be2 b5 14.O-O b4 15.Ncd1** (This is a developing move) **Qa5 16.Qc1 Rfe8 17.b3 Ra7 18.Nb2** (White has a bind on the c4 square; that is why Rfe8 was poorly motivated. Black should have played c4) **Qc7 19.Bh6 Bh8 20.Re1 Bc8 21.Qc2 Qb8 22.Rad1 a5 23.Bc1 Ned7**

24.Nc4 Nb6 25.Bb2 Bg7 26.f4 (White begins to bring pressure on the Kingside) **Nfd7 27.Nxb6 Qxb6 28.Bb5 f6 +/- 29.Ng4 Rf8 30.Ne3 Qd8 31.h4 Nb6 32.h5 Re7 33.hxg6 hxg6 34.e5 fxe5 35.fxe5 Bf5 36.Bd3 Rxe5** (After crunching to a depth of 26; Bxe5?? 37.Bxf5+-) **37.Bxe5 Bxe5 38.Nxf5 Qf6 39.Rf1 gxf5 40.Bxf5 Kg7 41.Qe4 Qg5 42.Rd3 Rh8 43.Be6 Bh2+ 44.Kh1 Bg3ch 45.Bh3 Be5 46.Rdf3 Qg6 47.Qe2 Nd7 48.Qa6 Nf6 49.Re1 Ne4 50.Qa7ch Kh6 51.Qe7 Ng3+ 52.Kg1 Re8 53.Qh4ch Qh5 54.Qxh5 Nxh5 55.Bg4 Bd4ch 56.Kf1 Rxe1ch 57.Kxe1 Nf6 58.Be6 Ba1 59.Ke2 c4 60.bxc4 Ne4 61.Bf5 Nc5 62.Rg3 Kh5 63.Rg6 Be5 64.Kf3 Nxa4 65.g3 Nc3 66.c5 Nb5 67.g4ch Kh4 68.Bd3 1-0**

1.d4 Nf6 2.c4 g6 3.Nc3 Bg7 4.e4 d6 5.f3 O-O 6.Bd3 e5 7.d5 Nh5 8.Nge2 Qh4ch 9.g3 Qh3 10.Kf2 a5 11.Qf1 Qd7 12.g4 Nf6 13.Ng3 Qe7 14.h4 Nfd7 15.h5 Nc5 16.Bc2 a4 17.Qd1 Bd7 18.Be3 Rd8 19.Rb1 Bf6 20.b4 axb3e.p. 21.axb3 Bg5 22. Qd2 Bxe3ch 23.Qxe3 Be8 24.hxg6 fxg6 25.Nf5! +/- gxf5 26.exf5 e4

27.b4 Ncd7 28.Nxe4 Ra2 29.Qb3 Rxc2ch 30.Qxc2 Nf6 31. Rh6
Nxe4ch 32. Qxe4 Qxe4 33. Fxe4 +-
5.Nge2 O-O 6.Ng3 Nbd7 7.f4 c5 8.d5 Nb6 9.a4 a5 10.Be2
e6 11.f5! gxf5 12.Bg5 Qe8 13.O-O h6 14.Bxf6 Bxf6 15.Bd3 f4
16.Nh5 Bd4ch 17.Kh1 Qe7 18.Nxf4 +/-Be5 19.Qb3 Nd7
20.Rf3 Bxf4 21.Rxf4 Ne5 22.Be2 Bd7 23.R1f1 Kg7 24.Nd1
Ng6 25.Qc3ch f6 26.R4f2 exd5 27.exd5 Qe5 28.Qb3 f5 29.Bh5
f4 30.Bxg6 Kxg6 31.Nc3 Rae8 32.h3 Kh7 33.Qxb7 Re7
34.Qb3 Qh5 35.Ne2 Re3 36.Qc2ch Bf5 37.Nxf4 Bxc2 38.Nxh5
Rxf2 39.Rxf2 Bd1 40.Nf6ch Kg6 41.Nd7 Bxa4 42.Rf6ch Kg5
43.Rxd6 Bxd7 44.Rxd7 Re4 45.b3 a4 46.bxa4 Rxc4 47.Rc7
Rxa4 48.Rxc5 Rd4 49.Kh2 h5 50.d6ch Kg6 51.Rc6 Kg5
52.Kg3 Rd3ch 53.Kf2 Kf5 54.Ra6 Rd5 55.Kg3 Rd4 56.Rb6
h4ch 57.Kf3 Ke6 58.d7ch Kxd7 59.Rg6 Ke7 60.Rg4 Rd3ch
61.Kf4 Kf6 62.Rxh4 1-0
5.Nf3 O-O 6.Bg5 Bg4 7.h3 Bxf3 8.Qxf3 c6 9.Qe3 Qa5
10.Qd2 c5 11.d5 a6 12.Bd3 b5 13.O-O b4 14.Nd1 Nbd7 15.f4
Qd8 16.Nf2 Nh5 17.g4 Nhf6 18.Bh4 a5 19.Rac1 Ne8 20.Be2 Bf6
21.g5 Bd4 22.Kg2 Ng7 23.Ng4 f6 24.Nh6ch Kh8 25.Bg4 Qe8
26.Rce1 Nb6 27.Qc2 Qb8 28.Bf2 Bxf2 29.Rxf2 Ra7 30.b3 a4
31.Qb2 Qd8 32.e5! +/- f5 33.Bf3 e6 34.R2e2 dxe5 35.Rxe5 exd5
36.cxd5 Rd7 37. Kg3 axb3 38. axb3 c4 39.Qd4 cxb3 40.Rb1 Nc8
41.Rxb3 Qb6 42. Qxb6 Nxb6 43. Rxb4 Nc8 44.Rb8 R8d8 45.Bd1
Nd6 46.Re7 Rxb8 47.Rxd7 Nge8 48.Ba4 Rc8 49.Kf3 Ra8 50.Bc6
Rb8 51.Nf7ch Nxf7 52.Rxf7 Kg8 53.Rd7 Rc8 54.Ke3 Ng7
55.Rb7 Rd8 56.Bd7 Kf8 57.Kd4 Ra8 58.Bb5 Ra1 59.Bc4 +6.75
61.Rb8ch +-
5.f3 O-O 6.Bd3 e5 7.d5 Nh5 8.Nge2 Qh4ch 9.g3 Qh3
10.Kf2 a5 11.a3 Nf6 12.Ng1 Qd7 13.Be3 Na6 14.Bc2 Qe7
15.Kg2 Nd7 16.h4 Nb6 17.Qe2 h5 18.Nh3 Kh7 19.Rhb1 Bh6
20.Bf2 Nc5 21.b4 axb4 22.axb4 Rxa1 23.Rxa1 Na6 24.Rb1 Bd7
25.Bd3 f6 26.Ng1 Ra8 27.Qd1 Bf8 28.Nge2 Qd8 29.Qb3 Kg7
30.Nc1 Be8 31.Bf1 Nd7 32.Nd3 Be7 33.Kg1 Rb8 34.Ra1 Ra8

35.Qb1 Bf8 36.Ra5 c5 37.dxc6e.p. bxc6 38.Qa2 Nc7 39.b5 c5
40.Nd5 Rb8 41.Ra7 Nxd5 42.exd5 Kg8 43.Nc1 Nb6 44.Nb3 Be7
45.Na5 Nc8 46.Ra6 Qd7 47.Nc6 Rb7 48.Be3 Kf8 49.Bd3 Nb6
50.Qa5 Qc7 51.Bh6ch Kf7 52.f4 Bd7 53.Nxe7 Kxe7 54.fxe5 dxe5
55.Qd2 Kf7 56.d6 Qb8 57.Be3 Qxd6 58.Bxg6ch Ke7 59.Qf2 Rc7
60.Bxh5 Be6 61.Be2 Bd7 62.Ra7 Rc8 63.Qf5 Kd8 64.Qg6 Rc7
65.Qg8ch Be8 66.Rxc7 Qxc7 67.h5 1-0

5.f3 O-O 6.Nge2 e5 7.d5 a5 8.Bg5 Na6 9.Qd2 Bd7 10.g4 h6
11.Be3 h5 12.g5 Nh7 13.O-O-O Nc5 14.Kb1 a4 15.Nb5 Bxb5
16.cxb5 Qe7 17.Rc1 Rfb8 18.h4 Nf8 19.Bh3 Nfd7 20.Rc2 Qe8
21.Nc1 Bf8 22.Rd1 Kg7 23.Bf1 Rd8 24.Rc3 Kg8 25.Qc2 Be7
26.Ra3 Kh7 27.Bc4 f6 28.Bf1 Kg7 29.Rc3 fxg5 30.hxg5 Kh7
31.Ne2 Ra7 32.Ng3 Kh8 33.Be2 Bf8 34.Rh1 Kg8 35.Nf5 Kh7
36.Nh4 Kg8 37.f4 exf4 38.Bxf4 b6 39.Re3 Ne5 40.Bxe5 dxe5
41.Bxh5 gxh5 42.Qe2 Bg7 43.g6 Rd6 44.Qxh5 Rf6 45.Nf5 Rxf5
46.Qxf5 1-0

1.d4 Nf6 2.c4 g6 3.Nc3 Bg7 4.e4 d6 5.Nf3 O-O 6.Bg5 Bg4
7.h3 Bxf3 8.Qxf3 c6 9.Qe3 Qb6 10.O-O-O Nbd7 11.g4 Rfe8
12.Kb1 Rad8 13.Qe2 e5 14.d5 cxd5 15.cxd5 Rc8 16.Rc1 Qa5
17.h4 +/- a6 18.h5 Rc7 19.f3 R8c8 20.hxg6 hxg6 21.Qe1 b5 22.a3
Ne8 23.Bd2 N8f6 24.Rh2 Qb6 25.Na2 Rxc1ch 26.Bxc1 Nb8
27.Be3 Qb7 28.g5 Nfd7 29.Bh3 Qc7 30.Nc1 Qc4 31.Bf1 Qc7
32.Nb3 Qd8 33.Bh3 Kf8 34.Qb4 Kg8 35.Qa5 Qe8 36.Ba7 Rc4
37.Bxb8 Nxb8 38.Qb6 b4 39.axb4 Nd7 40.Qxd6 Nb8 41.Bf1 Rc8
42.Nc5 Bf8 43.Qf6 Bg7 44.Qb6 Qe7 45.Rg2 Bf8 46.Bxa6 Nxa6
47.Qxa6 Rd8 48.Qb7 Qxb7 49.Nxb7 Rb8 50.Na5 Rxb4 51.Nc6
Ra4 52.Nxe5 1-0

5.Bd3 O-O 6.Nf3 c6 7.O-O Bg4 8.Be3 Nfd7 9.Be2 c5 10.d5
Qa5 11.Bd2 a6 12.Qc2 Qc7 13.h3 Bxf3 14.Bxf3 Re8 15.Rad1 Bd4
16.b3 Nf8 17.Ne2 Bg7 18.Bg4 b5 19.f4 Nbd7 20.Kh1 Rab8
21.Bf3 (Both sides have universal positions) Qb6 22.g4 bxc4
23.Qxc4 Qb5 24.Rc1 e6 25.Ng3 Bb2 26.Rb1 Bd4 27.Kg2 Nb6
28.Qc2 a5 29.dxe6 Nxe6 30.f5 Nc7 31.a4 Qa6 32.Be2 Qa7 33.Bf4

Red8 34.Qd3 Rd7 35.h4 Re8 36.h5 Qb7 37.Bf3 gxf5 38.Nxf5
Ne6 39.Bh2 Be5 40.Bxe5 dxe5 41.Qc3 Nf4ch 42.Kh1 Nc8
43.Qxc5 Qb6 44.Rc1 Rdd8 45.Qxb6 Nxb6 46.Rc5 Rd3 47.Rxa5
Rxb3 48.Rb5 Rxb5 49.axb5 Kf8 50.Ra1 Ne6 51.Kg2 Ng5 52.Kf2
Rc8 53.Ra6 Nd7 54.Ra7 Nb6 55.Rb7 Nc4 56.Kg3 Ke8 57.Be2
Nxe4ch 58.Kh4 Ned6 59.Bxc4 Nxb7 60.Bd5 Rc2 61.Bxb7 f6
62.Be4 Rh2ch 63.Kg3 Rb2 64.Kf3 Kf8 65.Bd3 Rb4 66.Ne3 e4ch
67.Bxe4 Rxb5 68.Bxh7 Kg7 69.Bg6 1-0
5.Be2 O-O 6.Be3 e5 7.d5 a5 8.g4 Na6 9.g5 Nd7 10.h4 Ndc5
11.Qd2 c6 12.O-O-O a4 13.h5 Qa5 14.f3 Bd7 15.Kb1 Rfd8
16.hxg6 hxg6 17.Bf1 Nc7 18.Rh2 Rdc8 19.Nge2 cxd5 20.Nxd5
Qxd2 21.Bxd2 Nxd5 22.cxd5 Rab8 23.Nc1 b6 24.Nd3 Ra8 25.Nb4
Rc7 26.Be2 R7c8 27.Nc2 Rab8 28.Ne3 Kf8 29.Nc4 Ke7 30.Rc1
b5 31.Na5 Ra8 32.Rc2 Rcb8 33.Rh7 Kf8 34.Nc6 Bxc6 35.dxc6
Rb6 36.Be3 Rxc6 37.Bxb5 Rcc8 38.R7h2 Ra5 39.Be2 Rb8 40.Bc4
Kg8 41.Bd2 Raa8 42.Bd5 Ra6 43.a3 Ne6 44.Be3 Ra5 45.Rc6 Bf8
46.Rc4 Kg7 47.Bxe6 fxe6 48.Rc7ch Kg8 49.Bd2 Raa8 50.Bc3 Bg7
51.Bb4 Ra6 52.Rd7 Bf8 53.Rhh7 Rc8 54.Rhf7 Rd8 55.Kc2 Rxd7
56.Rxd7 Kh8 57.Kd3 Kg8 58.Bc3 Bg7 59.Kc4 Rb6 60.Ra7 Rb8
61.Kd3 Rf8 62.Ke2 Rb8 63.Rxa4 d5 64.b4 Rc8 65.Bd2 Bf8 66.b5
dxe4 67.b6 exf3ch 68.Kxf3 Bd6 69.b7 e4ch 70.Kxe4 Rc5 71.Bf4
e5 72.Rd4 exd4 73.Bxd6 Rb5 74.b8(Q)ch Rxb8 75.Bxb8 1-0
5.Be2 O-O 6.Be3 e5 7.d5 a5 8.h4 Na6 9.g4 Nc5 10.f3 c6
11.h5 cxd5 12.cxd5 Bd7 13.Nh3 gxh5 14.g5 Ne8 15.Nf2 Rb8
16.Kd2!fxe4 b5 17.Qg1 f5 18.Rxh5 b4 19.Ncd1 a4 20.Qh1 a3
21.b3 fxe4 22.fxe4 Rf4 23.Rc1 Rb7 24.Kc2 Rc7 25.Kb1 Qe7
26.Rc2 Rc8 27.Bf1 Rc7 28.Bh3 Bb5 29.Bf5 Rxf5 30.exf5 Qf7
31.f6 Qg6 32.Rh4 Na6 33.Qe4 Qxe4 34.Rxe4 Rxc2 35.Kxc2 Bf8
36.Bd2 h6 37.f7ch Kxf7 38.gxh6 Nf6 39.Rh4 Bd7 40.Ne3 Kg8
41.h7ch Kh8 42.Nd3 Bg7 43.Nxb4 Nc7 44.Bc1 Nb5 45.Kd3 Ne8
46.Nbc2 Nd4 47.Nxd4 exd4 48.Nc4 Bf5ch 49.Ke2 d3ch 50.Kf3
Bxh7 51.Bxa3 Bf8 52.b4 Nc7 53.Bb2ch Kg8 54.a4 Be7 55.Rh2
Nxd5 56.b5 1-0

5.Be2 O-O 6.Be3 e5 7.d5 Na6 8.g4 Nc5 9.f3 a5 10.h4 c6
11.h5 a4 12.Nh3 cxd5 13.cxd5 gxh5 14.g5 Ne8 15.Nf2 Bd7
16.Rxh5 Qa5 17.Qd2 f6 18.Nb1 Qc7 19.Na3 Rc8 20.Nd3
Nxd3ch 21.Qxd3 Qd8 22.Qd2 Nc7 23.gxf6 Qxf6 24.Qa5 Be8
25.Rh3 Qd8 26.Rh1 Na6 27.Qxd8 Rxd8 28.Kd2 Bg6 29.Nc4
Bf6 30.Nb6 Nc5 31.Rag1 Be7 32.Kc3 Rf7 33.Kb4 Rg7 34.a3
Bf6 35.Rh3 Be8 36.Rxg7ch Kxg7 37.Rh2 Na6ch 38.Ka5 Nc7
39.Bh6ch Kf7 40.Bd1 Na8 41.Nxa4 Rc8 42.f4 Kg8 43.Bh5
exf4 44.Bxf4 Bxh5 45.Rxh5 Bd8ch 46.Kb4 Be7 47.Rh6 Rd8
48.Kc4 Nc7 49.Kd3 Bf8 50.Rh2 Ne8 51.Nb6 Nf6 52.a4 Re8
53.Re2 Nh5 54.Bh2 Nf6 55.a5 Ng4 56.Bf4 Kf7 57.b4 Ne5ch
58.Bxe5 dxe5 59.Rf2ch Kg7 60.Rg2ch Kf7 61.Nc4 h5 62.b5
h4 63.Rg4 h3 64.Rg3 h2 65.Rh3 Bc5 66.Rxh2 Kg7 67.Rh5
Rf8 68.Nxe5 1-0
  5.Be2 O-O 6.Bg5 Nbd7 7.Qc2 e5 8.d5 a5 9.h4 h6 10.Be3
Nc5 11.h5 Kh7 12.O-O-O a4 13.a3 Bd7 14.Kb1 Qe7 15.Rf1 Nb3
16.hxg6ch fxg6 17.Qd1 Nc5 18.Nf3 b6 19.Nd2 Rh8 20.g4 Kg8
21.g5 hxg5 22.Rxh8ch Bxg8 23.Bxg5 Bg7 24.Rg1 Qf7 25.Be3
Rb8 26.Rg2 Bh3 27.Rg3 Bd7 28.Qh1 Be8 29.Rg1 Bd7 30.Ka2
Ra8 31.Qh4 Nh7 32.Nf3 Qf6 33.Qg3 Be8 34.Rh1 Bd7 35.Qg2
Rb8 36.Nh2 Qf7 37.Bg4 Bxg4 38.Nxg4 Nf8 39.f4 Ncd7 40.f5
Nf6 41.Nxf6ch Bxf6 42.Rg1 Rd8 43.Nxa4 Rd7 44.fxg6 Qg7
45.Qg4 Qe7 46.Nc3 Qg7 47.Qf5 Bh4 48.Qh3 Bf6 49.Rf1 Re7
50.Nb5 Qh8 51.Qc8 Qg7 52.Bh6 Qxh6 53.Rxf6 Qg7 54.Rf2 Qh6
55.Qd8 Qg7 56.Rf5 Rd7 57.Rxf8ch Qxf8
  58.Qxd7 1-0
  5.Be2 O-O 6.Bg5 Na6 7.Qd2 c6 8.f3 Qa5 9.a3 Qc7 10.Bd1
(This gains a tempo) Nb8
  11.Nge2 c5 12.d5 Nbd7 13.O-O Ne5 14.b3 a6 15.a4 Re8
16.a5 Rb8 17.Bc2 Nh5 18.h3 Nd7 19.g4 Nhf6 20.Bh6 Bxh6
21.Qxh6 Rf8 22.Ng3 Ne8 (Black has a universal position) 23.Qe3
(White has returned to a universal position. White does not have a single pawn on its original square. Black has four pawns on the seventh.)

f6 24.f4 Rf7 25.Kg2 b6 26.axb6 Rxb6 27.h4 Rb8 28.Nd1 (This gains a tempo) Ng7 29.Rh1 Nf8 30.Nf2 e5 31.f5 Kh8 32.Rhf1 Rb7 33.h5 g5 34.Rxa6 Rxb3 35.Qxb3 Bxa6 36.Qa4 Qc8 37.Ra1 Bb7 38.h6 Ne8 39.Qb5 Rc7 40.Nh5 Nd7 41.Nd1 Qd8 42.Qa5 Qc8 43.Ba4 Qb8 44.Rb1 Kg8 45.Bc6 Kf7 46.Qb5 Bxc6 47.dxc6 Qxb5 48.cxb5 d5 49.cxd7 Rxd7 50.exd5 1-0

5.f3 O-O 6.Be3 Nbd7 7.Bd3 a6 8.a4 e5 9.d5 Nc5 10.Bc2 a5 11.Nge2 Nfd7 12.O-O b6 13.Qd2 Bb7 14.Rf2 Bf6 15.R1f1 Bh4 16.g3 Bf6 17.f4 exf4 18.gxf4 Qe7 19.b3 Rae8 20.f5 Kh8 21.Ng3 Qd8 22.Nb5 Be5 23.Kh1 Ba6 24.Nd4 Bb7 25.Bh6 Rg8 26.fxg6 fxg6 27.Nf3 Bf6 28.e5 dxe5 29.Ne4 Nxe4 30.Bxe4 Nc5 31.Ng5 Bxg5 32.Bxg5 Qxg5 33.Bxg5 Nxe4 34.Qe3 Nxf2ch 35.Rxf2 Rg7 36.Kg1 Kg8 37.Rf6 Bc8 38.c5 bxc5 39.Qxc5 Bf5 40.d6 cxd6 41.Qd5ch Kh8 42.Rxd6 Rc7 43.Qxa5 Rc1ch 44.Kg2 Kg7 45.Qa7ch Kg8 46.Qe3 Ra1 47.Qc5 Ra2ch 48.Kg3 h5 49.h4 Rc2 50.Qe3 Kh7 51.Ra6 Be6 52.a5 R8c8 53.Rxe6 R8c3 54.Re7ch Kg8 55.Qxc3 Rxc3ch 56.Kf2 Rc2ch 57.Kf3 Ra2 58.Rxe5 Kf7 59.b4 Ra3ch 60.Kf4 Kg7 61.Rb5 Kh6 62.Ke4 g5 63.hxg5ch 1-0

5.f3 O-O 6.Be3 Nbd7 7.Nge2 e5 8.d5 Nc5 9.Qd2 b6 10.g3 Re8 11.Bg2 a5 12.g4 Ba6 13.Nb5 Bxb5 14.cxb5 h5 15.g5 Nh7 16.O-O-O Rf8 17.Kb1 f6 18.h4 a4 19.Rhg1 fxg5 20.hxg5 Qd7 21.Nc3 Qe7 22.Bh1 Rf7 23.Qc2 Qd8 24.Rdf1 Qe7 25.Rg3 Rf4 26.R1g1 Ra7 27.Bg2 a3 28.b4 Nb7 29.Ne2 Rh4 30.Bh3 Nd8 31.Qc4 Ra8 32.Bd2 Kh8 33.Nc1 Nf7 34.Nd3 Rg8 35.Qc2 Rb8 36.Qc6 Rd8 37.Bc1 Kg8 38.Ne1 Rf4 39.Be6 Nf8 40.Bxf7ch Rxf7 41.Bxa3 Rc8 42.Ng2 Nd7 43.Nh4 Kh7 44.Bb2 Nf8 45.a4 Qd8 46.a5 bxa5 47.bxa5 Nd7 48.Ba3 Rb8 49.R3g2 Bf8 50.Rc2 Rf4 51.Rh2 Rf7 52.Ka2 Kg7 53.Rc2 Ra8 54.a6 Ra7 55.Kb1 Nb8 56.Qc4 Nxa6 57.bxa6 c5 58.Bc1 Qb6ch 59.Rb2 Qxa6 60.Qxa6 Rxa6 61.Bd2 Rc7 62.Rf1 Rf7 63.Kc2 Be7 64.R1b1 Bd8 65.Rb7 Ra2ch 66.R1b2 Rxb2ch 67.Rxb2 Rd7 68.Rb8 Kf7 69.Kd3 Be7 70.f4 exf4 71.Bxf4 Ra7 72.Rb3 Rd7 73.Rb6 Kg7 74.Kc4 Ra7 75.Bxd6 Bxg5 76.Nf3 Be3 77.Bxc5 1-0

5.Nf3 O-O 6.Bg5 Bg4 7.h3 Bxf3 8.Qxf3 Nfd7 9.Qe3 Re8
10.Be2 Nc6 11.Rd1 Nb4 12.Rd2 c5 13.d5 Bd4 14.Qg3 Qa5 15.O-
O Na6 16.a3 Nc7 17.Rb1 Rac8 18.Bf4 Qa6 19.Rc2 Red8 20.Bg5
Re8 21.b4 Be5 22.Qd3 Bd4 23.Ra2 b6 24.a4 Ne5 25.Qd2 f6 26.Bf4
Rb8 27.a5 Qc8 28.Nd1 bxa5 29.b5 e6 30.Ne3 exd5 31.exd5 a6
32.b6 Na8 33.Qxa5 Re7 34.Nc2 Qf5 35.Bg3 Reb7 36.Qxa6 Rxb6
37.Rb5 Rxb5 38.cxb5 Nb6 39.Nxd4 cxd4 40.Rd2 Qb1ch 41.Kh2
Qb4 42.Rc2 Ned7 43.Rc7 Re8 44.Bf3 Ra8 45.Qb7 Qxb5 46.Bxd6
Rb8 47.Qc6 Qxc6 48.bxc6 Ne5 49.Bxe5 fxe5 50.Bg4 Na8 51.Rb7
Rd8 52.c7 Nxc7 53.Rxc7 Rd6 54.Re7 e4 55.Rxe4 Kf8 56.Kg3 Kf7
57.Kf4 Kf6 58.Re5 d3 59.Ke4 Rd8 60.Rd5 Re8ch 61.Kxd3 1-0
5.Bd3 O-O 6.Nge2 Nc6 7.f4 Nd7 8.Be3 Nb4 9.Bb1 c5 10.a3
cxd4 11.Bxd4 Nc6 12.Bxg7 Kxg7 13.b4 Nb6 14.Ba2 e5 15.O-O
Be6 16.f5 Bxc4 17.f6ch Kh8 18.Bxc4 Nxc4 19.Rf3 g5 20.Nd5
Nb6 21.Ne3 Rc8 22.Qd2 Qd7 23.Rd1 Rg8 24.Nf5 Qe6 25.b5
Nc4 26.Qd5 Nd8 27.Ne7 Rc5 28.Qxe6 Nxe6 29.Nxg8 Kxg8
30.Rc3 h5 31.Rd5 Rc8 32.Ng3 Kh7 33.Nxh5 g4 34.Ng3 Kg6
35.Rd1 Rc5 36.a4 Kg5 37.Nf5 Nb2 38.R1c1 Nd3 39.R1c2 Nd4
40.Rxc5 dxc5 41.Rd2 c4 42.Ne3 Nc5 43.Nxc4 Kxf6 44.Rd1 Nxe4
45.Re1 Kf5 46.Ne3ch Ke6 47.Nxg4 f5 48.h4 Nc2 49.b6 axb6
50.Rb1 fxg4 51.Rxb6ch Kf5 52.h5 Nf6 53.a5 Nd4 54.Rxb7
Ne2ch 55.Kf1 Nd4 56.a6 1-0
5.Be2 O-O 6.Be3 Na6 7.f3 c5 8.d5 e6 9.Qd2 exd5 10.cxd5
Nc7 11.a4 b6 12.Bg5 h6 13.Be3 Kh7 14.g4 Nd7 15.h4 Ne5
16.Nh3 Re8 17.Nf2 Ba6 18.f4 Bxe2 19.Qxe2 Nd7 20.O-O-O
Bxc3 21.bxc3 b5 22.h5 g5 23.e5 gxf4 24.Bxf4 Rxe5 25.Bxe5 Nxe5
26.Ne4 bxa4 27.Qc2 Kh8 28.Rhf1 Qf8 29.Nf6 Qg7 30.Qxa4
Qg5ch 31.Qf4 Qxf4ch 32.Rxf4 Nb5 33.Ne4 Rg8 34.c4 Nd4
35.Rf2 Rxg4 36.Nxd6 Kg8 37.Ra2 a5 38.Kb1 Rg3 39.Re1 Rb3ch
40.Ka1 f6 41.Rxa5 Rb6 42.Rg1ch Kh7 43.Rb1 Nc2ch 44.Ka2
Nb4ch 45.Rxb4 Rxb4 46.Rxc5 1-0

In this game, white achieved an advantage of +/- despite the fact
that not a single piece or pawn had been exchanged. This evaluation

is based on the observation that white had a huge advantage in interior space allowing great wing to wing mobility. **5.f3 O-O 6.Bd3 e5 7.d5 Nh5 8.Nge2 Qh4ch 9.g3 Qh3 10.Kf2 a5 11.a3 Na6 12.Bc2 Nf6 13.Qf1 Qd7 14.Be3 Rb8 15.Qe1 Qh3 16.Nb5 b6 17.b4 axb4 18.axb4 Ra8 19.Qd2 Rd8 20.Bd3 Bf8 21.Nec3 Qd7 22.Na4 Qe7 23.Kg2 Bb7 24.Rhc1 Nd7 25.Nb2 Bg7 26.Ra4 h5 27.Bc2 h4 28.Nd3 Rf8 29.Nf2 Kh7 30.Bg5 f6 31.Be3 Rh8 32.Ra3 Kg8 33.R1a1 hxg3 34.hxg3 Kf7 35.Rb1 Rh5 36.Rh1 Rxh1 37.Nxh1 Kg8 38.Nf2 Nf8 39.Bd3 Qd7 40.c5 dxc5 41.bxc5 bxc5 42.Bc4 Kh8 43.Qb2 Rb8 44.Qa1 Ra8 45.Qb1 f5 46.Nc3 Bc8 47.Qa1 Qd6 48.Nd3 Bb7 49.Qb1 Bc8 50.Bxc5 +3.07 +-**

5.Nf3 O-O 6.Bg5 Bg4 7.h3 Bxg4 8.Qxf3 Nfd7 9.Qe3 Re8 10.Be2 c5 11.d5 Bd4 12.Qd2 a6 13.Be3 Bxe3 14.Qxe3 e6 15.O-O-O exd5 16.Rxd5 Nf6 17.Rd2 Qe7 18.f3 Nc6 19.g4 Nd4 20.g5 Nh5 21.Nd5 Nxe2ch 22.Rxe2 Qd7 23.f4 Rad8 24.Rf1 Rb8 25.Qf3 Rbd8 26.f5 Kh8 27.Ref2 Re5 28.fxg6 fxg6 29.Qb3 Rxe4 30.Qc3ch Kg8 31.Rf7 Qe6 32.Nxe7ch Qxe7 33.Rxe7 Rxe7 34.Qf3 Kg7 35.h4 Rb8 36.a3 Rc8 37.Kb1 R8e8 38.Ka2 Rd8 39.Qf2 Kg8 40.Qg2 Kg7 41.Qd2 Kg8 42.Rf3 Kh8 43.Re3 Rf7 44.Rd3 R7d7 45.Rb3 Ng7 46.Qd5 Rb8 47.h5 Nxh5 48.Rb6 Nf4 49.Qe4 Nh5 50.Rxd6 Rxd6 51.Qe5ch Kg7 52.Qxd6 Rf8 53.Qxc5 Rf7 54.Qc8ch Kg7 55.Qe8 Rf5 56.c5 Rf7 57.a4 Rf5 58.Qe4 Rf7 59.c6 bxc6 60.Qxc6 1-0

He who writes the rules wins. The easiest way for humans to defeat supercomputers is to change the rules:

1) Play consultation games. These are spectator friendly because the GM's will be encouraged to think out loud. We get to step inside the minds of the greatest players while they decide which moves to make. Spectators will be permitted to have laptops so they can anticipate what moves will be played.

2) Get rid of time delay; this benefits computers,

3) The five second rule---under no circumstance will computers be permitted to make a move in under five seconds. If they make a move in under five seconds, they lose half their remaining time. With the last rules change, think of how difficult it will be for computers to win a "simple" Rook and pawn ending. Humans will be able to use the time the computer spends five seconds before it can move to make a move in under a second. Some Rook and pawn endings may take 50 moves to win. Have a large countdown clock so the spectators will know that the computer will lose on time.

4) Once GM's beat a 3100 computer, they can step up to a 3200 computer. As they begin to beat stronger and stronger computers eventually they will have to face a 3500 computer.

With these rules changes, humans will beat supercomputers.

SUMMARY AND CONCLUSIONS

According to Magnus Carlsen, the current World Champion, super-computers are unbeatable. As my 29 wins against Fritz 15 in the King's Indian Defense demonstrate, the long-term problems the computer has is that it fails to contest space and tries to do everything with piece pressure alone.

One of the major findings of this book is that white can deny black counterplay in the King's Indian Defense, allow black to gain space on the Queenside, but this is not enough to prevent white from attacking in the center and Kingside. White just "churns" his pieces in a Universal Position, gains time and builds for a sacrificial attack in the center and Kingside. It is instructive that white typically is assured of a sacrificial attack once Black has lost any hope of counterplay.

White can contest the Alekhine Defense by meeting 1.e4 Nf6 with 2.Qe2 e5 3.f4 with a new way to play the King's Gambit.

I present a whole host of new plans in the 4.Ng5 variation of the Two Knight's Defense. This includes a winning attack against the Berliner Gambit, and a big plus in the Ulvestad, the Wilkes-Barre Traxler, and a new try by Black in the Fried Liver that yields complete equality. In several games featuring the "main line", white has excellent chances for a plus suggesting that Black must play aggressively or just stand worse.

When white combines the Evans Gambit with the 4.Ng5 variation of the Two Knight's Defense, he has a complete repertoire to meet the aggressive responses to 3.Bc4. It should be pointed out that Black can play quietly with 3.Bc4 Bc5 4.b4 Bb6.

The Latvian Gambit does not fare well against supercomputers. The most striking feature of the Latvian Gambit shows how Knight moves that cannot be achieved in less than a certain number of moves are all developing moves. What this means is that in a soon to be open position white will have a four tempo lead in development.

What is surprising to the author is how often I disagree with the analysis of Fritz 15, a 3170 computer. Fritz 15 is all too eager to simplify the position which often leads to positions that are impossible to win. Most of the time when Fritz would try to exchange pieces I would avoid these continuations so that I could gain time in a Universal Position.

Berliner Gambit

1.e4 e5 2.Nf3 Nc6 3.Bc4 Nf6 4.Ng5 d5 5.exd5 Nd4 6.c3 b5 7.Bf1
Nxd5 8.Ne4 Qh4 9.Ng3 Bg4 10.f3 e4 11.cxd4 Bd6 12.Qe2 O-O
13.fxg4 Bxg3+14.Kd1 c6 15.Nc3 Rfe8 16.a4 b4 17.Nxe4 f5
18.Qf3 fxe4 19.Qxg3 Qf6 20.Kc2 Qxd4 21.b3 e3 22.Bc4 Re4
23.Ra2 Qc5 24.d3 Re7 25.Re1 Kh8 26.Kb1 Nc3+ 27.Ka1 Nxa2
28.Kxa2 Qe5 29.Qxe5 Rxe5 30.d4 R5e8 31.Rxe3 Rxe3 32.Bxe3
Re8 33.Bd2 Re4 34.Kb2 Rxg4 35.g3 Rd4 36.Bxb4 Rd8 37.Kc2
h5 38.Bc3 Kh7 1-0:49

Fried Liver

1.e4 e5 2.Nf3 Nc6 3.Bc4 Nf6 4.Ng5 d5 5.exd5 Nxd5 6.Nxf7 Kxf7
7.Qf3+ Ke6 8.Nc3 Nb4 9.Qe4 c6 10.a3 Na6 11.f4 Nc7 12.O-O+
Kg8 13.Qf3 Qh4 14.Ne4 Be7 15.g3 Qh5 16.Ne4 Be7 17.Qd3 Rf8
18.Bd2 Bf5 19.Rae1 b5 20.Bb3 Qg4 21.a4 a6 22.c3 h3 23.Bc2
Bh4 24.g3 Bg5 25.Bxg5 Bxe4 26.Rxe4 Qxg5 27.axb5 axb5
28.Ree1 Rxf1+ 29. Qxf1 g6 30.Qh3 Ne7 31.Qd7 Ncd5 32.Be4
Kg7 33.Bxd5 cxd5 34.Rf1 Rf8 35.Rxf8 Kxf8 36.Qxb5 h5 37.Qb8+
Kg7 38.Qb7 h4 39.Kf2Qd2+ 40.Kf3 Kf7 41.Qa6 Qxh2 42.Qf6+
Ke8 43.gxh4 Qc2 44.Qh8+ Kf7 45.Qb8 Qe4+ 46.Kg3 Nf5+
47.Kf2 Nxh4 48.Qb7+ Ke6 49.Qc8+ Kf7 50.Qd7+ Kg8 51.e6
Qf3+ 52.Ke1 Ng2+ 53.Kd2 Qf2+ 54.Kc1 Ne3 55.Kb1 Nc4
56.Qc8+ Qf8 57.Qd7 Nb6 58.Qb7 Qf5+ 59.Ka1 Qxe6 60.Qb8+
Kf7 61.Qh2 Nc4 62.Qh7+ Kf6 63.Qh8+ Kg5 64.Qh1 Ne3 65.c4
dxc4 66.Qf3 Nc2+ 67.Ka2 Nb4+ 0-1

Fritz

1.e4 e5 2.Nf3 Nc6 3.Bc4 Nf6 4.Ng5 d5 5.exd5 Nd4 6.c3 Nf5
7.O-O Nxd5 8.d4 exd4 9.Qh5 g6 10.Qe2+ Be7 11.Qe5 f6 12.Qe4

c6 13.Ne6 Nd6!! 14.Nxd8 Nxe4 15.Re1 f5 16.f3 Kd8 17.fxe4 fxe4 18.cxd4 Nb4 19.Re2 Bg4 20.Rxe4 Bf5 21.Re2 Re8 22.Nc3 Nc2 23.g4 Nxa1 24.gxf5 gxf5 25.Bf7 Rf8 26.Bh5 Kd7 27.Kf1 Rg8 28.Bf7 Rg7 29.Be6+ Kc7 30.b3 f4 31.Bb2 f3 32.Rf2 Rf8 33.Bxa1 Rg6 34.d5 Bc5 35.Ne4 Bxf2 36.Nxf2 cxd5 37.Bxd5 Rg5 38.Be4 R8g8 39.Nh3 Rg2 40.Be5 Kb6 41.a4 Re8 42.Bd4+ Kc7 43.Bxf3 Rd2 44.Bf2 Rd3 45.Kg2 Rxb3 46.Nf4 Ra3 47.Nd5+ Kd6 48.Bg3+ Kc5 49.Nf6 Re7 50.Ne4+ Kc4 51.Bh4 Rg7+ 52.Kf2 Rxa4 53.Be2+ Kb4 54.Ke3 b5 55.Bf6 Ra3+ 56.Bd3 Rd7 57.Bd4 Rxd3+ 58.Kxd3 a5 59.h4 a4 60.Nc3 a3 0-1

King's Indian Defense

1.d4 Nf6 2.c4 g6 3.Nc3 Bg7 4.e4 d6 5.Nf3 O-O 6.Bg5 Bg4 7.h3 Bxf3 8.Qxf3 Nfd7 9.O-O-O h6 10.Be3 c5 11.Qe2 cxd4 12.Bxd4 Bxd4 13.Rxd4 Nc6 14.Rd1 Qa5 15.f4 Rad8 16.g4 e5 17.Qd2 Kh7 18.f5 Nd4 19.h4 Rc8 20.Kb1 a6 21.g5 h5 22.b3 Nb6 23.Ne2 Qxd2 24.Rxd2 Nxe2 25.Bxe2 +-

Berliner Gambit

1.e4 e5 2.Nf3 Nc6 3.Bc4 Nf6 4.Ng5 d5 5.exd5 Nd4 6.c3 b5 7.Bf1 8.Ne4 Qh4 9.Ng3 Bg4 10.f3 e4 11.cxd4 Bd6 12.Bxb5+ Kd8 13.O-O gxf3 14.Rxf3 Rb8 15.a4 a6 16.Bf1 Re8 17.Nc3 c6 18.d3 f5 19.Nce2 Re6 20.Rf2 g5 21.Qd2 Ne3 22.Qa5+ Bc7 23.Qc5 Bd6 24.Qa7 Bxe2 25.Rxe2 Re7 26.Qxe7+ Bxe7 27.Bxe3 Bd6 28.Bf2 Kd7 29.R1e1 Qh6 30.Rc2 g4 31.d5 cxd5 32.d4 f4 33.Nf5 Qg6 34.Bd3 Rb7 35.Rc3 Qxc3 36.bxc3 Kxd6 37.Re5 Rb1+ 38.Kf1 Rxa4 39.Rg5 g3 40.hxg3 fxg3 41.Rxg3 a5 42.Rg7 h5 43.Rh7 Rc4 44.Rxh5 Kd6 45.Rh8 Kb7 46.Rf8 Rc6 47.Rf2 Ka6 48.Ra2 Rf6+ 49.Ke2 Re6+ 50.Kd2 Ka5 51.Bf2 Rg6 52.g3 Rg4 53.Ra3 Rg8 54.Ke3 Rg7 55.Kf3 Rh7 56.g4 Rf7+ 57.Kg3 Rg7 58.Be3 1-0

Berliner Gambit
1.e4 e5 2.Nf3 Nc6 3.Bc4 Nf6 4.Ng5 d5 5.exd5 Nd4 6.c3 b5 7.Bf1
Nxd5 8.Ne4 Qh4 9.Ng3 Bg4 10.f3 e4 11cxd4 Bd6 12.Qe2 Be6
13.Qxb5+ Kf8 14.fxe4 Nb4 15.Nc3 a5 16.e5 Qxd4 17.Kd1 c6
18.Qa4 Qxe5 19.Be2 Rb8 20.Re1 Qd4 21.Bf3 Qb6 22.Rxd6 fxe6
23.a3 Nd3 24.Qxc6 Qxc6 25.Bxc6 Ke7 26.Kc2 Ne1+ 27.Kb1 Nd3
28.Be4 Nxc1 29.Kxc1 Rb6 30.Kc2 g6 31.Nf1 R8b8 32.Rb1 Bf4
33.h3 Rf8 34.Bf3 Rbb8 35.Ne3 Bxe3 36.dxe3 Kf6 37.b3 Ke7 38.a4
Rc8 39.Be2 Rd6 40.Bc4 Rdd8 41.Rf1 Rc5 42.e4 Re5 43.Rf3 Rd7
44.g4 g6 45.Bd3 Rc5 46.Kd2 Rh8 47.Bc4 g5 48.h5 R5c8 49.Ke3
Rc5 50.e5 Rhf8 51.Rxf8 Rxf8 52.Kc5 Rf3 53.Nb5 Re3 54.Kb6 Rxe4
55.Kxa5 Rxg4 56.Kb6 1-0

Fried Liver
1.e4 e5 2.Nf3 Nc6 3.Bc4 Nf6 4.Ng5 d5 5.exd5 Nxd5 6.Nxf7 Kxf7
7.Qf3+ Ke6 8.Nc3 Nb4 9.a3 Nxc2+ 10.Kd1 Nxa1 11.Nxd5 Qh4
12.Nxc7+ Kd7 13.Qf7+ Qe7 14.Qxe7 Bxe7 15.Nxa8 Kd6 16.d4
Bf5 17.dxe5+ Kc5 18.Ba2 Rxa8 19.Ke2 Nc2 20.Rd1 Rd8 21.Rxd8
Bxd8 22.Bd2 g5 23.g3 Kc6 24.f3 g4 25.f4 b5 26.Bf7 Kd7 27.Bd5
Bb6 28.Bc3 Nd4+ 29.Kf2 a5 30.Bg8 h6 31.Bd2 Nf3+ 32.Be3
Bxe3+ 33.Kxe3 Nxh2 34.Kf2 Nf3 35.Ke3 Ne1 36.Bd5 Nc2+
37.Kf2 Kc7 38.Bg2 Kb6 39.Bf1 Kc5 40.Be2 b4 41.axb4+ Kxb4
42.Ba6 Kb3 43.Be2 Kxb2 44.Bb5 Kc3 0-1

Fried Liver
1.e4 e5 2.Nf3 Nc6 3.Bc4 Nf6 4.Ng5 d5 5.exd5 Nxd5 6.Nxf7 Kxf7
7.Qf3 9.a3 Nxc2+ 10.Kd1 Nxa1 11.Nxd5 Qa4 12.Nxc7+ Kd7
13.Qf7+ Qe7 14.Qxe7+ Bxe7 15.Nxa8 Kd6 / 16.d4 Bf5 17.dxe5+
Kc5 18..Bf7 Rxa8 19.Ke2 Nc2 20.Rd1 Rd8 21.b4+ Kb5 22.Rxd8
Bxd8 23.Kd1 Nd4 24.Be3 Nc6 25.f4 Ka4 26.Bc1 g5 27.g3 gxf4
28.gxf4 Nd4 29.Be8+ b5 30.Be3 Bb6 31.Kd2 Nb3+ 32.Ke2 Kxa3
33.Bf7 Kxb4 34.e6 Bd8 35.Bxa7 Nc5 36.Bb6 Bxb6 37.e7 Bd7
38.e8(Q) Bxe8 39.Bxe8 Kc4 40.f5 Bd8 0-1

Berliner Gambit

1.e4 e5 2.Nf3 Nc6 3.Bc4 Nf6 4.Ng5 d5 5.exd5 Nd4 6.c3 b5 7.Bf1
Nxd5 8.Ne4 Qh4 9.Ng3 Bg4 10.f3 e4 11.cxd4 Bd6 12.Qe2 O-O
13.fxg4 Bxg3+ 14.Kd1 c6 15.Nc3 Rfe8 16.a4 b4 17.Nxe4 f5
18.Qf3 fxe4 19.Qxg3 Qf6 20.Kc2 Qxd4 21.b3 e3 22.Bc4 Re4
23.Ra2 R8e8 24.Rf1 Qc5 25.d3 R4e7 26.Kb1 Kh8 27.Rc2 Nc3+
28.Rxc3 bxc3 29.Re1 Qd4 30.Kc2 Qf6 31.Qf3 Qh4 32.Re2 Qxh2
33.Ba3 Rb7 34.Qxc6 R7b8 35.Bc5 Rbd8 36.Ba7 Qg2 37.Kxc3
Qd1 38.Qf3 Qa1+ 39.Kb4 Rb8+ 40.Bxb8 Rxb8+ 41.Bb5 Qd4+
42.Ka3 Qa1_43.Ra2 Qc1+ 44.Kb4 Qe1+ 45.Kc4 Qc1+ 46.Kd4
Rd8+ 47.Ke4 Qxb3 48.Kxe3 Qg8 49.Qf4 Ra8 50.Qe4 1-0

Berliner Gambit

1.e4 e5 2.Nf3 Nc6 3.Bc4 Nf6 4.Ng5 d5 5.exd5 Nd4 6.c3 b5 7.Bf1
Nxd5 8.Ne4 Qh4 9.Ng3 Bg4 10.f3 e4 11.cxd4 Bd6 12.Bxb5+ Kd8
13.O-O exf3 14.Rxf3 Rb8 15.a4 a6 16.Bf1 Re8 17.Nc3 c6 18.d3
f5 19.Nce2 Re6 20.Rf2 g5 21.Qd2 Ne3 22.Qa5+ Bc7 23.Qc5 Bd6
24.Qa7 Bxe2 25.Rxa2 Re7 26.Qxe7+ Bxe7 27.Rxe3 Bd6 28.Nxf5
Qxh2+ 28.Kf2 g4 29.Nxd6 Qxd6 30.Re4 Qf6+ 31.Kg3 h5 32.Bf4
Rb7 33.Rc1 Re7 34.Be2 Rxe4 35.dxe4 Qe6 36.Bxa6 Qxe4
37.Bg5+ Ke8 38.Rxc6 Qxd4 39.Kh4 Qa4 40.Rd6 Qb4 41.Rd8+
Kf7 42.g3 Ke6 43.Rd2 Qb3 44.Bd3 Qb4 45.Kxh5 Qc5 46.Kxg4
1-0

Some players may have felt cheated that I did't checkmate Fritz 15;
here is a likely continuation of the attack

67...Rb8 68.Rb1 Nc6 69.d7 Rd8 70.Rb6 Rxd7 71.Rxc6 Rxb7
72.Bd4 Kf5 73.Rxf6+ Ke4 74.Rxh6 Kf5 75.g4+ Ke4 76.g5 Rb3
77.g6 Rb8 78.g7 Rg8 79.Kg4 Kd3 80.Rh8 Rxg7+ 81.Bxg7 Kd2
82.Kf3 Kd3 83.Rh7 Kd2 84.Ke4 Kd1 85.Rh2 Kc1 86.Bh6+ Kb1
87.Kd5 Ka1 88.Kxc4 Kb1 89.Kb3 Ka1 90.Rh1#

I'm sure that even though White had an advantage of +6.80 some readers would argue that I had overlooked some spectacular defensive move by Fritz 15. As the above move sequence shows the win is trivial.

Grandmasters are so afraid of computers that they will not play computers unless the computer gives them odds of two pawns or the exchange. You will observe my only advantage is that I had the advantage of the first move only.

Moody (1600 my "floor") Fritz 15 (3170)

1.d4 Nf6 2.c4 g6 3.Nc3 Bg7 4.e4 d6 5.f3 O-O 6.Bg5 c5 7.d5 a6 8.Qd2 Qa59.Be2 Re8 (Nfd7/f5?) 10.Bd1 (To get Fritz out of book) b5 11.Be2 bxc4 12.Bxc4 Nfd7 13.Bb3 Ne5 14.Nge2 Nbd7 15.O-O Rb8 16.Rab1 Nb617.Qd1 Bd7 18.Kh1 Bb5? 19.Bc1 Ned7 20.Nxb5 axb5 21.a3 Nc4 22.f4! Qa6 23.Rf3! Rb7 24.Qf1 Ra8 25.Nc3 Ncb6 26.Qe1(Qh4) Rbb8 27.h4 Nc4? 28.Bxc4! bxc4 29.h5! Rb3 30.hxg6 fxg6 31.Qh4 Qb7 32.Ra1 Bd4 33.f5 gxf5 (Ne5 34.Rh3 +/-) 34.Rg3+ (The computer has no feel for the attack and doesn't fully appreciate what is meant by having pieces in the "King's Field") Kh8 35.Bh6 Bf6 36.Qh5 f4? 37.Bxf4 Qc8 38.Rf1 (Fritz missed this move) Qe8 39.Qh6 Qf7 40.Qh3! Rb7 41.e5! +/- dxe5 42.Bg5 Rf8 43.d6 Qe8 44.Ne4 c3 45.Bh6 Rg8 46.Rxg8+ Qxg8 47.bxc3 Qg6 (+2.33)48.Nxf6 exf6 49.Rf3 Qe8 50.Kh2 e4 51.Rg3 Ne5 52.Qf5 Rf7 53.a4(To anchor the Queen) Qd7 54.Qxe4 Qb7 55.Qe2 Qe6 56.Qb5 Qxb5 57.axb5 (+3.02) Rd7 58.b6 Rb7 59.Kh3 c4 60.Be3 h6 61.Bd4 Kh7 62.Kh4 Rd7 63.Re3 Nc6 64.Bc5 Ne5 65.Re1 Kg6 66.Ra1 Rd8 67.b7 +6.80

If Fritz is playing defensively at 3170, White is playing offensively at the 3300 level. Fritz is in zugzwang.

ACKNOWLEDGMENTS

The foundation for this book started in 1984 with my first letters to Grandmaster Lev Alburt. Through the years, Lev has provided a sounding board and been a contributor to the growth of theory in many openings outside his opening praxis. Thanks for your patience, Lev! Several individuals contributed to the growth of theory in the Two Knights Defense, most notably ICM van der Tak, GM Alburt, GM Reshevsky, FM Craig Mar. and NM Alon Bochman. NM Eric Schiller provided a very weighty database for this opening.

The Universal Attack was analyzed by IM Gerard Welling, and the databases from IM Colin Leach and Bill Townsend proved especially useful. In summary the overwhelming body of theory presented here and the practical results are primarily the work of the author, with constructive review and comment from many sources.

Many thanks to my family for allowing me the time to be creative. Their support has been the moving force behind my ability to write this book.

Thanks to the crew at Howe Caverns, who made the workplace an enjoyable experience and a respite from the rigors of writing. Special thanks to Andy, Matt. Sara, Ashton, Carol, Paul, Shane, Jaime, Jo Ann, Holly, and Ellen.